Forced Mobility of EU Citizens

Forced Mobility of EU Citizens is a critical evaluation from an empirical perspective of existing practices of the use of transnational criminal justice instruments within the European Union. Such instruments include the European Arrest Warrant (EAW), prisoner transfer procedures and criminal law-related deportations.

The voices and experiences of people transferred across internal borders of the European Union are brought to the fore in this book. Another area explored is the scope and value of EU citizenship rights in light of cooperation between not just judicial authorities of EU Member States but criminal justice systems in general, including penitentiary institutions. The novelty of the book lays not only in the fact that it focuses on a topic that so far has been under-researched, but it also brings together academics and studies from different parts of Europe – from the West (i.e. the expelling countries) and the East (the receiving countries, with a special focus on two of the jurisdictions most affected by these processes – Poland and Romania). It therefore exposes processes that have so far been hidden, shows the links between sending and receiving countries, and elaborates on the harms caused by those instruments and the very idea of 'justice' behind them. This book also introduces a new element to deportation studies as it links to them the institution of the European Arrest Warrant and EU law transfers targeting prisoners and sentenced individuals.

With a combination of legal, criminological and sociological perspectives, this book will be of great interest to scholars and students with an interest in EU law, criminal law, transnational criminal justice, migration/immigration and citizenship.

José A. Brandariz is a professor of criminal law and criminology at the University of A Coruña, Spain. He is a former associate editor of the *European Journal of Criminology* (2018–2022) and a former member of the executive board of the European Society of Criminology (2016–2019). He has published some 20 books and 150 journal articles and book chapters, and has been visiting professor and visiting research fellow at various international universities and research institutes, such as Bologna (Italy), Buenos Aires (Argentina), Coimbra (Portugal), Chicago (USA), Freiburg (Germany), Northern Arizona (USA), Pompeu Fabra (Spain), Turin (Italy) and Warsaw (Poland), among others. Professor Brandariz has particularly focused his research on migration enforcement, bordered penalty and citizenship issues in the past decade. Having participated in various EU-funded projects, he recently co-coordinated a Spanish team participating in two supranational research actions on EU criminal justice cooperation procedures (2017–2020).

Witold Klaus is a professor at the Institute of Law Studies, Polish Academy of Sciences, and Head of the Department of Criminology and of the Centre for Migration Law Research. He is also a research fellow in the Centre of Migration Research at the University of Warsaw. He is a lawyer, criminologist, migration researcher and NGO activist. He is a former executive secretary of the Polish Society of Criminology (2008–2018) and serves as editor-in-chief to the oldest Polish criminological journal 'Archiwum Kryminologii' (Archives of Criminology). He held scholarships from the British Academy (UK), the Max Planck Institute for Foreign and International Criminal Law (currently the Max Planck Institute for the Study of Crime, Security and Law, Germany) and the US government. His main areas of academic interests include refugee and immigrant rights, deportation studies, crimmigration, victimology and victimisation of vulnerable groups in society. Currently, he leads a project on experiences of Poles deported from the UK and the EU in the aftermath of their contact with the criminal justice system (funded by National Science Centre, Poland).

Agnieszka Martynowicz is a senior lecturer in Criminology at Edge Hill University (EHU) in England. She is currently the 'Features' editor for *Justice, Power and Resistance* (journal, Bristol University Press) and a member of the Editorial Committee of 'Archiwum Kryminologii' (Archives of Criminology). Dr Martynowicz is a core member of the Migration Working Group – North West (EHU) and a long-standing member of the European Group for the Study of Deviance and Social Control. Before entering an academic career in 2016, she worked as a researcher and policy officer in a number of statutory and voluntary sector organisations, including the Northern Ireland Human Rights Commission in Belfast, the Institute for Conflict Research (Belfast) and the Irish Penal Reform Trust in Dublin. Between 2011 and 2016, she worked as an independent research and evaluations consultant, delivering projects with organisations such as the Irish Council for Civil Liberties and the European Prison Litigation Network. She is an author and co-author of numerous publications relating to prisons and prisoners' rights, migration and migrant rights, 'crimmigration', children's rights, and youth justice.

Directions and Developments in Criminal Justice and Law

www.routledge.com/Directions-and-Developments-in-Criminal-Justice-and-Law/book-series/DDCJL

The ways in which crime is constructed in society is of time-honored interest to criminologists across the globe. The ever-changing landscape of what is criminal and what is not affects scholars and policymakers in their approach to the body of law defining prohibited conduct, how that law evolves, and the modes by which it is administered. Rule of law cannot exist without a transparent legal system, strong enforcement structures, and an independent judiciary to protect against the arbitrary use of power. Critical consideration of the mechanisms through which societies attempt to make the rule of law a reality is essential to understanding and developing effectual criminal justice systems. The *Directions and Developments in Criminal Justice and Law* series offers the best research on criminal justice and law around the world, offering original insights on a broadly defined range of socio-legal topics in law, criminal procedure, courts, justice, legislation, and jurisprudence. With an eye toward using innovative and advanced methodologies, series monographs offer solid social science scholarship illuminating issues and trends in law, crime, and justice. Books in this series will appeal to criminologists, sociologists, and other social scientists, as well as policymakers, legal researchers, and practitioners.

9. **Criminal Justice Responses to Domestic Abuse in Northern Ireland**
   Ronagh J.A. McQuigg

10. **Prison Segregation: The Limits of Law**
    Eleanor Brown

11. **Domesticating International Criminal Law**
    Reflections on the Italian and German Experiences
    Florian Jeßberger, Chantal Meloni and Maria Crippa

12. **Forced Mobility of EU Citizens**
    Transnational Criminal Justice Instruments and the Management of 'Unwanted' EU Nationals
    Edited by José A. Brandariz, Witold Klaus and Agnieszka Martynowicz

Forced Mobility of EU Citizens

Transnational Criminal Justice Instruments and the Management of 'Unwanted' EU Nationals

Edited by José A. Brandariz, Witold Klaus and Agnieszka Martynowicz

Routledge
Taylor & Francis Group
LONDON AND NEW YORK

First published 2024

by Routledge
4 Park Square, Milton Park, Abingdon, Oxon OX14 4RN

and by Routledge
605 Third Avenue, New York, NY 10158

Routledge is an imprint of the Taylor & Francis Group, an informa business

 Funded by Institute of Law Studies, Polish Academy of Sciences.

British Library Cataloguing-in-Publication Data
A catalogue record for this book is available from the British Library

ISBN: 978-1-032-18453-1 (hbk)
ISBN: 978-1-032-18450-0 (pbk)
ISBN: 978-1-003-25458-4 (ebk)

DOI: 10.4324/9781003254584

Contents

Tables

Contributors

José A. Brandariz is a professor of criminal law and criminology at the University of A Coruña, Spain. He is a former associate editor of the *European Journal of Criminology* (2018–2022) and a former member of the executive board of the European Society of Criminology (2016–2019). He has published some 20 books and 150 journal articles and book chapters, and has been visiting professor and visiting research fellow at various international universities and research institutes, such as Bologna (Italy), Buenos Aires (Argentina), Coimbra (Portugal), Chicago (USA), Freiburg (Germany), Northern Arizona (USA), Pompeu Fabra (Spain), Turin (Italy) and Warsaw (Poland), among others. Professor Brandariz has particularly focused his research on migration enforcement, bordered penalty and citizenship issues in the past decade. Having participated in various EU-funded projects, he recently co-coordinated a Spanish team participating in two supranational research actions on EU criminal justice cooperation procedures (2017–2020).

Theodora E.D. Ene is a licensed social worker and a lecturer at University of Bucharest with over 20 years' experience in social work-related fields, social work education and international social work. Her research interests span the following fields: probation, CSR, volunteering, non-profit sector and social services management. Dr Ene is a member in the Commission for Professional Approval and Certification of the National College of Social Workers of Romania (since 2012).

Valeria Ferraris holds a PhD in criminology and she is an associate professor of Sociology of Law and Sociology of Deviance at the University of Turin in Italy. Her research interests focus on migration management and control, administrative detention, migration and crime and urban security. She has been a visiting researcher at the University of Oslo (Norway) and at the University of A Coruña, Spain, as well as being an honorary lecturer at the Catholic University in Lyon and at the University of Hong Kong. She participated in several EU funded projects, and she is currently one of the experts in the EU programme 'Urban Innovative Actions'. She is the co-chair of the Working Group on Immigration, Crime and Citizenship of the European Society of Criminology.

Helene O.I. Gundhus is a professor in criminology at Department of Criminology and Sociology of Law at the Faculty of Law, University of Oslo and currently Head of the Department. She obtained a PhD in criminology from the University of Oslo in 2006. Gundhus was a project member of 'Crime Control at the Borderlands of Europe', headed by professor Katja Franko, University of Oslo. From 2015 to 2021 she has worked on a study on digitalisation of policing in Norway, addressing risk management and precautionary logics in the police. She has published widely on issues relating to police methods and technology, police professionalism, crime prevention and security, migration control and transnational policing.

Witold Klaus is a professor at the Institute of Law Studies, Polish Academy of Sciences, and Head of the Department of Criminology and of the Centre for Migration Law Research. He is also a research fellow in the Centre of Migration Research at the University of Warsaw. He is a lawyer, criminologist, migration researcher and NGO activist. He is a former executive secretary of the Polish Society of Criminology (2008–2018) and serves as editor-in-chief to the oldest Polish criminological journal 'Archiwum Kryminologii' (Archives of Criminology). He held scholarships from the British Academy (UK), the Max Planck Institute for Foreign and International Criminal Law (currently the Max Planck Institute for the Study of Crime, Security and Law, Germany) and the US government. His main areas of academic interests include refugee and immigrant rights, deportation studies, crimmigration, victimology and victimisation of vulnerable groups in society. Currently he leads a project on experiences of Poles deported from the UK and the EU in the aftermath of their contact with criminal justice system (funded by National Science Centre, Poland).

Agnieszka Martynowicz is a senior lecturer in Criminology at Edge Hill University (EHU) in England. She is currently the 'Features' editor for *Justice, Power and Resistance* (journal, Policy Press) and a member of the Editorial Committee of 'Archiwum Kryminologii' (Archives of Criminology). Dr Martynowicz is a core member of the Migration Working Group – North West (EHU) and a long-standing member of the European Group for the Study of Deviance and Social Control. Before entering an academic career in 2016, she worked as a researcher and policy officer in several statutory and voluntary sector organisations, including the Northern Ireland Human Rights Commission in Belfast, the Institute for Conflict Research (Belfast) and the Irish Penal Reform Trust in Dublin. Between 2011 and 2016, she worked as an independent research and evaluations consultant, delivering projects with organisations such as the Irish Council for Civil Liberties and the European Prison Litigation Network. She is an author and co-author of numerous publications relating to prisons and prisoners' rights, migration and migrant rights, 'crimmigration', children's rights and youth justice.

Stefano Montaldo is an associate professor of EU law at the University of Turin. His research activity mainly focuses on EU institutional law, the protection of fundamental rights in Europe, EU migration law and judicial cooperation in criminal matters. He is the deputy director of the MA in European Legal Studies and member of the board of the journal *European Papers*.

Martin Nøkleberg holds a PhD in criminology from the Department of Criminology and Sociology of Law (IKRS), University of Oslo. He is currently working as an associate professor at Western Norway University of Applied Sciences, Department of Welfare and Participation. His research focuses on maritime port and airport security, plural policing, securitisation of critical infrastructure, and inter-organisational collaboration and network processes.

Gabriel Oancea, PhD, is a probation counsellor at the Bucharest Probation Service and associate lecturer at the University of Bucharest, Faculty of Sociology and Social Work. He teaches effective methods used in offenders' supervision and rehabilitation and aspects related to the specifics of social work in criminal justice. Dr Oancea is involved in research on the effectiveness of preventive measures and transfer of prisoners and probationers within the European Union.

Justyna Włodarczyk-Madejska is a criminologist and holds PhD in law. She is an assistant professor in the Department of Criminology, Institute of Law Studies Polish Academy of Sciences and in the Institute of Justice. Member of the Polish Society of Criminology and European Society of Criminology. She serves as an Executive Editor to the 'Archives of Criminology' – the oldest Polish criminological journal. Her academic interests focus on juvenile justice and delinquency, offending in old age and criminological aspects of international judicial cooperation.

Dominik Wzorek is a PhD candidate in law (Criminology) and works as a research assistant in Department of Criminology, Institute of Law Studies Polish Academy of Sciences. He holds an MA in Law and Bachelor's Degree in Sociology from Jagiellonian University in Cracow, Poland. He was also awarded the title of Master of Laws (LL.M) at Ruprecht-Karl University in Heidelberg, Germany. His research interests include qualitative and quantitative methods in criminology, life-course criminology and criminal, penal and sentencing policy.

Acknowledgement

The book is an element of the research project titled 'Experiences of Poles Deported from the UK in the Context of the Criminal Justice System Involvement', which was made possible thanks to the funding from National Science Centre, Poland (under Grant No. UMO-2018/30/M/HS5/00816).

Transnational criminal justice instruments and the management of 'unwanted' EU nationals

An introduction

José A. Brandariz, Witold Klaus and Agnieszka Martynowicz

Introduction: comprehensiveness and diversity

The assumption on which this edited collection is based may seem intriguing – if not puzzling. This book brings together discussions of several law enforcement and criminal justice devices that at first sight appear to be heterogeneous. Initially, the collection explores several EU law instruments aimed at enabling the cross-border cooperation of national criminal justice authorities in prosecuting and punishing criminal offences in cases where actors from different jurisdictions are involved. These legal arrangements are a critical part of the ambitious judicial cooperation agenda implemented by EU authorities in the past two decades, under the umbrella of the area of freedom, security and justice (see Title V of Part 3 of the Treaty on the Functioning of the European Union) (Fijnaut, 2019). The enactment of the European Arrest Warrant (Council Framework Decision 2002/584/JHA of 13 June 2002; hereinafter EAW) was an early and significant milestone in these cooperation efforts (Barbosa et al., 2022; Fichera, 2011; Klimek, 2015). The EAW has markedly altered the texture and operation of cross-border criminal justice in Europe, being widely and increasingly utilised in many jurisdictions (see European Commission, 2021).

Successful as the EAW has apparently been, it is only one of a long list of legal instruments aimed at boosting judicial cooperation in criminal matters (Klip, 2021; Mitsilegas, 2022). Legislative acts added to this list in recent years are, for example, the Directive (EU) 2016/1919 of 26 October 2016 on legal aid for suspects and accused persons in criminal proceedings and for requested persons in European Arrest Warrant proceedings (Contissa et al., 2022), and Regulation (EU) 2018/1805 of 14 November 2018 on the mutual recognition of freezing orders and confiscation orders (Bernardi & Rossi, 2019; see also Schunke, 2017). In the framework of this law-making endeavour, there are some mutual trust-based procedures that show a close relation with the EAW. They pertain to a specific sphere of the EU justice agenda focusing on the detention and transfer of prisoners. More precisely, three Framework Decisions form this legislative sphere, namely Council Framework Decision 2008/909/JHA of 27 November 2008 on the transfer of prisoners (hereinafter FD 909), Council Framework Decision 2008/947/JHA of 27 November 2008

DOI: 10.4324/9781003254584-1

on the transfer of probationers and individuals sentenced to noncustodial penalties (hereinafter FD 947), and Council Framework Decision 2009/829/JHA of 23 October 2009 on the European supervision order and alternatives to pre-trial detention (hereinafter FD 829; Flore et al., 2012; Klimek, 2017; Marguery, 2018; Montaldo, 2020). These three legal instruments share a common, pivotal trait with the EAW, that is, they all result in the forced mobility of EU citizens.

As the title of this collection bears witness to, this forced mobility dimension is vital to grasp the consequences and implications of judicial cooperation tools in empirical terms. The empirical focus taken here provides evidence that the aforementioned EU law instruments have close proximity with the various forms of removal and deportation regulated by EU and national legal provisions. As is further elaborated in the chapters that follow, criminal justice arrangements and immigration law arrangements are combined in varied and changeable ways in different jurisdictions in coercively dealing with EU nationals (see also Brandariz, 2022).

Although this perspective is relatively new, there is no shortage of academic studies exploring these criminal justice and law enforcement instruments, especially the EAW (see e.g. Barbosa et al., 2022; Graat, 2022; Klip et al., 2022). However, the extant literature is manifestly unbalanced in this field. Forced mobility instruments have been mainly scrutinised from a legal viewpoint, chiefly owing to their prominence in the EU law domain. Despite their relevance, existing studies leave many aspects of these law enforcement phenomena unaddressed. For one, they provide little-to-no information on how EAW procedures and prisoner transfer procedures, as well as forced return measures, are being enforced on the ground, and what are their consequences for the daily lives of criminalised EU nationals. Since these legal procedures have long been transposed into national legal orders, this is a significant research lacuna. This collection contributes to filling this omission by examining forced mobility procedures from an empirical viewpoint, relying on fieldwork carried out in various jurisdictions. In this regard, the book brings fresh perspectives, by elaborating socio-legal, penological and deportation studies' view on the topics under exploration. These perspectives significantly supplement the legal analyses currently at the centre of transnational justice studies by providing a comprehensive exploration of forced mobility practices that examine the operation of measures targeting EU nationals from an innovative and fresh perspective.

In sum, this book aims to provide a comprehensive analysis of forced mobility practices, examining connections between legal and policy instruments that have been underexplored so far. In addition, it endeavours to bring diversity into this academic field. Various scholars have claimed that studies exploring the relationship between borders, citizenship and penalty have been almost exclusively focused on a handful of Global North jurisdictions (Bosworth et al., 2018; Van der Woude et al., 2017). Seeing this limitation as a significant shortcoming, the book's contributions are largely authored by scholars based in relatively peripheral European jurisdictions, which sometimes are overlooked in academic conversations.

In this regard, this collection is aligned with southern criminology proposals (Carringtonet al., 2016, 2019), which compellingly claim that current debates in criminology and socio-legal studies could be significantly enriched by pushing the boundaries of global academic conversations, involving scholars from disregarded, peripheral regions. This proposal does not have a geographical nature. Carrington and her collaborators (2019: 184) highlight that "Southern criminology is not just a 'Southern' thing . . . it resonates well beyond any geographical divide". In fact, the southern criminology project has an epistemological ambition, since it has to do with the unbalanced economy of academic knowledge; in their own words, "the Southernising of criminology is one step in the journey toward the development of a robust transnational criminology that . . . enhance(s) the democratisation of knowledge, a journey toward cognitive justice" (Carrington et al., 2019: 188).

This collection unambiguously joins these efforts at democratisation of knowledge. Specifically, peripheral voices are pivotal in this case as the authors included herein map out the stratifications characterising belonging, citizenship and ultimately rights in Europe and Schengenland.

Go East!

Back in the mid-nineteenth century, the US publisher Horace Greeley popularised the slogan "Go West, young man" to encourage US residents to colonise the American West (Fuller, 2004). Not only then, but all throughout the last centuries, the West has frequently epitomised the notion of a promising land full of opportunities. It is also true for Europe. The perception of Central and Eastern Europeans about the European and American West was – and still is – linked with the notion of prosperity, success, and wealth. On the other hand, eastern neighbours are seen as less civilised, not developed enough, being part of the 'Wild East'. Thus, there is an attempt to escape from the 'East' – both geographically, and when it comes to emigrants, literally, that is, physically by migration (Melegh, 2006: 115–116). European forced mobility practices on the other hand head in the opposite direction, compelling EU citizens to go back east. In fact, forced mobility regimes in Europe and the transnational justice instruments explored in this collection cannot be grasped without thoroughly examining the vital part played in them by eastern EU citizens and eastern EU jurisdictions.

The legislative act regulating EU citizenship rights, the Directive 2004/38/EC, was passed on 29 April 2004. Two days later, ten countries (including eight Central and Eastern European states) became new EU Member States in the widest enlargement of the EU to date. EU expansion into the 'east' was further reinforced with the subsequent accessions of Bulgaria and Romania in 2007 and Croatia in 2013. However, these processes of formal inclusion into the political structures were not necessarily based on equality of the then 'new' EU citizens in access to the benefits of membership. The way in which the 2004 and 2007 enlargements altered power relations within the EU and impacted patterns of belonging and membership has been widely scrutinised (see e.g. Currie, 2008). The differential, probationary status given to new Member States was corroborated by various freedom of movement restrictions imposed on their citizens for some time in the mid-2000s to late 2000s (Hristova, 2008; Shimmel, 2006).

There are also quite visible traces of this peculiar status in the transnational justice and forced mobility procedures analysed in this book. Invariably, Eastern Europeans make up the lion's share of the EU citizens forcefully returned, as well as those targeted by transfer procedures and – to a lesser extent – by an EAW (except for Polish nationals as in Poland EAW is a key instrument in transnational judicial cooperation – see Klaus, Włodarczyk-Madejska and Wzorek in this volume). Consequently, the chapters contained in this collection bring to the fore the significance of the aforementioned legal practices for eastern EU jurisdictions and eastern EU citizens.

Echoing southern criminology scholars' claim regarding the figurative nature of geographical references, 'the East' appears to be somehow misplaced in a north/south divide. In fact, it is adrift between the south and the north (Klaus forthcoming), unveiling the constructed texture of these apparently binary notions. This 'being in-between' resonates with the contradictory representations of Eastern EUropean countries adopted and promoted by European elites, which see them concurrently as relatively untrustworthy Member States *and* increasingly pivotal pieces of the EUropean (geo)political and economic architecture.

In addition, there is no self-evident definition of 'the East' and 'Eastern European countries'. The division between the West and the East was created during the Enlightenment (Wolff, 1994), and its very purpose was to divide the 'enlightened' Western Europe from its wilder and 'barbaric' outskirts – as the westerners perceived those territories. That segregation deepened further during the communist regimes in the (former) Soviet Bloc and the Cold War. And despite many attempts of the Central and Eastern European societies and governments to see themselves and foremost be seen as a part of the West, the label of 'East' sticks hard and the Western countries and their citizens are not willing to give it up (Galasińska & Radziwinowiczówna, 2021; Melegh, 2006).

But beyond the authoritarian political regimes ruling them in the second half of the twentieth century, the 11 'new' EU Member States of Eastern and Central Europe now have little in common. More than three decades after the fall of the Berlin Wall, they differ markedly in social and economic indicators measuring, for example, the risk of poverty and social exclusion,[1] Gross National Income (GNI) per capita[2] and human development,[3] as well as in political aspects[4] and governance indicators.[5] Interestingly, national differences in economic performance and workforce needs have made these jurisdictions also diverge in terms of human mobility. While certain countries such as Slovakia are barely affected by immigration flows, others such as Romania and especially Poland[6] have become key countries of destination in recent years.[7] Curiously, Poland and Romania are the only two jurisdictions that have remained countries of emigration in recent years – although the significance in this regard is clearly declining in the Polish case.[8] All in all, only Croatia, Latvia, Lithuania and Romania had a five-year negative net migration rate from 2016 to 2020.

Despite this diversity and the economic development of many eastern countries in recent past,[9] the relevant national populations are the best evidence of the stratifications eroding EU citizenship and EU citizenship rights. In fact, these eastern national groups, and particularly Romanians, Bulgarians and – to a certain extent – Poles have long been treated as second-class citizens (Gul-Rechlewicz, 2020; Juverdeanu, 2021; Ulceluse & Bender, 2022), and the legal and policy arrangements prioritising them as primary targets of forced mobility practices are part and parcel of these stratification efforts. Eastern Europeans are targeted by law enforcement agencies as a potential threat to the public safety and often face profiling by nationality. They are perceived by many law enforcement agencies as criminals and thus are much often stopped and searched, and vehicles with plates from those countries have come under greater scrutiny for allegedly crime-related reasons (Brouwer et al., 2018; van der Woude & van der Leun, 2017). All that leads to the conclusion that legal provisions enshrining EU citizenship rights and safeguards have manifestly failed to bridge the extra-legal cleavages giving shape to hierarchies of belonging and rights.

There is also an evident racialisation dimension underlying these processes. Despite their EU citizenship, Roma constitute a group particularly targeted by state coercion measures, including transnational justice practices and forced returns (De Genova, 2019; Fekete, 2014; van Baar et al., 2019). However, the scope of the racialisation processes operating in this sphere goes far beyond the Roma people. Discrimination patterns affect wider Eastern European communities, showing that there are various shades of whiteness, as the critical literature has insightfully contended (Aliverti, 2018; Bhui, 2016; Parmar, 2020). In fact, there is no way to understand racialisation processes in EUrope without taking into account the pivotal part that varied Eastern European populations have long been playing in those processes (Fox, Moroşanu & Szilassy, 2012; Franko, 2020). Still, racialisation has an intersectional texture in this context. In fact, the groups primarily targeted by the law enforcement practices explored in this collection are not only racialised because of being from Eastern Europe; they are also segregated due to their lower socio-economic class: they are relatively poor, uneducated or with lower levels of educational attainment, frequently have criminal records and carry out unskilled jobs away from their home country (Morgan, 2022; Brouwer et al., 2018).

There is no doubt that migration policy in general is highly class-selective and that people from lower socio-economic classes are less welcomed in the Global North (and West) and perceived by both societies and politicians as more 'problematic' when it comes to integration in host countries (Bonjour & Chauvin, 2018). The fact remains, however, that they constitute the vast majority of migrants globally. This is also true for the emigration from Eastern Europe to the former EU15 countries, which was primarily driven by the wish of improvement of economic situation of people who decided to move. Of course, not only people from the lower socio-economic classes emigrate, but regardless of their social position in the country of origin, in a host country many tend to join the lower-middle or working class. In some instances, life experiences such as the inability to cover the costs of accommodation and becoming homeless result in their joining the 'underclass' (Morgan, 2021: 25–26). And here the prejudice against the lower class (Garland, 2001; Schuilenburg, 2008) meets race/nationality, resulting in racialised responses which go beyond ethnicity or 'race'. They show "how hierarchies of whiteness and class serve to reproduce social hierarchies by creating and maintaining internal borders between the more and less white" (Webster, 2008: 296).

This last point is particularly relevant to understanding of the biased practices operating in this field. The criminalisation practices affecting Eastern Europeans are vital in masking the stratification processes at play and in stripping racialised individuals of their EU citizenship rights and safeguards (Brandariz, 2021; Vrăbiescu, 2021). Drawing on the relatively ambiguous regulation of the Citizenship Rights Directive[10] (see e.g. Articles 27(2) and 33(1)), the risk and public security stigmas associated with criminal offending are allowing othering processes to prevail over EU citizenship protections.

Exploring the interrelation between transnational justice and forced mobility across Europe

The chapters forming this collection explore in more detail the aforementioned aspects of transnational justice and forced mobility practices. Beginning with the discussion of prisoner and pre-trial transfer procedures, Brandariz (Chapter 1) tackles the complex questions relating to the implementation of EU mutual cooperation instruments in the area of 'management' of 'offenders' under three legal instruments, namely FD 909, FD 947 and FD 829. Utilising data from a variety of statistical sources combined with policy and practice reviews, the author shows that – apart from a minority of EU Member States making use of FD 909 – the other two of those instruments lay largely dormant in the area of judicial cooperation. This, he further argues, potentially fails to improve the legal and material conditions of EU citizens serving non-custodial sentences or being held on remand outside of their country of citizenship. The chapter contrasts this under-utilisation of transfers in the context of the criminal justice process with an increasing use of deportations regulated by the EU Citizenship Directive, which, while designed in the legislation as an exceptional measure with high threshold of protection, has been gaining significant momentum in certain EU countries in most recent past. While all the instruments under review have been designed as measures to react 'against noncitizen offending', it is clear that deportations under the latter Directive are now akin to an immigration rather than criminality control device.

Continuing the topic of prisoner transfers, Ferraris (in Chapter 2) discusses the process of transposition of Framework Decision 909 in Italy, highlighting Italian authorities' attempted use of this legal device to create conditions to transfer foreign national prisoners *out* of Italy to deal with long-criticised overcrowding problems in the country's prison system. As the data presented in the chapter shows, these transfers have been particularly targeted at Romanian prisoners, constituting the largest group of 'foreign national offenders' in Italian prisons. The chapter lays bare the failure of both transposition and its practical implementation to achieve this aim, together with highlighting the disproportionate use of FD 909 to target one specific national group. Oancea and Ene (Chapter 3) provide an empirically evidenced critique of the notion of 'transfer for rehabilitation' and social reintegration, the stated aims of the FD 909. Based on research with prisoners transferred from other EU states to serve their sentences in Romania, the authors outline the challenges faced by them in the overcrowded and under-funded conditions in the country's penitentiary institutions, which often lack the resources needed to support 'rehabilitation'. The authors also provide ample evidence of the damaging impact of transfers on family ties, progression within the prison regimes, and – ultimately – on chances of successful reintegration into society post-release.

Having looked at policy and practical implications of transfer procedures under what can generally be grouped as 'sentenced transfers', the next set of chapters focus on the analysis of the workings of the EAW. Arguably the best-known instrument of intra-EU law enforcement cooperation, the EAW has previously been scrutinised in legal commentary; however, questions about the fairness and 'just nature' of its implementation have been raised much less frequently. This section of the book, therefore, begins with Klaus considering the questions around *just punishment* and *justice* in EAW context (Chapter 4). He offers detailed theoretical exploration of those terms and their complex and often politicised meaning, expanding the discussion into the transnational context. The theory is then tested against the empirical evidence of experiences of decision-makers (judges), law enforcement officials and individuals transferred under the EAW to Poland from a variety of EU jurisdictions. In the course of the discussion, the chapter considers the gravity of offences for which people are transferred, the time it often takes between the offence and the EAW, and the reasons for which decision-makers in the Polish criminal justice system certify the issuing of warrants while also delving into their understanding of the meaning of justice in this context. Klaus concludes that in a system based on legalism, formalism and bureaucratic procedures, 'justice' is sacrificed in the transnational process of implementing the EAW.

In some contrast, Montaldo outlines in Chapter 5 what could be considered as resistance by the Italian law makers to the very idea of the EAW. The chapter starts with a detailed analysis of the Court of Justice of the European Union cases relating to the refusal grounds in the execution of the EAW. Recalling the initial transposition of the Framework Decision into Italian law in 2005, the author debates the significant departures in Italian law from the very idea of mutual recognition of judicial decisions and mutual trust, in particular by expanding the grounds on which the EAW could be refused by Italian courts. However, as the chapter shows, both the initial transposition and the subsequent reforms of the Italian implementing laws raised significant questions about discriminatory use of the EAW against non-Italian EU nationals, leading to a conclusion that it is used not just as a mutual cooperation instrument but as a measure of immigration control.

Staying within the broad theme of the implementation of the EAW as an instrument of mutual cooperation and trust, in Chapter 6, Włodarczyk-Madejska and Wzorek query whether the EAW is the 'rigorous, efficient and expeditious' way of enforcing 'cross-border proceedings in criminal matters' that it was initially designed to be. The chapter begins with the exploration of the notion of *efficiency* and how it can be understood in the context of the assessment of the EAW from this perspective. Indicators of *efficiency* are then tested against empirical evidence from a review of Polish court case files, supplemented with interview data from, among others, law enforcement practitioners, judges, probation officers, prison and border guard staff, civil society experts and those directly affected by EAW transfers, the arrestees. Analysing the speed with which EAWs are issued, the accuracy of court rulings, offences for which EAWs are issued and cost of EAW, the authors conclude that while the EAW can be considered *efficient* on the metrics used, some changes – such as refraining from using the EAW for very minor offences – could be implemented to improve its utility.

Having looked at some of the technical aspects of the EAW, the next two chapters delve into what can be called the *lived experience* aspect of its implementation. First, in Chapter 7, Klaus, Włodarczyk-Madejska and Wzorek reflect on the effects of executing the EAW on the lives of Polish emigrants returned to Poland on foot of the EAW procedure. Poland continues to issue one of the highest numbers of EAWs in the EU due to the legalism identified by Klaus in Chapter 4. While those transferred under the EAW to Poland constitute around 2 per cent of all 're-emigrants', their experiences are not insignificant. The research on which the chapter is based showed that in making their initial decision to move abroad, most wanted their story of emigration to be a 'new start', often driven by the desire to improve their financial circumstances and life chances. Importantly for some, in the context of this book, their reason to move was linked to previous convictions and the need to escape both the stigma and pressures to reoffend. As such, emigration was often mentioned as path to desistance. For others still, however, the 'escape' was to avoid the criminal justice process, whether a court case or prison time. Whatever the reason to move abroad, transfer under the EAW interferes abruptly with lives both lived and planned, often engendering feelings of being a 'failed migrant' in front of family and friends.

The focus on *lived experience* continues in Chapter 8, where Martynowicz links prior disruption to family lives caused by EAW process in cases of Polish male prisoners in Northern Ireland to contemporary changes in residence status of EU nationals after UK's exit from the European Union. The chapter lays bare the often life-changing consequences of arrests and transfers of (in this case, male) family members on the whole family unit, often sustained financially and emotionally by the relationship with the arrestee. However, the chapter delves further into the potential consequences of 'criminal past' – including prior EAW transfers – for the future of secure residence of the affected individuals and their families, up to and including the threat of becoming undocumented under the post-Brexit immigration arrangements.

Finally, and as a fitting closing chapter, Nøkleberg and Gundhus provide a discussion of the *Schengen Agreement* as a European criminal justice instrument. Taking as a starting point the establishment of the Schengen area as one of free movement of people, goods, services and capital, the authors note that the cost of 'freedom' has been the securitisation of, in particular, the external borders of the Member States. The chapter also notes that the agreement does not limit the monitoring of intra-Schengen cross-border mobility; in fact, given the reintroduction of physical borders during the Covid-19 pandemic, the chapter asks whether the whole idea of 'borderless Schengen' is now in crisis.

Conclusion: re-erecting internal walls – an increasingly Saturnian Europe?

The EAW and other judicial cooperation devices have long been cherished as manifestations of the emergence of a cross-national model of criminal justice (König et al., 2021; Ouwerkerk, 2021). However, at least some of these legal measures, especially transfer procedures and forced returns, are also fuelling the re-bordering processes gaining momentum across Europe, against the backdrop of a devaluated EU citizenship status. The re-bordering character of the transnational justice and forced mobility measures examined in this collection reveal that they are part of far wider changes that are markedly altering sovereign relations inside the EU. In fact, several recent crises paved the way for new re-bordering arrangements to surface across Europe. Obviously, the Brexit referendum has been a watershed moment in the recent development of the EU project. Indeed, Brexit has had a significant impact on EU national populations living in the UK, and more precisely on Eastern European groups (Cambien et al., 2020, Mindus, 2017). With regard to transnational cooperation, however, the EAW was immediately replaced by its almost mirror instrument, a 'Surrender' process, introduced as a part of the EU–UK Trade and Cooperation Agreement, becoming available from 1 May 2021 (for more, see Martynowicz in this volume). There are some, but really small differences between those two legal institutions (more safeguards are in place in the surrender), but in general the purpose of both legal instruments is the same and their procedures are similar (Grange et al., 2021).

Having said that, the changes eroding the supranational ambitions of the EU project and leading to the re-erection of walls inside Europe go well beyond the Brexit conundrum. Even before the coronavirus pandemic, EU Member States were increasingly relying on the powers to temporarily reintroduce border control at internal borders pursuant to Articles 25 ff. of the Schengen Borders Code (Regulation (EU) 2016/399 of 9 March 2016) (Gülzau, 2021; Salomon & Rijpma, 2021). The number of cases in which those re-bordering measures were adopted rose from 34 between 2006 and 2014, up to 91 between 2015 and 2019. Needless to say, these powers were increasingly normalised in the framework of the pandemic, when internal borders were reintroduced 196 times in 2020 and 2021. In addition, while these exceptional measures used to be in force for hours or days in the 2000s and early 2010s, they have been enforced for months on end in the recent past.[11]

Metaphorically, there is a certain Saturnian dimension in these re-bordering efforts. Since at least the mid-2010s, cross-border cooperation has been superseded by competition and lack of solidarity in the field of border and mobility management policies. Recent deportation changes are a good evidence of this shift. Return measures targeting so-called Dubliners, that is, asylum seekers whose international protection applications must be assessed in a different EU country than that in which they stay pursuant to the Dublin III Regulation (Regulation (EU) No 604/2013 of 26 June 2013), have been gaining significant traction since the mid-2010s (Picozza, 2017). While they accounted for 8.41 per cent of the deportations enforced in the EU in 2016, their share soared to 16.75 per cent in 2019 and to 29.3 per cent in 2020.[12]

In short, forced mobility arrangements scrutinised in this book, such as forced returns and certain transfer procedures, cannot be disconnected from other similar re-bordering strategies that are greatly contributing to re-erecting of internal borders inside Schengenland, thereby undermining the deeply democratic potential of a cooperative, borderless Europe.

*****

This edited collection traces its origins to two events. First, some of the chapters emanate from contributions presented by authors at an international conference titled 'Unwanted Citizens of EU Member States', which took place in Liverpool (UK) in August 2019. Generously funded by the British Academy under the project 'Polish migrants deported from the UK' (Grant No: VF1\101178) and organised under the auspices of Edge Hill University, the Migration Working Group North-West and the Institute of Law Studies of the Polish Academy of Sciences, the event brought together the three editors of this book and kick-started their conversations on the then much less known area of scholarly activity in border studies, the forced mobility of EU nationals *within* the European Union. Second, a very significant number of chapters in this book are based on findings of the research project titled 'Experiences of Poles Deported from the UK in the Context of the Criminal Justice System Involvement', which was made possible thanks to the funding by National Science Centre, Poland (under Grant No. UMO-2018/30/M/HS5/00816). As editors, we very much thank the funders, as well as the participants in the aforementioned research project and international conference, and especially the scholars authoring the book chapters for their contribution to this collective reflection on the intersection between transnational justice and forced mobility practices in current EUrope. It is our hope that the conversations about such mobility within 'Fortress Europe' in all its guises shall continue, aided by the empirical knowledge presented in this book.

Notes

1 Six eastern EU Member States had percentages of person at risk of poverty or social exclusion significantly lower than the EU average in 2021, especially the Czech Republic, Slovenia, Slovakia and Poland. By contrast, five eastern EU countries ranked above average, particularly Romania and Bulgaria (source: Eurostat. Income and living conditions database; https://ec.europa.eu/eurostat/web/income-and-living-conditions/data/database; accessed 2 November 2022).

2 Not a single eastern EU country had a GNI per capita – measured in purchasing power standard – higher than the EU average in 2020, although the Czech Republic and Slovenia were relatively close to that average. Bulgaria and to a lesser extent Croatia ranked very low in this regard (source: Eurostat. National accounts database; https://ec.europa.eu/eurostat/web/national-accounts/data/database; accessed 2 November 2022).

3 Human Development Index (HDI) data show that ten out of 11 eastern EU Member States had a very high development in 2021, with Slovenia, Estonia and the Czech Republic heading this group. By contrast, Bulgaria had the lowest HDI score of all EU countries and was included within the list of countries with high – rather than very high – human

development (source: United Nations Development Programme; https://hdr.undp.org/content/human-development-report-2021-22; accessed 2 November 2022).

4 No eastern EU jurisdiction was part of the selective list of full democracies published by The Economist' 2021 Democracy Index (see www.eiu.com/n/campaigns/democracy-index-2021/?utm_source=economist&utm_medium=daily_chart&utm_campaign=democracy-index-2021; accessed 3 November 2022). Although all of them are considered as flawed democracies, Estonia, the Czech Republic and Slovenia have scores far higher than those of Croatia, Hungary and Romania.

5 The World Bank's 2021 Worldwide Governance Indicators also show a significant gap between the high scores of Estonia, the Czech Republic and Lithuania and those of Romania and Bulgaria, which lag far behind other eastern EU jurisdictions in every governance indicator (see https://info.worldbank.org/governance/wgi/Home/Reports; accessed 3 November 2022).

6 Poland ranks sixth of all EU28 Member States in the number of immigrants received from 2016 to 2020, below Germany, the UK, Spain, France and Italy. Evidently, this position as country of destination has been further reinforced in the framework of the Russian invasion of Ukraine in 2022. Actually, according to OECD data Poland was ranked second (just beyond the US) as the country which received the biggest number of newly arrived seasonal workers in 2021 (OECD, 2022).

7 Eurostat. International migration and citizenship database; see https://ec.europa.eu/eurostat/web/migration-asylum/international-migration-citizenship/database; accessed 3 November 2022.

8 Romania and Poland ranked respectively fifth and sixth of all EU Member States in the number of emigrants from 2016 to 2020.

9 Ten out of 11 Eastern EU countries are clearly above EU average in terms of GDP growth from 2010 to 2019. Poland, Lithuania, Estonia, Romania and Slovakia have respectively ranked third to seventh of all EU Member States in this regard (source: Eurostat. National accounts database. https://ec.europa.eu/eurostat/web/national-accounts/data/main-tables; accessed 7 November 2022).

10 Directive 2004/38/EC of the European Parliament and of the Council of 29 April 2004 on the right of citizens of the Union and their family members to move and reside freely within the territory of the Member States amending Regulation (EEC) No 1612/68 and repealing Directives 64/221/EEC, 68/360/EEC, 72/194/EEC, 73/148/EEC, 75/34/EEC, 75/35/EEC, 90/364/EEC, 90/365/EEC and 93/96/EEC.

11 European Commission; see https://home-affairs.ec.europa.eu/document/download/11934a69-6a45-4842-af94-18400fd274b7_en?filename=Full%20list%20notifications_27102022.pdf; accessed 7 November 2022.

12 Source: Eurostat. Managed migration database. Some EU countries have put particular efforts in targeting so-called Dubliners for intra-EU deportation in recent years, namely Denmark, Hungary, Sweden and especially Slovenia.

References

Aliverti A. (2018). Strangers in our Midst: The Construction of Difference through Cultural Appeals in Criminal Justice Litigation. In: Bosworth M., Parmar A. & Vázquez Y. (eds) *Race, Criminal Justice and Migration Control: Enforcing the Boundaries of Belonging*. Oxford: Oxford University Press, pp. 127–141.

Barbosa R., Glerum V., Kijlstra H., Klip A., Peristeridou C., Wąsek-Wiaderek M. & Zbiciak A. (2022). *European Arrest Warrant: Practice in Greece, the Netherlands and Poland*. Den Haag: Eleven.

Bernardi A. & Rossi F. (eds) (2019). *Improving Confiscation Procedures in the European Union*. Napoli: Jovene.

Bhui H.S. (2016). The Place of 'Race' in Understanding Immigration Control and the Detention of Foreign Nationals. *Criminology and Criminal Justice* 16(3): 267–285.

Bonjour S. & Chauvin S. (2018). Social Class, Migration Policy and Migrant Strategies: An Introduction. *International Migration* 56(4): 5–18.

Bosworth M., Franko K. & Pickering S. (2018). Punishment, Globalization and Migration Control: 'Get Them the Hell Out of Here'. *Punishment and Society* 20(1): 34–53.

Brandariz J.A. (2021). The Removal of EU Nationals: An Unaccounted Dimension of the European Deportation Apparatus. *Central and Eastern European Migration Review* 10(1): 13–33.

Brandariz J.A. (2022). Criminalization or Instrumentalism? New Trends in the Field of Border Criminology. *Theoretical Criminology* 26(2): 285–303.

Brouwer J., van der Woude M. & van der Leun J. (2018). (Cr)immigrant Framing in Border Areas: Decision-making Processes of Dutch Border Police Officers. *Policing and Society* 28(4): 448–463.

Cambien N., Kochenov D. & Muir E. (2020). *European Citizenship under Stress: Social Justice, Brexit and Other Challenges*. Leiden: Brill.

Carrington K., Hogg R., Scott J., Sozzo M. & Walters R. (2019). *Southern Criminology*. Abingdon: Routledge.

Carrington K., Hogg R. & Sozzo M. (2016). Southern Criminology. *British Journal of Criminology* 56(1): 1–20.

Contissa G., Lasagni G., Caianiello M. & Sartor G. (eds) (2022). *Effective Protection of the Rights of the Accused in the EU Directives: A Computable Approach to Criminal Procedure Law*. Leiden: Brill.

Currie S. (2008). *Migration, Work and Citizenship in the Enlarged European Union*. Farnham: Ashgate.

De Genova N. (2019). The Securitization of Roma Mobilities and the Re-bordering of Europe. In: van Baar H., Ivasiuc A. & Kreide R. (eds) *The Securitization of the Roma in Europe*. London: Palgrave Macmillan, pp. 29–44.

European Commission (2021). *Commission Staff Working Document. Statistics on the Practical Operation of the European Arrest Warrant – 2019*. 6 August 2021. SWD(2021) 227 final. Retrieved from ec.europa.eu/info/sites/default/files/law/search_law/documents/eaw_statistics_2019_swd_2021_227_final_08_2021_en.pdf (accessed 31 October 2022).

Fekete L. (2014). Europe against the Roma. *Race & Class* 55(3): 60–70.

Fichera M. (2011). *The Implementation of the European Arrest Warrant in the European Union: Law, Policy and Practice*. Antwerp: Intersentia.

Fijnaut C. (2019). *A Peaceful Revolution: The Development of Police and Judicial Cooperation in the European Union*. Antwerp: Intersentia.

Flore D., Bosly S., Honhon A. & Maggio J. (eds) (2012). *Probation Measures and Alternative Sanctions in the European Union*. Antwerp: Intersentia.

Fox J.E., Moroşanu L. & Szilassy E. (2012). The Racialization of the New European Migration to the UK. *Sociology* 46(4): 680–695.

Franko K. (2020). *The Crimmigrant Other: Migration and Penal Power*. Abingdon: Routledge.

Fuller T. (2004). "Go West, Young Man" – An Elusive Slogan. *Indiana Magazine of History* 100(3): 231–242.

Galasińska A. & Radziwinowiczówna A. (2021). 'The Vile Eastern European': Ideology of Deportability in the Brexit Media Discourse. *Central and Eastern European Migration Review* 10(1): 75–93.

Garland D. (2001). *The Culture of Control. Crime and Social Order in Contemporary Society*. Oxford University Press.

Graat J. (2022). *The European Arrest Warrant and EU Citizenship: EU Citizenship in Relation to Foreseeability Problems in the Surrender Procedure*. Cham: Springer.

Grange E., Keith B. & Kerridg S. (2021). Extradition Under the EU – UK Trade and Cooperation Agreement. *New Journal of European Criminal Law* 12(2): 213–221.

Gul-Rechlewicz V. (2020). Immigrants in the Netherlands: Second-class Citizens? The Polish Case. *Studia Europejskie* 24(3): 109–128.

Gülzau F. (2021). A "New Normal" for the Schengen Area. When, Where and Why Member States Reintroduce Temporary Border Controls? *Journal of Borderlands Studies*. Epub ahead of print. Online on 17 November 2021. https://doi.org/10.1080/08865655.2021.1996260

Hristova A. (2008). "Welcome to Europe, Which Has Always Been Yours": Are Bulgarians and Gypsies Second Class Citizens? *Georgia Journal of International and Comparative Law* 36: 677–704.

Juverdeanu C. (2021). The Different Gears of EU Citizenship. *Journal of Ethnic and Migration Studies* 47(7): 1596–1612.

Klaus, W. (forthcoming). Eastern Europe – Adrift between the North and the South. Deportation and Detention from the Polish Perspective. In: Fabini G., Fernandez-Bessa C., Ferraris V. & Brandariz J.A. (eds) *Border Criminologies from the Periphery: Cross-national Conversations on Bordered Penality*. Routledge.

Klimek L. (2015). *European Arrest Warrant*. Cham: Springer.

Klimek L. (2017). *Mutual Recognition of Judicial Decisions in European Criminal Law*. Cham: Springer.

Klip A. (2021). *European Criminal Law: An Integrative Approach*. 2nd edn. Antwerp: Intersentia.

Klip A., Glerum V., Peristeridou C., Barbosa R. & Kijlstra H. (2022). *Improving the European Arrest Warrant*. Den Haag: Eleven.

König J., Meichelbeck P. & Puchta M. (2021). The Curious Case of Carles Puigdemont – The European Arrest Warrant as an Inadequate Means with Regard to Political Offenses. *German Law Journal* 22(2): 256–275.

Marguery T. (2018). *Mutual Trust under Pressure, the Transferring of Sentenced Persons in the EU: Transfer of Judgments of Conviction in the European Union and the Respect for Individual's Fundamental Rights*. Nijmegen: Wolf Legal Publisher.

Melegh A. (2006). *On the East-West Slope: Globalization, Nationalism, Racism and Discourses on Central and Eastern Europe*. Budapest: Central European University Press.

Mindus P. (2017). *European Citizenship after Brexit: Freedom of Movement and Rights of Residence*. London: Palgrave.

Mitsilegas V. (2022). *EU Criminal Law*. 2nd ed. Oxford: Hart.

Montaldo S. (ed.) (2020). *The Transfer of Prisoners in the European Union: Challenges and Prospects in the Implementation of Framework Decision 2008/909/JHA*. Den Haag: Eleven/Giappichelli.

Morgan B. (2021). *Still Here: Defending the Rights of Homeless EU Citizens after Brexit and Covid-19*. London: Public Interest Law Centre.

Morgan B. (2022). What Fresh Hell? UK Policies Targeting Homeless Migrants for Deportation after Brexit and Covid-19. *Critical Social Policy* 42(1): 150–159.

OECD. (2022). International Migration Outlook 2022. *Organisation for Economic Co-operation and Development*. www.oecd-ilibrary.org/social-issues-migration-health/international-migration-outlook-2022_30fe16d2-en

Ouwerkerk J. (2021). Are Alternatives to the European Arrest Warrant Underused? The Case for an Integrative Approach to Judicial Cooperation Mechanisms in the EU Criminal Justice Area. *European Journal of Crime, Criminal Law and Criminal Justice* 29(2): 87–101.
Parmar A. (2020). Arresting (non)Citizenship: The Policing Migration Nexus of Nationality, Race and Criminalization. *Theoretical Criminology* 24(1): 28–49.
Picozza F. (2017). 'Dubliners': Unthinking Displacement, Illegality, and Refugeeness within Europe's Geographies of Asylum. In: De Genova N. (ed.) *The Borders of "Europe": Autonomy of Migration, Tactics of Bordering*. Durham, NC: Duke University Press, pp. 233–254.
Salomon S. and Rijpma J. (2021) A Europe without Internal Frontiers: Challenging the Reintroduction of Border Controls in the Schengen Area in the Light of Union Citizenship. *German Law Journal* 1–29.
Schuilenburg M. (2008). Citizenship Revisited – Denizens and Margizens. *Peace Review: A Journal of Social Justice* 20(3): 358–365.
Schunke M. T. (2017). *Extended Confiscation in Criminal Law: National, European and International Perspectives*. Antwerp: Intersentia.
Shimmel N. (2006). Welcome to Europe, But Please Stay Out: Freedom of Movement and the May 2004 Expansion of the European Union. *Berkeley Journal of International Law* 24(3): 760–800.
Ulceluse M. & Bender F. (2022) Two-tier EU citizenship: Disposable Eastern European Workers during the COVID-19 Pandemic. *Organization* 29(3): 449–459.
van Baar H., Ivasiuc A. & Kreide R. (eds) (2019) *The Securitization of the Roma in Europe*. London: Palgrave Macmillan.
van der Woude M., Barker V. & van der Leun J. (2017) Introduction: Crimmigration in Europe. *European Journal of Criminology* 14(1): 3–6.
van der Woude M. & van der Leun J. (2017). Crimmigration Checks in the Internal Border Areas of the EU: Finding the Discretion That Matters. *European Journal of Criminology* 14(1): 27–45.
Vrăbiescu I. (2021). *Deporting Europeans: The Racialized Mobility of Romanians in France*. Lanham, MD: Lexington Books.
Webster C. (2008). Marginalized White Ethnicity, Race and Crime. *Theoretical Criminology* 12(3): 293–312.
Wolff L. (1994). *Inventing Eastern Europe: The Map of Civilization on the Mind of the Enlightenment*. Stanford, CA: Stanford University Press.

1 Foiled transnational justice?

An exploration of the failures of EU judicial cooperation procedures

José A. Brandariz[1]

Introduction

Back in the late 2000s, EU institutions gave a significant boost to their cooperation in criminal matters agenda. That impulse was not new. On the contrary, judicial cooperation efforts had already led to noteworthy results, such as the passage of the Council Framework Decision 2002/584/JHA of 13 June 2002 creating the European Arrest Warrant (hereinafter EAW). Subsequently, these efforts received new impetus in the 2010s when EU institutions enacted a number of legislative acts regarding common minimum standards for criminal proceedings (e.g. Directive (EU) 2016/1919), exchange of information between criminal justice agencies of EU Member States (e.g. Directive 2014/41/EU on the European investigation order), protection of crime victims (e.g. Directive 2012/29/EU), confiscation and freezing of assets (e.g. Regulation (EU) 2018/1805 on freezing orders and confiscation orders), and mutual recognition of judgements, among other aspects.

Several framework decisions issued in the last years of the first decade of the century shaped a specific sphere of this EU justice agenda, that of detention and transfer of prisoners. In fact, judicial cooperation in this area was fostered through the passage of three framework decisions: Council Framework Decision 2008/909/JHA of 27 November 2008 on the transfer of prisoners (hereinafter FD 909), Council Framework Decision 2008/947/JHA of 27 November 2008 on the transfer of probationers and individuals sentenced to non-custodial penalties (hereinafter FD 947), and Council Framework Decision 2009/829/JHA of 23 October 2009 on the European supervision order and alternatives to pre-trial detention (hereinafter FD 829). Much more recently, this legislative package was supplemented with the publication of the European Commission's *Handbook on the transfer of sentenced persons and custodial sentences in the European Union* in November 2019. The goals to be pursued by these transfer procedures appear to be particularly ambitious, as presented by the recitals of the corresponding framework decisions. Beyond references to 'the protection of victims and the general public' (FD 947, recital 8; see also FD 947, recital 24 and FD 829, recital 3), FD 909 and FD 947 are both aimed at reintegration of the sentenced individual into society, not least by enabling them 'to preserve family, linguistic, cultural and other ties' (FD 947, recital 8; see also FD 909, recital 9, and FD 947, recital 24). The goals to be served by FD 829

DOI: 10.4324/9781003254584-2

procedures dealing with pre-trial measures are even more ambitious, since they 'aim at enhancing the right to liberty and the presumption of innocence', as well as promoting 'the use of non-custodial measures as an alternative to provisional detention' (recital 4). Moreover, FD 829 provisions are expected to 'ensure that a person subject to criminal proceedings who is not resident in the trial state is not treated any differently from a person subject to criminal proceedings who is so resident' (recital 5).

Despite the thrust given by EU authorities to these judicial cooperation procedures, more than one decade after the enactment of the three FDs, it is still doubtful whether they have succeeded in consolidating transfer procedures. There are good reasons to adopt a glass half-empty viewpoint in this regard. Section 2 of this chapter will show that EU institutions have long acknowledged that the FDs on transfer procedures have been failing to meet their expectations, particularly FD 947 and FD 829. Both institutional and academic actors have put significant efforts into pinpointing why these legal procedures are not widely used across EU jurisdictions. In the framework of this exploration, legal factors have largely taken centre stage. This chapter, though, casts a light on certain extra-legal aspects that have been clearly underexplored. For these purposes, Section 3 examines a law enforcement measure relatively similar to the transfer procedures under study which has been gaining significant momentum across Europe, the deportation orders targeting EU nationals. Drawing on the lessons to be inferred from this 'success story', the last, concluding section scrutinises the role played by certain factors, crucially among them the judicial nature of FD 909, FD 947 and FD 829 procedures in hampering their consolidation.

Before moving into Section 2, some brief methodological notes are in order. This chapter relies on a number of secondary quantitative data on transfer procedures and deportation measures which have been largely overlooked in the institutional and academic conversations on these topics (see FRA, 2016). However, it also builds on primary data collected in the framework of two research projects funded by the Directorate-General Justice and Consumers of the European Commission and is aimed at scrutinising the conditions hindering the regular utilisation of transfer measures, 'Mutual Trust and Social Rehabilitation into Practice – RePers' (2017–2019; www.eurehabilitation.unito.it/repers_project) and 'Trust and Social Rehabilitation in Action – Trust and Action' (2018–2020; www.eurehabilitation.unito.it/trust_action). These research actions were carried out by a cross-national consortium formed by scholars, criminal justice practitioners and government officials from Italy, Romania and Spain. I participated in this three-year research effort as a member of the University of A Coruña's ECRIM team. In the framework of the RePers and Trust and Action projects, national teams carried out a variety of research activities that resulted in the publication of a collective book presenting the main conclusions of these projects (Montaldo, 2020b; see also Fernández-Bessa, Ferraris & Damian, 2020). These data and conclusions, though, are of limited use for the purposes of this chapter, since they were largely focused on legal obstacles preventing transfer procedures from gaining momentum across European jurisdictions. Still, those EU research actions involved a number of so-called 'mutual learning' activities engaging Italian, Romanian and Spanish scholars, practitioners and government officials in a cross-national conversation on FD 909, FD 947 and FD 829 pitfalls.[2] The data collected in the framework of these organised conversations are of particular importance for the exploration presented in this chapter. In fact, those lively debates allowed participant observers to grasp the underlying, non-legal factors impeding the increasing consolidation of transfer procedures.

1. An unpromising beginning: the troublesome implementation of transfer procedures

EU officials have long been concerned over the implementation and actual impact of transfer regulations. Various evaluation documents reflect this institutional concern. In early 2014, the first official report on the implementation of the three FDs (European Commission, 2014) pinpointed several obstacles obstructing the regular utilisation of transfer procedures. After having praised the many positive aspects of these legal regulations, the report pointed out that 'member States have little practical experience in the application of the Framework Decisions so far'. More precisely, it noted that "the limited figures available show that the Transfer of Prisoners is already used whereas no transfers have yet taken place under Probation and Alternative Sanctions and European Supervision Order" (European Commission, 2014, p. 6). Apparently, a key reason for this limited application of transfer practices was the delayed transposition process. The report stressed that "at the time of writing, respectively 10, 14 and 16 Member States have not yet transposed the Framework Decisions" (European Commission, 2014, p. 5), although all EU Member States were obliged to have transposed them into their legal orders before either early December 2011 (FD 909 and FD 947) or early December 2012 (FD 829).

Institutional concerns persisted for a few more years. The EU Agency for Fundamental Rights (FRA) published a comprehensive report on the human rights aspects of transfer procedures in 2016 (FRA, 2016). In this document, the FRA portrayed a relatively bleak scenario. The report recognised that "The Framework Decisions have not been frequently utilised" (p. 32). This limited use led the FRA to put forward several recommendations aimed at consolidating transfer measures. Implementation shortcomings seemed to be particularly worrying in the case of the uncharted European Supervision Order, with regard to which the report stressed that "the EU and its Member States need to assess the instrument's non-application" (p. 34).

Recent institutional evaluations are less sombre than mid-2010s European Commission and FRA reports. In an assessment of the field of mutual recognition in criminal matters released in May 2019, the Romanian Presidency of the Council of the EU openly mentions FD 909 as one of the legal instruments in this area that "are used relatively often". In stark contrast, though, this official memorandum points out that FD 947 and 829 "are used less frequently" (Council of the EU, 2019b, p. 3). This pitfall led the Council's Presidency to single out the "identification of gaps in the application of mutual recognition instruments and possible solutions to fill these gaps" (p. 5) as one of the critical tasks to be urgently carried out in this sphere of judicial cooperation in criminal matters. A contemporary Council's Presidency document selecting the three FDs as critical topics to be addressed in the ninth round of mutual evaluations of the measures taken to fight against organised crime also highlighted that FD 947 and FD 829 "have not been sufficiently implemented" and "are less used in practice than other mutual recognition instruments" (Council of the EU, 2019a, p. 3 and p. 5).

Although these EU Council documents unambiguously put the spotlight on the hindrances preventing the FDs on non-custodial measures and alternatives to pre-trial detention from being widely used, it is not clear whether its assessment on the current FD 909 scenario is too optimistic or not. Whereas comprehensive, harmonised data on the application of these transfer procedures are still missing (FRA, 2016), the scattered data provided by national databases and the SPACE I programme of the Council of Europe are not particularly promising. This impression is corroborated when these data are compared with those related to the utilisation of the EAW, which has been considered as the benchmark in terms of best practices in the field of judicial cooperation (see Council of the EU, 2019b). EU Member States issued no less than 20,226 EAWs in 2019, following a significant rise initiated in 2011 (source: European Commission, 2021).[3] It is certainly true that the execution rate is actually low (34.2 per cent from 2015 to 2019),[4] and that the EAW landscape is markedly unbalanced, with just four countries (Poland, Germany, France and Romania) accounting for 55.7 per cent of the EAWs issued from 2005 to 2019. However, it is not adventurous to conclude that this pivotal legal instrument makes up the gold standard of success in the field of mutual recognition.

Against this backdrop, the scale and scope of FD 909 prisoner transfers seem relatively insignificant. The Council of Europe's SPACE I programme[5] has been releasing data on the utilisation of these transfers in recent years. Although these SPACE I data are grossly incomplete, the general picture is reasonably clear. The number of FD 909 transfers either received or carried out is markedly insignificant (from 0 to 5 cases per year) in various European countries, such as Croatia, Ireland,[6] Malta, Portugal and Slovenia. Other jurisdictions such as Cyprus and Norway have very rarely acted as executing states,[7] that is, as the jurisdictions receiving transfers.

Some European jurisdictions are a bit more active in this field; still, the number of transfer procedures carried out per year in these countries is counted in the dozens (e.g. Luxembourg and Sweden; Czech Republic, Lithuania and Poland in their capacity as executing states; Norway acting as issuing state,[8] that is, as the jurisdiction requesting the transfer to be accepted). Drawing on SPACE I data, there are only two exceptions to this general landscape. The Spanish criminal justice system has been intensively participating in these FD 909 procedures as an issuing state in the recent past, averaging 158.5 transfers annually from 2015 to 2019.[9] Spain ranks also relatively well as an executing state, with 56.7 transfers received per year from 2013 to 2019. In addition, Romania has been turned into the country of destination of prisoner transfers par excellence, with an average of 982 transfer procedures annually concluded from 2014 to 2019. However, Romania's role as an issuing state is much more insignificant. In fact, Romania averaged only 8.8 transfers per year as an issuing state from 2015 to 2019 (see also Fernández-Bessa, Ferraris & Damian, 2020).[10]

Additional data provided by national databases do not differ significantly from this general image. In stark contrast to its leading role in the EAW sphere, Germany seems to be making a moderate use of FD 909 transfers.[11] Italy, in turn, averaged no more than 99.3 outward transfers per year from 2014 to 2017 (Ferraris, 2019; see also Fernández-Bessa, Ferraris & Damian, 2020). Sweden has annually completed 45.5 FD 909 transfers as an issuing state and 9.3 transfers as an executing state from 2015 to 2020 (source: Kriminalvården, 2018, 2021).[12] Belgium, in turn, on average carried out 41.6 FD 909 transfers as an issuing state from 2013 to mid-2018 (Hofmann & Nelen, 2020; Nelen & Hofmann, 2019; see also Service Public Fédéral Justice, 2017, 2020). By contrast, the Austrian criminal justice system has been more active in this field, with 129.3 outward transfers annually carried out from 2018 to 2020 (source: Federal Ministry of Justice; see www.parlament.gv.at/PAKT/VHG/XXVII/AB/AB_03718/index.shtml#; accessed 10 January 2022). Although no complete data are publicly available, there is evidence to infer that the Netherlands should also be included in this group of countries relatively involved in FD 909 transfers, especially as an executing state.[13] Surprisingly, UK criminal justice agencies have used these transfer procedures more sparingly; on average, the UK completed 58.5 transfer cases per year as an issuing state from 2013 to 2018 and 14.3 cases per year as an executing state from 2012 to 2018 (source: Ministry of Justice; see questions-statements.parliament.uk/written-questions/detail/2019–02–12/220146; accessed 10 January 2022).[14]

Beyond these cross-national variations, the main conclusion to be drawn from the available data is that FD 909 transfer procedures are hardly relevant in most European jurisdictions and that in many of them their significance is close to none. In fact, the low number of FD 909 transfers starkly contrasts with those of issued and enforced EAWs. What is more, the scope and actual significance of current FD 909 practices should be assessed by comparing them with the scale of the group potentially affected by those transfers, that of EU nationals imprisoned abroad (see also European Commission, 2014; Fernández-Bessa, Ferraris & Damian, 2020; FRA, 2016; Hofmann & Nelen, 2020). According to SPACE I data (Aebi & Tiago, 2018), at least 32,266 EU national prisoners were incarcerated in a different EU28 country in January 2018, accounting for 29.9 per cent of the noncitizen prison population and for 5.9 per cent of the total prison population.[15] EU national prisoner contingents are particularly relevant in Austria, Cyprus, Ireland and Luxembourg, where they account for more than 10 per cent of the incarcerated population. In stark contrast to this prison demography scenario, at least in Cyprus and Ireland FD 909 transfers are very rarely utilised. Considered through this comparative lens, it is evident that FD 909 transfers are having a very limited impact on noncitizen prison populations, as has been acknowledged by various national administrations (Ferraris, 2019; see also questions-statements.parliament.uk/written-questions/detail/2018–11–13/190835; accessed 11 January 2022).

In short, almost one decade after the continent-wide legal transposition of FD 909 provisions, there are very few – if any – reasons to be optimistic with regard to the degree of utilisation of FD 909 procedures. Still, the judicial cooperation scenario is even more concerning in the case of FD 947 and FD 829 procedures, which seem to be applied even more sparingly. Data on the utilisation of these measures are scanter than in the case of FD 909 practices. Yet the Spanish General Council of the Judiciary reports that Spanish courts issued 3.5 FD 947 procedures and 4 FD 829 procedures per year, and received 2.5 FD 829 procedures per year from 2015 to 2020 (see www.poderjudicial.es/cgpj/es/Temas/Estadistica-Judicial/Estadistica-por-temas/Aspectos-internacionales/Cooperacion-con-organos-judiciales-extranjeros/Solicitudes-de-cooperacion-tramitadas-directamente-por-los-organos-judiciales/; accessed 11 January 2022). Romania, in turn, annually carried out 7.4 FD 947 transfers as an issuing state from 2014 to 2019 (source: SPACE II. Council of Europe; see wp.unil.ch/space/space-ii/annual-reports/; accessed 11 January 2022). Certain data also show that Germany is having a very low profile with 947 transfers.[16] Sweden has been relatively more active in this field, averaging 17.4 FD 947 cases per year as an issuing state but only 3.6 FD 947 cases per year as an executing state from 2016 to 2020 (Kriminalvården, 2018, 2021). In contrast to other national cases, the Netherlands stands out for its involvement in FD 947 procedures, but mainly as an issuing state.[17]

These extremely low numbers show that the official reports monitoring the implementation of FD 947 and FD 829 are right, that is, these transfer procedures are failing to improve the legal and material conditions of the many EU citizens serving non-custodial sentences or being in pre-trial detention abroad. More than 12 years after the passage of both framework decisions, no transposition issues are impeding the regular implementation of FD 947 and FD 829 measures (Council of the EU, 2021a, 2021b; see also Montero Pérez de Tudela et al., 2019).[18] Consequently, the factors preventing these transfer measures from being widely used across Europe are unrelated to transposition issues. The last section of this chapter will be devoted to scrutinising those factors. Before then, the next section examines what might be considered as a ‘success story’ – so to speak[19] – in the cross-national management of noncitizen offending in Europe, that is, the increasing utilisation of deportations targeting EU nationals.

2. A contrasting ‘success story’: the deportation of EU nationals

There are remarkable differences between judicial cooperation transfers and deportations targeting EU citizens. To begin with, FD 909, FD 947 and FD 829 procedures are expected to be regularly implemented and utilised by European criminal justice agencies. By contrast, the deportation practices regulated by the Citizenship Rights’ Directive (Directive 2004/38/EC of the European Parliament and of the Council of 29 April 2004 on the right of citizens of the Union and their family members to move and reside freely within the territory of the Member States; hereinafter CRD) are legally considered as exceptional measures. Paradoxically, though, transfer procedures have been used sparingly, whereas CRD deportations have gained significant momentum across many EU countries in the recent past.

This law enforcement shift is certainly intriguing from an EU law perspective, since CRD deportations are regulated as exceptional restrictions to the freedom of movement rights attributed to EU citizenship. Indeed, pursuant to chapter VI of the CRD these coercive return orders can only be enforced for serious reasons of public policy and public security, that is, essentially when the corresponding EU citizen is considered to be a serious threat to fundamental social interests (Guild, Peers & Tomkin, 2014).

This uncontested legal nature, though, does not mirror what has been happening on the ground, in terms of the actual extent of these allegedly exceptional deportation orders. In many EU jurisdictions, CRD deportations are far from being a marginal phenomenon. In fact, they are an increasingly pivotal part of European immigration enforcement systems.

Spain is one of the EU countries in which this shift is particularly evident. The Spanish immigration enforcement apparatus averaged 409.4 CRD deportations enforced per year from 2010 to 2018, a period in which their share mounted from 2 per cent of all deportations in 2010 to 10.5 per cent in 2017 (Brandariz, 2021a). Germany has also been enforcing an increasing number of CRD deportations in recent years, averaging 1048.7 deportations per year from 2012 to 2020 (6.1 per cent of all forced returns; source: German Parliament; www.proasyl.de/thema/fakten-zahlen-argumente/statistiken/; accessed 14 January 2022). In the Netherlands, some 6.2 per cent of the noncitizens returned from 2016 to 2020 were EU nationals; in other words, some 310 CRD deportations were annually enforced over this five-year period (source: Dutch Statistics Service; data.overheid.nl/dataset/immigratie-dtenv-vertrek#panel-resources; accessed 14 January 2022).

In other European jurisdictions, though, CRD deportations are playing a relatively minor – and sometimes declining – part in national immigration enforcement systems. Greece annually carried out 385.2 CRD deportations from 2014 to 2019 (2.7 per cent of all forced returns; source: Greek Data Office; see catalog.data.gov.gr/dataset/apela-seis-mh-nomimwn-metanastwn-ana-yphkoothta; accessed 14 January 2022). In Italy, 67.5 deportations targeting Romanian nationals were annually enforced from 2017 to 2020 (source: National Prison Ombudsman; see www.garantenazionaleprivatiliberta.it/gnpl/it/pub_rel_par.page; accessed 14 January 2021).

In stark contrast to this second group of countries, in various EU jurisdictions CRD deportations have gained significant momentum in the recent past, being turned into a vital piece of their immigration enforcement systems. In Belgium, at least 19 per cent of the forced returns carried out in 2019 and 2020 were CRD deportations, mainly based on the previous perpetration of a criminal offence (source: Belgian Federal Immigration Office; dofi.ibz.be/fr/themes/figures/rapports-annuels; accessed 14 January 2022).[20] The Norwegian immigration enforcement system, in turn, has carried out on average 1099.3 CRD deportations per year from 2013 to 2020 (source: Norwegian Directorate of Immigration; www.udi.no/en/statistics-and-analysis/annual-reports/; accessed 14 January 2022). This significant number of removals targeting EU nationals accounts for 24.5 per cent of the returns enforced over these eight years. In a national system in which immigration enforcement practices are guided by the need to meet certain annual quotas (Franko, 2020), the impact of CRD deportations is so remarkable in Norway that deportation rates were higher than 400 EU national deportees per 100,000 EU national residents from 2014 to 2016.

CRD deportations are extensively used as well in two additional European jurisdictions, France and the UK. In Britain, removal practices have been on the decline in the recent past, and CRD deportations have not been an exception to this rule. However, the momentum gained in the UK by these deportations targeting EU nationals is almost unparalleled across Europe. On average, the British immigration enforcement system deported 3,551 EU nationals per year from 2013 to 2020; CRD deportations accounted for 38.4 per cent of all forced returns carried out over this period (source: UK Home Office; see www.gov.uk/government/statistics/immigration-statistics-year-ending-december-2020/how-many-people-are-detained-or-returned; accessed 18 January 2022). Also in France CRD deportations are playing a pivotal role within the national deportation regime since the early 2010s (Vrăbiescu, 2021a, 2021b). Although the astonishing number of EU nationals deported in the first years of the last decade has not been matched recently (see Eremenko, El Qadim & Steichen, 2017; Lafleur & Mescoli, 2018), France averaged 4,230 CRD deportations per year from 2010 to 2020, which account for 20.8 per cent of all returns carried out over these 11 years (source: French Home Office; see www.immigration.interieur.gouv.fr/Info-ressources/Etudes-et-statistiques/Statistiques/Essentiel-de-l-immigration/Chiffres-cles; accessed 19 January 2022). Deportation rates in France have been slightly higher than 200 deportees per 100,000 EU national residents in recent years, but they were close to 500 deportees per 100,000 EU national residents in the early 2010s.

In short, the particularly large contingents of EU citizens deported from European countries such as France and the UK, as well as from Belgium, Germany, the Netherlands, Norway, Spain and elsewhere across the continent show that CRD deportations are far from being exceptional legal measures. The apparently rights-based EU law regulation of these deportation orders has not prevented them from being widely used in many jurisdictions.

This immigration enforcement scenario stands in stark contrast to the poor performance of FD 909 and – especially – FD 947 and FD 829 measures. Consequently, the next section will focus on the lessons to be drawn from this 'successful' deportation experience to grasp the obstacles hampering the regular utilisation of transfer procedures.

However, before addressing that research question, an additional clarification is in order. In principle, there seems to be a loose connection between FD transfer procedures and CRD deportations. The former are a critical tool of judicial cooperation in criminal matters and therefore a legal instrument to be used by criminal justice agencies. The latter are a specific exception to the freedom of movement rights EU citizens are entitled to. The significant amplification of their scope, though, has turned CRD deportations into something close to an immigration control device, in the sense that they are massively utilised to remove unwanted (EU national) noncitizens.

Consequently, these notable differences might make any comparison between those legal measures particularly futile. Still, a thorough exploration unveils that despite their diverse legal nature FD transfers and CRD deportations are closely interrelated. Both of them have become – more or less – vital pieces of institutional efforts aimed at reacting against noncitizen offending. That is especially evident in the case of FD transfers, which try to combine institutional interests of criminal justice agencies in prosecuting EU national offenders, holding them accountable and making them serve their sentences with human rights concerns and rehabilitation purposes (Martufi, 2018; Montaldo, 2019, 2020a; see also FRA, 2016). By contrast, crime-fighting purposes are not manifest in the case of CRD deportations. In fact, although these deportation orders can be part of a criminal sentence (Article 33(1) of the CRD), Article 27(2) of the CRD establishes that "previous criminal convictions shall not in themselves constitute grounds for taking" such forced return measures.[21]

Notwithstanding this legal regulation, CRD deportations have been recruited for crime prevention efforts (Brandariz, 2021a). In the framework of the crimmigration turn-changing immigration control practices in various global north jurisdictions (Stumpf, 2006, 2015; van der Woude, van der Leun & Nijland, 2014), law enforcement agencies are giving increasing preference to criminalised noncitizens in organising their detention and deportation regimes (Stumpf, 2013; Wonders, 2017). CRD deportations have not been immune to this shift. There is much evidence showing that CRD deportations actually garnered traction when they began to be treated primarily as measures to coercively deal with EU national offenders. This is especially the case in the two countries that have spearheaded the expansion of CRD deportation practices, France and the UK (Bosworth, 2011; Kaufman, 2015; Turnbull & Hasselberg, 2017). However, both there and elsewhere across Europe, a significant part of the EU national deportees is made up of former prisoners having been in pre-trial detention or having completely or partly served their imprisonment sentences. This phenomenon has been confirmed in many European jurisdictions, such as Austria (see Heilemann, 2019), Belgium (Breuls, 2017; Service Public Fédéral Justice, 2020), the Czech Republic (source: European Migration Network Contact Point in the Czech Republic; ec.europa.eu/home-affairs/emn-annual-reports_en; accessed 17 January 2022), Finland (Könönen, 2020), Norway (Aas, 2014; Franko, 2020), Spain (Brandariz & Fernández-Bessa, 2017), Sweden (Barker, 2018), and the UK (Turnbull, 2017). Hence, thousands of EU national prisoners that FD transfer procedures fail to manage are being channelled into CRD deportations on a continental scale. In some countries, the gap between both law enforcement procedures is shockingly wide. In the UK, the proportion between CRD deportations enforced against former EU national prisoners and FD 909 transfers carried out as an issuing state was 57.8 to 1 from 2013 to 2018 (sources: UK Home Office; UK Ministry of Justice).

In other cases, these deportation practices contribute to circumvention of regular criminal justice procedures in a different way. In a conspicuous manifestation of the instrumentalism characterising immigration enforcement policies (Brandariz, 2021b; Sklansky, 2012),[22] CRD deportations are also being used to quickly get rid of alleged troublesome EU national groups instead of funnelling them into the time- and resource-consuming criminal justice adjudication processes (Brandariz, 2021b; see also Aliverti, 2020). Deportation practices in France are a telling example of this instrumentalism rationale (see also Maslowski, 2015; Vrăbiescu, 2021a, 2021b).

In sum, there are good reasons to think that academic conversations on transfers may have much to gain from closely scrutinising the consolidation of CRD deportations. That exploration may actually lead to consider FD transfers pitfalls under a new light. The shortcomings affecting FD 909, FD 947 and FD 829 procedures have been mostly considered as a legal issue, that is, as obstacles of legal nature requiring legal remedies. The CRD deportation impulse suggests that legal aspects are only part of the story, a may not even constitute the vital part (see also Hofmann & Nelen, 2020; Nelen & Hofmann, 2019). The conclusions to be drawn from that comparative perspective are explored in the last, concluding section.

3. Regulations, actors, logistics: the obstacles hampering the consolidation of transfer procedures

The scant utilisation of FD 909, and especially FD 947 and FD 829 procedures, has been a motive of concern for both institutions and academic communities. The various stakeholders engaging in a conversation on the obstacles preventing transfer procedures from being widespread have largely adopted legal viewpoints. This is unsurprising, since those transfers are sophisticated legal procedures mainly involving judicial actors. Therefore, the legal lens has led officials and scholars to put the spotlight on the shortcomings of EU law provisions and national regulations. This is the path followed, for example, by the 2019 European Commission's *Handbook on the transfer of sentenced persons*, which provides recommendations on how the corresponding legal requirements should be understood to facilitate transfers. This legal guidance task is also carried out by other bodies, crucially among them Europris (see www.europris.org/topics/framework-decision-909/; accessed 1 February 2022) and the European Judicial Network (hereinafter EJN; see www.ejn-crimjust.europa.eu/ejn/libcategories/EN/7/-1/0; accessed 3 February 2022). Moreover, academic voices have given particular relevance to legal obstacles and have proposed solutions focusing on legal reforms and the interpretation of legal provisions. These recommendations chiefly address procedural issues related to, for example, decentralised competence and the need for cooperation, the assessment of the potential transferee's opinion, the certificate, the translation, the description of the corresponding sentence, the evaluation of social rehabilitation needs, the role to be played by prison conditions in making a decision on transfer requests (see Marguery, 2018), and the coordination with the EAW (Durnescu, 2017; Klimek, 2017; Montaldo, Damian & Brandariz, 2020; Montero Pérez de Tudela et al., 2019; Nelen & Hofmann, 2019).

However, the apparently resilient nature of the pitfalls preventing transfers from being widely used seems to have led EU institutions to adopt a broader perspective on FD 909, 947 and 829 shortcomings. The 2019 Council of the EU's document outlining a way forward in the field of mutual recognition (Council of the EU, 2019b) is a good example of this wide viewpoint. This policy report assumes that legal factors may be playing a critical role in hindering the regular, unobstructed application of mutual recognition instruments. More precisely, in addressing the infrequent utilisation of FD 947 and FD 829 procedures, the Council highlights that "it is also important to establish whether the less frequent application of the two Framework Decisions might not simply be the consequence of insufficient harmonisation of substantial procedural provisions and of the differences in the transposition processes" (Council of the EU, 2019b, p. 16). In addition, the document gives significant weight to awareness obstacles and promotes an ambitious training agenda. In fact, the Council of the EU stresses that "it is important to establish whether the less frequent application of the two Framework Decisions (FD 2008/947/JHA and FD 2009/829/JHA) is due to the fact that practitioners are not aware of the legal possibilities they offer/do not have enough experience in their application" (Council of the EU, 2019b, p. 16). Certainly, awareness-raising and training strategies are widely mentioned. They have been recommended by many stakeholders examining the application of transfer procedures (see e.g. Council of the EU, 2019a; see also Durnescu, 2017; Fernández-Bessa, Ferraris & Damian, 2020; Montero Pérez de Tudela et al., 2019). However, those aspects fail to grasp why some mutual recognition instruments are widely consolidated while others are not. Concerning the comparison proposed in this chapter, training and awareness-raising issues cannot explain either why CRD deportations are thriving or FD transfers are facing apparently unsurmountable obstacles to be generally applied.

Consequently, there are good reasons to venture beyond these already beaten paths in addressing the topic under study. Specifically, "practical and operational aspects" (Council of the EU, 2019a, p. 6) need to be particularly scrutinised (see also Hofmann & Nelen, 2020; Nelen & Hofmann, 2019). Institutional actors seem to be moving in that direction. The aforementioned Council of the EU's document embraces an audit culture in emphasising the need to identify "gaps in the application of mutual recognition instruments and possible solutions to fill these gaps" (2019b, p. 5). That laudable perspective is also adopted by the FRA (2016), which strongly recommends collecting and analysing data on the non-application of transfer procedures. These pragmatic audit efforts may bring to the fore non-legal factors that negatively condition the utilisation of FD transfers. Some of these factors have been recurringly pointed out by the literature, be it grey literature or academic literature. Long processing times are one of these practical issues significantly challenging transfer procedures, especially in cases involving short custodial or non-custodial sentences (FRA, 2016; Nelen & Hofmann, 2019). Communication issues are also crucial, as has been recognised by the 2019 European Commission's *Handbook on the transfer of sentenced persons*. Indeed, the permanent communication between judicial authorities may greatly contribute to the smooth application of mutual recognition procedures (Montero Pérez de Tudela et al., 2019).

Moving beyond these critical aspects, the Council of the EU singles out the institutional framework as a key additional dimension to be seriously considered. Specifically, it stresses the need to enhance "the institutional framework which allows for a proper functioning of judicial cooperation in criminal matters at EU level" (Council of the EU, 2019b, p. 5). In this regard, the Council recommends heightening the involvement of Eurojust and the EJN, as well as their cooperation with COPEN, the Working Party on Judicial Cooperation on Criminal Matters. However, consolidating a continent-wide transfer system has already proven to be an extremely arduous task. Therefore, more actors should be brought to cooperate in this joint effort. In this regard, prison authorities are critical to foster the utilisation of FD 909 and FD 829 procedures (Durnescu, Montero & Ravagnani, 2017; Montaldo, Damian & Brandariz, 2020), no less than probation officials are pivotal to give a boost to FD 947 measures.

All these proposals should be taken into serious consideration to expand the scope of transfer procedures. Specifically, the institutional aspects the Council of the EU reports have recently referred to are particularly crucial. The experience of the very few countries in which 909 transfers are regularly utilised (i.e. Romania and the Netherlands) demonstrates the pivotal role to be played by political will and institutional resources in enabling judicial cooperation in this field (Leerkes & van Houte, 2020). Nonetheless, the comparative gaze examining CRD deportations also suggests exploring logistical aspects. In fact, in any subfield of the criminal justice system that has a cross-national, potentially global nature (Franko, 2017, 2020) logistical issues are of utmost importance (see Walters, 2018, 2022). The comparison with the 'successful' CRD deportations brings to the fore an additional dimension, that is, professional cultures and the character of the institutional actors involved in these EU-wide criminal justice procedures. In fact, the main structural difference between FD transfers and CRD deportations is that the former are essentially judicial procedures, whereas in the latter judicial players are largely absent.

Judicial ethnographies and publications exploring the professional cultures of judicial actors do not rank very high in criminology studies. In stark contrast to what happens with regard to, for example, policing, top criminology handbooks and textbooks largely overlook these topics or address them mainly from a legal perspective (see e.g. Liebling, Maruna & McAra, 2017; Newburn, 2017). Yet the judicial texture of FD transfer procedures is a critical issue to be much further scrutinised. The fieldwork carried out in the framework of the RePers and Trust and Action mutual learning activities back in 2018 and 2019 suggests that at least two specific points should be considered here: the judicial mindset and its professional ethos, and the structure of incentives promoting the involvement of judicial actors in supranational mutual recognition procedures.

Judges and magistrates, as well as public prosecutors and other judicial officials usually have a markedly corporative mindset, which makes the judiciary relatively reluctant to change and partly impervious to critique (Anitua, 2017; Ferrari, 2004). In fact, courts frequently operate as 'closed communities' (Hester & Eglin, 2017). This feature interacts with an additional trait which is of particular importance with respect to judicial cooperation measures. The increasing authority and force of transnational law is putting under strain national legal systems and criminal justice agencies, which essentially have a national character (see Cotterrell, 2017). Evidently, this strain is also having an impact on judicial actors. To be true, RePers and Trust and Action mutual learning activities showed that many judicial actors are willing and even eager to engage in this emerging EU-wide dimension of their criminal justice tasks. Exceptions aside, though, judicial actors are still closely tied to legal education, legal conceptions, and constitutions and statutory law of national nature. In fact, the extant literature has already highlighted that the diversity of legal cultures may actually obstruct the consolidation of transfer procedures (Conway, 2018; Fernández-Bessa, Ferraris & Damian, 2020). The already mentioned mutual learning activities laid bare the limited capacity of judicial participants to alter their national legal conceptions and to challenge the legal solutions consolidated in their jurisdictions.[23]

These professional ethos obstacles are further compounded by incentive issues and organisational impediments. Judicial authorities and court personnel use to be compelled by 'organisational imperatives' conditioning their activities. In fact, in carrying out their professional tasks, they constantly have to deal with organisational issues such as "the resources available, the time at hand, the working relationships that must be sustained between setting co-inhabitants, the division of labour, the flow of cases, etc." (Hester & Eglin, 2017, p. 178). In this regard, rank-and-file judges and prosecutors, which in many countries are involved in either issuing or executing transfer cases, are largely overwhelmed by demanding caseloads (Blay & González, 2020; Campesi, Pannarale & Pupolizio, 2017; Jurka, 2017). Understandably, they tend to be uneager to further expand their caseloads. For organisational reasons, judges are generally willing to engage in cross-national procedures that may assist in bringing cases to completion. That is the main reason why EAW procedures were consolidated and notably widespread in a short period of time. The European Investigation Order seems to be garnering increasing traction for these same reasons. In these cases, there are evident incentives for national judges to join mutual cooperation efforts. The scenario is markedly different when what is at stake has no connection to caseloads and investigative tasks but rather to relatively vague rehabilitation concerns and the harms the criminal legal system inflicts onto EU nationals sentenced and imprisoned abroad. In these cases, which encompass FD 909, FD 947 and especially FD 829 procedures, the incentives to engage in the frequently taxing cross-jurisdictional procedures are negligible (Neira Pena, 2020; see also Montero Pérez de Tudela et al., 2019).

In sum, both recent CRD deportation changes and the fieldwork conducted in the framework of the RePers and Trust and Action projects show that legal reforms are not the main issue to be considered to give a boost to transfer procedures. Both legal remedies and awareness-raising and training efforts are actually needed, but they alone cannot overcome the analysed obstacles. The measures to be taken relate not only to regulations but also to actors and logistics. With regard to the institutions and authorities involved in these procedures, the already mentioned FRA report poses a compelling question. In reminding that 'effective communication is essential for cooperation', the report openly wonders "Is the 'school English' of a German judge or prison official sufficient to communicate effectively with an Irishman about the alternatives to detention or the comparative elements of the sanctioning systems in Germany and Ireland?" (FRA, 2016, p. 47). That rhetorical question deeply resonates with the kind of cultural and legal-cultural barriers we encountered in carrying out the RePers and Trust and Action mutual learning activities.

The Italian criminologist Dario Melossi (2005, 2014) persuasively claims that sharing a common language – regardless of whether it is a mother tongue or not – is a first, decisive step in giving shape to a European public, to a continent-wide public sphere. The question posed by the FRA report some years ago may be understood in pragmatic terms, as referring to the practical hurdles hampering the communication between national authorities. However, it may also have a deeper meaning. Supranational legal procedures unavoidably need criminal justice practitioners with a supranational inclination who may be willing to foster the EU judicial cooperation agenda. That is a pivotal aspect to be targeted by EU institutions' strategies to promote the application of mutual recognition instruments.

Notes

1 This chapter is a deferred outcome of the projects 'Mutual Trust and Social Rehabilitation into Practice – RePers' and 'Trust and Social Rehabilitation in Action – Trust and Action', funded by the European Union Justice Programme 2014–2020 (www.eurehabilitation.unito.it). The content of this chapter represents the views of the authors only and is their sole responsibility. The European Commission does not accept any responsibility for use that may be made of the information it contains.

2 The Trust and Action project's plans to carry out mutual learning activities were severely disrupted by the emergence of the coronavirus pandemic. However, before that the RePers and Trust and Action projects led to the organisation of three inspiring mutual learning meetings gathering 30–40 officials, practitioners and scholars each. These meetings were held in Bucharest in October 2018, Madrid in March 2019 and Rome in July 2019. Mutual learning activities were subsequently moved online, dramatically eroding their usefulness for participant observation purposes.

3 EU national criminal justice agencies issued 6,894 EAWs in 2005 and 6,889 EAWs in 2006, whilst the number of warrants issued in 2011 was 9,784 (source: European Commission 2021).

4 This is an underestimation, because a small number of EU countries do not supply data on executed EAWs. Whether this execution rate is slightly or significantly misleading, it means that 6,015 EAWs were executed per year from 2015 to 2019.

5 See wp.unil.ch/space/space-i/annual-reports/ (accessed 7 January 2022).

6 Hurley (2021) informs that Ireland enforced only 1 transfer as an executing state and 14 transfers as an issuing state from 2016 to 2020. These data, though, bring all prisoner transfer programmes together. Therefore, FD 909 data are even lower.

7 Article 1(d) of the FD 909 describes 'executing state' as 'the Member State to which a judgement is forwarded for the purpose of its recognition and enforcement'.

8 Article 1(c) of FD 909 defines 'issuing state' as 'the Member State in which a judgement is delivered'.

9 This is actually a four-year estimation, because SPACE I did not publish 2016 data.

10 For the same reason mentioned in the previous endnote, this is a four-year estimation.

11 The German administration provided data on transfer and other rendition practices carried out in Germany in a parliamentary answer released in July 2018 (see dserver.bundestag.de/btd/19/035/1903596.pdf; accessed 10 January 2022). Although this official report recognises that no specific FD 909 data are available, the total number of cases is relatively low (217.7 cases per year when Germany is an issuing state and 93.9 cases per year when Germany is an executing state from 2010 to 2016) and decreased

over time. More precise data are available with regard to North Rhine-Westphalia. This pivotal German state averaged 68.5 outgoing transfers and 18.5 incoming transfers in 2016–2017 (Hofmann and Nelen 2020; Nelen and Hofmann 2019).

12 These averages are somewhat underestimated, because they do not count transfers between Scandinavian jurisdictions, which are regulated by a regional agreement rather than by FD 909.

13 The Netherlands averaged 154 FD 909 cases as an executing state from 2012 to 2017, although it is estimated that only 40–60 per cent of these transfers are finally enforced. The number of outgoing cases is significantly lower (30.8 cases per year from 2012 to 2017) (Nauta, van Aalst and Özgül 2018; see also Hofmann and Nelen 2020; Nelen and Hofmann 2019).

14 The UK is not taking part anymore in any of the three analysed instruments of mutual cooperation since January 2021.

15 These numbers are slightly underestimated, because SPACE I data did not include Belgian and Scottish data in 2018. Since then, the gap is even wider because SPACE I reports have not provided German data on EU national prisoners in recent years.

16 Nelen and Hofmann (2019; see also Hofmann and Nelen 2020) report that the German state of North Rhine-Westphalen received 19 FD 947 requests and issued only 1 FD 947 request from 2015 to mid-2018.

17 The number of outgoing FD 947 requests was above 100 cases in 2016 and 2017, but no data on actually enforced transfers are available. Regarding incoming requests, they were 17 in 2016 and 27 in 2017, but it is again unclear how many of these cases led to transfer enforcement (Nauta, van Aalst and Özgül 2018; see also Hofmann and Nelen 2020; Nelen and Hofmann 2019).

18 Official communications inform that 26 EU Member States had already transposed FD 947 and FD 829 provisions by mid-2021. Whether or not the remaining Member State, Malta, had also transposed these EU legislative acts was then unclear (Council of the EU 2021a, 2021b).

19 Evidently, this description of the impulse of deportation practices targeting EU nationals as a 'success story' is metaphorical. The severe harm caused by these border control practices to the individual rights, living conditions and life prospects of EU nationals prevent this phenomenon from being seriously considered as a 'success' in the field of law enforcement.

20 This is actually an underestimation because the Belgian Federal Immigration Office only provides data on the five EU national groups most affected by CRD deportations. On the impact of crime-based deportation orders on the increasing traction garnered by CRD deportations in Finland see Könönen 2020.

21 On this, see CJEU Case C-554/13 *Z. Zh. and I. O.* [2015] ECLI:EU:C:2015:377.

22 Instrumentalism considerations are deeply embedded in the impetus recently given to CRD deportations. National deportation regimes are particularly focused on enforcing removals to neighbouring countries. Two top deporting countries, such as Mexico and the United States, are evidence of this specialisation of deportation practices (Campos-Delgado 2021; Golash-Boza 2018; Gómez Cervantes and Menjívar 2018). This instrumental arrangement seems to be playing a part also in the case of both intra-EU deportations (Brandariz 2021a) and – at least in certain European countries – criminal justice transfers (Hofmann and Nelen 2020).

23 This willingness to defend the national legal order was particularly conspicuous in one of the mutual learning activities, when one of the judicial participants vividly advocated the decision of his national Supreme Court in issuing an EAW against a top politician, when that EAW request had been just overturned by a high court of another EU Member State.

Some government officials participating in these mutual learning activities, in turn, were particularly disinclined to question the arrangements adopted by their national administration in the field of FD transfer procedures.

References

Aas K F (2014) Bordered Penality: Precarious Membership and Abnormal Justice. *Punishment & Society* 16(5): 520–541.

Aebi M F and Tiago M (2018) *SPACE I – 2018 – Council of Europe Annual Penal Statistics: Prison Populations*. Strasbourg: Council of Europe.

Aliverti A (2020) Patrolling the 'Thin Blue Line' in a World in Motion: An Exploration of the Crime-Migration Nexus in UK Policing. *Theoretical Criminology* 24(1): 8–27.

Anitua G I (2017) *La justicia penal en cuestión: Aproximación genealógica al poder de juzgar*. Madrid: Iustel.

Barker V (2018) *Nordic Nationalism and Penal Power: Walling the Welfare State*. Abingdon: Routledge.

Blay Gil E and González Sánchez I (2020) *Los jueces penales: Una introducción al studio de la profesión*. Madrid: Iustel.

Bosworth M (2011) Deportation, Detention and Foreign-National Prisoners in England and Wales. *Citizenship Studies* 15(5): 583–595.

Brandariz J A (2021a) The Removal of EU Nationals: An Unaccounted Dimension of the European Deportation Apparatus. *Central and Eastern European Migration Review* 10(1): 13–33.

Brandariz J A (2021b) Criminalization or Instrumentalism? New Trends in the Field of Border Criminology. *Theoretical Criminology* 26. https://doi.org/10.1177/13624806211009158.

Brandariz J A and Fernández-Bessa C (2017) The Managerial Turn: The Transformation of Spanish Migration Control Policies since the Onset of the Economic Crisis. *The Howard Journal of Crime and Justice* 56(2): 198–219.

Breuls L (2017) Portraying Forced Removal as a Means for Crime Control. On Immigration Policy Communication in Belgium. *Lo Squaderno* 44: 39–42.

Campesi G, Pannarale L and Pupolizio I (2017) *Sociologia del diritto*. Milano: Le Monnier.

Campos-Delgado A E (2021) Bordering Trough Exemption: Extracontinental Migration Flows in Mexico. *International Journal for Crime, Justice and Social Democracy* 10(3): 30–40.

Conway G (2018) Prospects and Problems for European Legal Cooperation Concerning Prisoners. *European Journal of Probation* 10(2): 136–159.

Cotterrell R (2017) *Sociological Jurisprudence: Juristic Thought and Social Inquiry*. London: Routledge.

Council of the EU (2019a) *9th Round of Mutual Evaluations – Scope of the Evaluation and Contributions to the Questionnaire*. 13 February 2019. 6333/19. Retrieved from data.consilium.europa.eu/doc/document/ST-6333–2019-INIT/en/pdf (accessed 7 January 2022).

Council of the EU (2019b) *The Way Forward in the Field of Mutual Recognition in Criminal Matters – Policy Debate*. 27 May 2019. 9728/19. Retrieved from data.consilium.europa.eu/doc/document/ST-9728–2019-INIT/en/pdf (accessed 7 January 2022).

Council of the EU (2021a) *Implementation of Council Framework Decision 2008/947/JHA of 27 November 2008 on the Application of the Principle of Mutual Recognition to Judgments and Probation Decisions with a View to the Supervision of Probation Measures and Alternative Sanctions*. 17 June 2021. 9907/21. Retrieved from db.eurocrim.org/db/en/doc/3631.pdf (accessed 12 January 2021).

Council of the EU (2021b) *Implementation of Council Framework Decision 2009/829/JHA of 23 October 2009 on the Application, between Member States of the European Union, of the Principle of Mutual Recognition to Decisions on Supervision Measures as an Alternative to Provisional Detention*. 17 June 2021. 9909/21. Retrieved from db.eurocrim.org/db/en/doc/3632.pdf (accessed 12 January 2021).

Durnescu I (2017) Framework Decisions 2008/947 and 2009/829: State of Play and Challenges. *Era Forum* 18: 355–363.

Durnescu I, Montero Perez de Tudela E and Ravagnani L (2017) Prisoner Transfer and the Importance of the 'Release Effect.' *Criminology & Criminal Justice* 17(4): 450–467.

Eremenko T, El Qadim N and Steichen E (2017) Southern Europeans in France: Invisible Migrants? In: Lafleur J M and Stanek M (eds) *South-North Migration of EU Citizens in Times of Crisis*. New York: Springer, pp. 123–148.

European Commission (2014) *Report from the Commission to the European Parliament and the Council on the Implementation by the Member States of the Framework Decisions 2008/909/JHA, 2008/947/JHA and 2009/829/JHA on the Mutual Recognition of Judicial Decisions on Custodial Sentences or Measures Involving Deprivation of Liberty, on Probation Decisions and Alternative Sanctions and on Supervision Measures as an Alternative to Provisional Detention*. 5 February 2014. COM(2014) 57 final. Retrieved from eur-lex.europa.eu/legal-content/EN/TXT/PDF/?uri=CELEX:52014DC0057&from=EN (accessed 7 January 2022).

European Commission (2021) *Commission Staff Working Document. Statistics on the Practical Operation of the European Arrest Warrant – 2019*. 6 August 2021. SWD(2021) 227 final. Retrieved from ec.europa.eu/info/sites/default/files/law/search_law/documents/eaw_statistics_2019_swd_2021_227_final_08_2021_en.pdf (accessed 7 January 2022).

Fernández-Bessa C, Ferraris V and Damian A (2020) Implementation Strategies: Distinctive Features, Advances and Shortcomings in the Application of Framework Decision 2008/909/JHA in Italy, Romania and Spain. In: Montaldo S (ed.) *The Transfer of Prisoners in the European Union: Challenges and Prospects in the Implementation of Framework Decision 2008/909/JHA*. Den Haag: Eleven/Giappichelli, pp. 121–140.

Ferraris V (2004) *Diritto e società: Elementi di sociologia del diritto*. Roma-Bari: Laterza.

Ferraris V (2019) Il trasferimento dei detenuti comunitari: l'ennesimo tentativo fallito di riduzione del sovraffollamento. *Antigone: XV rapporto sulle condizioni di detenzione*. Retrieved from www.antigone.it/quindicesimo-rapporto-sulle-condizioni-di-detenzione/il-trasferimento-dei-detenuti-comunitari/ (accessed 10 January 2021).

FRA (2016) *Criminal Detention and Alternatives: Fundamental Rights Aspects in EU Cross-Border Transfers*. Wien: FRA. Retrieved from fra.europa.eu/sites/default/files/fra_uploads/fra-2016-criminal-detention-and-alternatives_en.pdf (accessed 6 January 2022).

Franko K (2017) Criminology, Punishment, and the State in a Globalized Society. In: Liebling A, Maruna S and McAra L (eds) *Oxford Handbook of Criminology*. Oxford: Oxford University Press, pp. 353–372.

Franko K (2020) *The Crimmigrant Other: Migration and Penal Power*. Abingdon: Routledge.

Golash-Boza T (2018) Raced and Gendered Logics of Immigration Law Enforcement in the United States. In: Bosworth M, Parmar A and Vázquez Y (eds) *Race, Criminal Justice and Migration Control: Enforcing the Boundaries of Belonging*. Oxford: Oxford University Press, pp. 229–244.

Gómez Cervantes A and Menjívar C (2018) Mass Deportation, Forced Removal, Immigrant Threat, and Disposable Labor in a Global Context. In: Martínez Jr. R, Hollis M E and Stowell J I (eds) *The Handbook of Race, Ethnicity, Crime, and Justice*. Hoboken, NJ: Willey Blackwell, pp. 527–546.

Guild E, Peers S and Tomkin J (2014) *The EU Citizenship Directive: A Commentary*. Oxford: Oxford University Press.

Heilemann S (2019) *Austria. Annual Policy Report 2018*. Wien: International Organization for Migration.

Hester S and Eglin P (2017) *A Sociology of Crime*. 2nd edn. New York: Routledge.

Hofmann R and Nelen H (2020) Cross-border Cooperation in the Execution of Sentences between the Netherlands, Germany and Belgium: An Empirical and Comparative Legal Study on the Implementation of EU Framework Decisions 2008/909/JHA and 2008/947/JHA. *Crime Law and Social Change* 74(4): 381–404.

Hurley D (2021) Criminal Justice (Mutual Recognition of Custodial Sentences) Bill No. 103 of 2021. *Oireachtas Library & Research Service: Bill Digest*. Retrieved from data.oireachtas.ie/ie/oireachtas/libraryResearch/2021/2021–09–22_bill-digest-criminal-law-mutual-recognition-of-custodial-sentences-bill-2021_en.pdf (accessed 10 January 2022).

Jurka R (2017) European Supervision Order – Is It the Ballast for Law Enforcement or the Way Out of the Deadlock? *Journal of Eastern European Criminal Law* 1: 31–45.

Kaufman E (2015) *Punish and Expel: Border Control, Nationalism, and the New Purpose of the Prison*. Oxford: Oxford University Press.

Klimek L (2017) *Mutual Recognition of Judicial Decisions in European Criminal Law*. New York: Springer.

Könönen J (2020) Legal Geographies of Irregular Migration: An Outlook on Immigration Detention. *Population, Space and Place* 26(5): 1–11.

Kriminalvården (2018) *Årsredovisning 2017*. Norrköping: Kriminalvården. Retrieved from www.kriminalvarden.se/globalassets/publikationer/ekonomi/kriminalvardens-arsredovisning-2017.pdf (accessed 11 January 2022).

Kriminalvården (2021) *Årsredovisning 2020*. Norrköping: Kriminalvården. Retrieved from www.kriminalvarden.se/globalassets/publikationer/ekonomi/kriminalvardens-arsredovisning-2020.pdf (accessed 11 January 2022).

Lafleur J M and Mescoli E (2018) Creating Undocumented EU Migrants through Welfare: A Conceptualization of Undeserving and Precarious Citizenship. *Sociology* 52(3): 480–496.

Leerkes A and van Houte M (2020) Beyond the Deportation Regime: Differential State Interests and Capacities in Dealing with (Non-)Deportability in Europe. *Citizenship Studies* 24(3): 319–338.

Liebling A, Maruna S and McAra L (eds) (2017) *The Oxford Handbook of Criminology*. 6th edn. Oxford: Oxford University Press.

Marguery T (2018) Towards the End of Mutual Trust? Prison Conditions in the Context of the European Arrest Warrant and the Transfer of Prisoners Framework Decisions. *Maastricht Journal of European and Comparative Law* 25(6): 704–717.

Martufi A (2018) Assessing the Resilience of 'Social Rehabilitation' as a Rationale for Transfer: A Commentary on the Aims of Framework Decision 2008/909/JHA. *New Journal of European Criminal Law* 9(1): 43–61.

Maslowski S (2015) The Expulsion of European Union Citizens from the Host Member State: Legal Grounds and Practice. *Central and Eastern European Migration Review* 4(2): 61–85.

Melossi D (2005) Security, Social Control, Democracy and Migration within the 'Constitution' of the EU. *European Law Journal* 11: 5–21.

Melossi D (2014) The Borders of the European Union and the Processes of Criminalization of Migrants. In: Body-Gendrot S, Hough M, Kerezsi K, Lévy R and Snacken S (eds) *The Routledge Handbook of European Criminology*. London: Routledge, pp. 513–550.

Montaldo S (2019) Offenders' Rehabilitation and the Cross-border Transfer of Prisoners and Persons Subject to Probation Measures and Alternative Sanctions: A Stress Test for EU Judicial Cooperation in Criminal Matters. *Revista Brasileira de Direito Processual Penal* 5(2): 925–960.

Montaldo S (2020a) Framework Decision 2008/909/JHA and Fundamental Rights Concerns: In Search of Appropriate Remedies. In: Montaldo S (ed.) *The Transfer of Prisoners in the European Union: Challenges and Prospects in the Implementation of Framework Decision 2008/909/JHA*. Den Haag: Eleven/Giappichelli, pp. 37–60.

Montaldo S (ed.) (2020b) *The Transfer of Prisoners in the European Union: Challenges and Prospects in the Implementation of Framework Decision 2008/909/JHA*. Den Haag: Eleven/Giappichelli.

Montaldo S, Damian A and Brandariz J A (2020) The Road Ahead: Proposals for Improving the Implementation of Framework Decision 2008/909/JHA. In: Montaldo S (ed.) *The Transfer of Prisoners in the European Union: Challenges and Prospects in the Implementation of Framework Decision 2008/909/JHA*. Den Haag: Eleven/Giappichelli, pp. 141–162.

Montero Pérez de Tudela E, García Ruiz C R, Arenas García L, Martín Ríos B and Fernández-Pacheco Alises G (2019) *Literature Review on the Council Framework Decision 2008/947/JHA of 27 November 2008 and the Council Framework Decision 2009/829/JHA of 23 October 2009*. Retrieved from probationobservatory.eu/wp-content/uploads/2019/06/PONT-Literature-review-final-PDF-1.pdf (accessed 3 February 2022).

Nauta O, van Aalst M and Özgül P (2018) *RAPPORT — Evaluatie Wet wederzijdse erkenning en tenuitvoerlegging vrijheidsbenemende en voorwaardelijke sancties (Wets)*. Amsterdam: WODC. Retrieved from repository.wodc.nl/bitstream/handle/20.500.12832/2361/2847_Volledige_Tekst_tcm28–332074.pdf?sequence=2&isAllowed=y (accessed 3 February 2022).

Neira Pena A (2020) The Reasons behind the Failure of the European Supervision Order: The Defeat of Liberty Versus Security. *European Papers* 5(3): 1493–1509.

Nelen H and Hofmann R (2019) *Cross-Border Cooperation in Sentencing: A Process Evaluation of the Execution of Sentences in the Netherlands, Belgium, and Germany*. Retrieved from cris.maastrichtuniversity.nl/ws/portalfiles/portal/40684457/CrossBes_Proces_evaluation_July_2019.pdf (accessed 3 February 2022).

Newburn T (2017) *Criminology*. 3rd edn. London: Routledge.

Service Public Fédéral Justice (2017) *Justice en chiffres 2011–2016*. Bruxelles: Service Public Fédéral Justice. Retrieved from justitie.belgium.be/sites/default/files/jic_fr-2016.pdf (accessed 10 January 2022).

Service Public Fédéral Justice (2020) *Justice en chiffres 2015–2019*. Bruxelles: Service Public Fédéral Justice. Retrieved from justitie.belgium.be/sites/default/files/jic-fr-2015–2019.pdf (accessed 10 January 2022).

Sklansky D A (2012) Crime, Immigration, and Ad Hoc Instrumentalism. *New Criminal Law Review* 15(2): 157–223.

Stumpf J (2006) The Crimmigration Crisis: Immigrants, Crime, and Sovereign Power. *American University Law Review* 56(2): 367–419.

Stumpf J (2013) The Process Is the Punishment in Crimmigration Law. In: Aas K F and Bosworth M (eds) *The Borders of Punishment: Migration, Citizenship, and Social Exclusion*. Oxford: Oxford University Press, pp. 58–75.

Stumpf J (2015) Crimmigration: Encountering the Leviathan. In: Pickering S and Ham J (eds) *The Routledge Handbook on Crime and International Migration*. London: Routledge, pp. 237–250.

Turnbull S (2017) Immigration Detention and the Racialized Governance of Illegality in the United Kingdom. *Social Justice* 44(1): 142–164.

Turnbull S and Hasselberg I (2017) From Prison to Detention: The Carceral Trajectories of Foreign-National Prisoners in the United Kingdom. *Punishment & Society* 19(2): 135–154.

van der Woude M, van der Leun J and Nijland J A (2014) Crimmigration in the Netherlands. *Law and Social Inquiry* 39(3): 560–579.

Vrăbiescu I (2021a) *Deporting Europeans: The Racialized Mobility of Romanians in France*. London: Lexington.

Vrăbiescu I (2021b) Devised to Punish: Policing, Detaining and Deporting Romanians from France. *European Journal of Criminology* 18(4): 585–602.

Walters W (2018) Aviation as Deportation Infrastructure: Airports, Planes, and Expulsion. *Journal of Ethnic and Migration Studies* 44(16): 2796–2817.

Walters W (2022) *Viapolitics: Borders, Migration, and the Power of Locomotion*. Durham, NC: Duke University Press.

Wonders N A (2017) Sitting on the Fence – Spain's Delicate Balance: Bordering, Multiscalar Challenges, and Crimmigration. *European Journal of Criminology* 14(1): 7–26.

2 Enhancing social rehabilitation or finding a back door to reduce prison overcrowding?

The failed implementation of FD 909 in Italy

Valeria Ferraris

Introduction: objectives and methodology[1]

This chapter aims to provide a contribution to the limited literature on the implementation within the EU Member States of Council Framework Decision 2008/909/JHA of 27 November 2008 on the application of the principle of mutual recognition to judgements in criminal matters imposing custodial sentences or measures involving deprivation of liberty for the purpose of their enforcement in the European Union (hereafter FD 909). It focuses on the overall functioning of this criminal cooperation mechanism within Italy and on the role of the various parties involved in so-called active procedures, namely cases where a sentenced person is transferred from Italy to another country. The analysis of FD 909 is particularly interesting with regard to Italy as it is one of the few cases where Italy transposed an EU legislative act well ahead of the deadline, in this case 5 December 2011. This unusual diligence on the part of the Italian legislator in transposing the Decision is evident when considering that the other two Framework Decisions on the mutual recognition of decisions relating to the transfer of sentenced persons – Council Framework Decision 2008/947/JHA of 27 November 2008 on the transfer of probationers and individuals sentenced to non-custodial penalties, and Council Framework Decision 2009/829/JHA of 23 October 2009 on the European supervision order and alternatives to provisional detention – were transposed very late in 2016, five and four years after the deadline.[2]

The Italian legislator clearly deviated from the original scope of FD 909. As clarified later in the chapter, Italian secondary legislation and its implementation demonstrate an attempt to adapt the EU act to respond to other national priorities, unrelated to the objectives underpinning the EU legislation. In particular, the Italian legislator identified in FD 909 an instrument to reduce prison overcrowding. Overcrowding is an endemic problem of Italian prisons (Aebi et al., 2019, p. 180) that was put under the maximum spotlight when in 2013 the European Court of Human Rights (ECtHR) in the so-called Torreggiani case[3] condemned Italy for inhuman treatment and overcrowding in prison facilities and demanded that Italy reduces its prison population in order to comply with its human rights obligations.

The decision was of paramount importance because the applicants alleged the violation of article 3 of the European Convention on Human Rights (ECHR),

DOI: 10.4324/9781003254584-3

freedom from torture and inhuman or degrading treatment or punishment, due to overcrowding and the prison conditions (lack of hot water, inadequate lighting and ventilation) and the Strasbourg judges recognised that overcrowding was not a problem limited to the applicants but a systemic and structural problem leading to several hundred of applications pending before the court regarding the compatibility of the detention conditions with ECHR requirements. Recognising the problem as structural, the Court gave Italy one year to reduce prison overcrowding and improve detention conditions, underlining that the recourse to detention should be reduced and that in cases where detainees suffered these conditions, they should be compensated. In response, the Italian government adopted a series of legislative remedies to reduce the entry flows to prisons and increased the possibilities for early release, to improve the living condition by implementing an open prison regime and renovating facilities, and to introduce a compensatory remedy for the detainees who had been subjected to detention conditions contrary to their dignity.

The transfer of EU prisoners – in the mind of the Italian legislator – could have contributed to the post-Torreggiani goal because, even though EU prisoners constitute between 5 and 7 per cent of the prison population in Italy (see Table 2.2), about 70 per cent of them belong to one single nationality, Romanian. Therefore, the Italian legislator identified Romanian detainees as the target of FD 909 procedure hoping it could be feasible to transfer a significant number of them, assuming, as explained later, that most of these detainees fell into the scope of the Framework Decision. Despite this purpose being pursued by the Italian authorities, the result in terms of the number of transferred prisoners was actually very poor. Initially, the Italian authorities acted without consideration of the personal situation of the detainees, who were deemed to be transferable merely due to their nationality. It had also become clear that the judicial authorities who, at the local level, had the duty to activate the FD 909 procedure, had very little dedicated time to deal with such cases, leading to mistakes which significantly hampered the process. Finally, the marginalisation of the detainees in the procedure and the lack of legal assistance did not allow for a successful transfer even in cases where the transfer corresponded to the will of the prisoner in question.

The study on which this chapter is based consisted of a classic socio-legal study aimed at analysing the implementation of a specific regulation. Therefore, the initial phase of the work involved obtaining and analysing the law and the secondary legislation approved by the Italian legislator to implement the FD 909. Thereafter, thanks to the authorisation granted by the Ministry of Justice, the study analysed 362 mutual recognition procedures opened under FD 909 in 2016 and 2017; 289 files were analysed for 2016 and 73 for 2017. The 2016 files concerned 20 executing States,[4] while 2017 files involved ten Member States.[5]

The procedures to be analysed were randomly chosen. I had access to the international cooperation office of the Ministry of Justice and could directly read the documents of the chosen procedures. This direct access also meant that I was able to observe the daily routine of this office.[6] For each procedure, the following information was collected: the judicial authority involved, the executing State, the nationality of the detainee, the opinion of the detainee, the crime committed, the exchange between Italy and the executing State; and the result of the procedure. This data collection allowed to draw some conclusions on the meaning given to social rehabilitation in the letter of the law and in the daily practice, the strategies adopted by the executing States, the role and expertise of the Italian judicial authorities, the role of the detainees and their lawyers, the role played by the judicial deportation measures in the transfer procedure; and the outcome of the transfer procedure.

Alongside the analysis of case files, statistical data were requested on the status changes of the files (openings, pending cases, type of outcome), classified by the Member State involved and the acting prosecutor. The fieldwork had been carried out in 2018 but many files, despite the considerable length of time that had passed, were still open, and thus still subject to potential future developments.

1. Framework decision 2008/909/JHA on the transfer of prisoners and Italian transposition

The Framework Decision on the transfer of prisoners, approved after a lengthy negotiation and just before the entry into force of the Lisbon Treaty in December 2009, replaced – for European citizens – the 1983 Council of Europe Convention on the transfer of sentenced persons. Despite 66 ratifications, many from non-Member States of the Council of Europe, and some – unsuccessful – attempts at modification of the conditions for transfers in 1997, the Convention had received little attention across the EU and its limited application had proven to be unsatisfactory, mainly because of its lengthy and cumbersome procedures (see on these difficulties, European Commission, 2004; Froment, 2002, pp. 132–133). The Framework Decision sought to overcome the application difficulties of the 1983 Convention, envisaging a more streamlined procedure, to be concluded in a defined timescale and characterised, in general, by greater automatism.

In a nutshell, the FD 909 aims at responding to the issue of the increased number of EU citizens sentenced and detained in a Member State different from the one of origin by providing a smooth and fast procedure of mutual recognition that should allow the detainees to be transferred to their own country, provided that this transfer contributes to their social rehabilitation (Montaldo, 2018). What social rehabilitation means is not defined by the FD 909, which just mandates Member States to take into account "such elements as, for example, the person's attachment to the executing State, whether he or she considers it the place of family, linguistic, cultural, social or economic and other links to the executing State". (FD 909/2008/JHA Preamble 9; see also Oancea and Ene in this volume). In international transfer conventions, rehabilitation assumes the meaning of reintegration, as re-entry into society (De Wree, Vander Beken & Vermeulen, 2009). It is also assumed, as specified by the European Commission's *Handbook on the transfer of sentenced persons and custodial sentences in the European Union* issued in November 2019 (hereinafter Handbook 2019),[7] that social rehabilitation prospects increase in a community where the detainees can communicate with others in common language and where they can count on a network of support composed of relatives and friends.

However, since the approval of FD 909 (De Wree, Vander Beken & Vermeulen, 2009; Mitsilegas, 2009; Vermeulen et al., 2011), the centrality of the social rehabilitation has been questioned, given that the procedure adopted marginalised the opinion of the detainees and is driven by efficiency goals. The procedure is characterised by speed and simplification, particularly when compared to the one regulated by the Council of Europe provisions. The State which sentenced the person to be transferred sends the judgement,[8] together with a standard form (known as certificate) summarising the judgement, the opinion of the detainee, the reasons that justify the transfer and other information relevant to the case. The consent of the detainee to the transfer is not required in the majority of cases; specifically, consent is not required in cases where the transfer takes place to the State of the person's nationality or to the State in which they live, to which they would be deported at the end of the sentence or from which they fled or returned (Article 6 FD 909). These three grounds cover almost all the situations that involve a detainee that could be transferred to another Member State. The only case of some statistical relevance in which the consent of the detainee is required concerns the case of a sentenced EU national who lives in another Member State different from the one of their nationality (e.g. a Romanian citizen convicted in Italy who lives in Belgium). The certificate contains a section where the person to be transferred can express their opinion, but the possibilities of objecting to the transfer are very limited. However, a positive opinion of the detainee could be a way to smooth the transfer and avoid obstacles.

The application of the mutual recognition principle means that, once the procedure has been initiated by the issuing State by sending the necessary documentation, the competent authority of the executing State must recognise and enforce the decision. Unlike under the Council of Europe Convention mentioned earlier, the executing State is virtually obliged to recognise the decision. Indeed, the Framework Decision prescribes the grounds for non-recognition by the executing State (Article 9 FD 909) which are defined cases, almost all of technical nature, linked to procedural defects or the operation of the *ne bis in idem* principle, leaving no room for discretion or reasons of opportunity. The aim of the EU legislator to encourage recognition to the greatest possible extent also appears clear from the broad room left for partial recognition and execution of the sentence to avoid the fully fledged refusal by the judicial authorities of the executing state (Article 10 FD 909).

1.1 Italian transposition law

The FD 909 was transposed in Italy with the Legislative Decree no. 161 of 7 September 2010 adopted in conformity with the Delegation Law no. 88 of 7 July 2009 (2008 Community law). The Italian law follows the Framework Decision closely, without any significant additions.

The competent authorities are the Ministry of Justice and the judicial authority. For the recognition abroad of Italian sentences, the Ministry sends to the foreign authority the judgement and the certificate previously received from the local judicial authorities (specifically, the public prosecutor) and then deals with the official correspondence and carries out the exchange activities with the authorities of the other Member State. The transfer can occur for any crime punishable with a sentence of at least three years of imprisonment (article 5, par. 2 Legislative Decree 161/2010), a broader provision than that of the FD 909. The Italian legislator thus extends the possibilities of prisoner transfers to another European country. Conversely, for so-called passive procedures, the crimes for which the transfer from other countries to Italy is permitted are exclusively those listed in the FD 909.

The Italian law also establishes that the residual sentence should not be less than six months, there must be no grounds for suspension of its execution, the transfer must facilitate the social rehabilitation of the sentenced person, and the individual must be located either in Italy or in the territory of the State of execution (article 5, par. 1 and 2 Legislative Decree 161/2010). In accordance with Article 4 of FD 909, Article 5(3) of Legislative Decree 161/2010 identifies the State to which the transfer may take place, namely the Member State: (1) in which the sentenced person lives and of which he/she is a citizen, (2) to which the sentenced person must be removed, and (3) to which the sentenced person has consented to be transferred. The rules on the opinion of the detainee follow the provisions of FD 909. In line with FD 909, the authority proceeds with the transfer on its own initiative as well as at the request of the sentenced person or the executing State and subject to consulting the executing State in order to acquire the necessary information (Article 6 Legislative Decree 161/2010).

2. Italian secondary legislation: the desperate search for a solution to prison overcrowding

As highlighted earlier, Italy transposed the FD 909 on time and almost verbatim, except for some limited additions. However, when focusing the analysis on the Italian secondary legislation, the picture becomes much more intriguing. Many circulars have been issued, revealing a strongly proactive approach to transfer procedures by several Departments of the Italian Ministry of Justice. To guarantee the functioning of this cooperation mechanism, the government promoted three main actions: (1) preliminary screening activities of detainees who may be candidates for transfer, (2) repeated reminders sent to public prosecutors regarding the priority that should be given to transfer procedures, and (3) strengthening the bilateral cooperation with Romania, being the Member State from which most EU prisoners in Italy originate.

The first circular issued by the General Affairs Department dated 2 May 2012 (Ministero della Giustizia, 2012) recalls the most significant points of the then-new regulation, highlighting the changes compared to the Council of Europe Convention and, in particular, the fact that recognition is no longer dependent on the detention status of the sentenced person and the need for consent in the majority of cases. Social rehabilitation is not cited as a guiding principle. Two circulars issued in 2014 – namely, the circular of the Department of Prison Administration of 18 April 2014 (Ministero della Giustizia, 2014a) and that of the Department for Justice Affairs of the Ministry of Justice of 22 April 2014 (Ministero della Giustizia, 2014b) – clearly reveal the intention of the Ministry of Justice to foster quick transfers. The first circular, which is addressed to public prosecutors, underlines that "prisoner transfer procedures to their country of origin is a **priority**".[9] Furthermore, the Directors of Italian prisons are required to cooperate with public prosecutors, immediately sending the list of prisoners that are supposed to meet the transfer requirements, a copy of the sentence if available and an individual fiche that contains information on the legal status of the detainee and on their working and family situation. What is worth to underline here is the efficient approach (as we will see, not necessarily effective) of the prison administration, which chose to implement a screening of prisoners in order to assist public prosecutors in preparing their requests.

Shortly thereafter, on 28 April 2014, the Department for Justice Affairs of the Ministry of Justice sent to public prosecutors its circular, which – as well as reiterating the key points of the Framework Decision and the transposing legislative decree – contains an incipit which reads (at page 1):

> In the context of the implementation by the Italian State of the action plan following the *Torreggiani v. Italy* judgment of 8 January 2013 of the Strasbourg Court, a meeting was held last 16 April at this Ministry with a view to encouraging greater use by the Italian judicial authorities of the judicial cooperation mechanism introduced by Framework Decision 909/2008, in order to achieve, in respect of the re-education function of the penalty, a distribution across the European Union of the foreign population currently present in Italian prisons.

The transfer of EU prisoners was thus positioned in the context of measures to reduce overcrowding and as part of a solution to the issues raised by the European Court of Human Rights in relation to the inhuman and degrading treatment caused by Italian prison conditions. Another interesting aspect of the Circular is its reference to the indicators developed by case law to assess the absence of "effective and stable bonds of the prisoner in Italy" (p. 4) in order to confirm that social rehabilitation prospects are greater in another Member State. A crucial criterion is identified, in particular, as the "inadequate comprehension or use of the Italian language" (p. 4).

On April 2015 a new circular from the Prison Administration (Ministero della Giustizia, 2015) addressed to the directors of prisons explained once again the rules for the identification of potential candidates for FD 909 transfer. The circular stated that the prison administration had already drafted a list of 1,044 detainees falling into the scope of the application of FD 909 and had forwarded it to the judicial authorities. Therefore, the Directors were invited to send to the judicial authorities all the available and updated information on these detainees. Furthermore, for the first time, it mentioned "the intensification and strengthening of collaboration with the Romanian authorities" and "the need for our country to incentivise that transfer tool, given the high number of Romanian prisoners confined in Italian prisons and the consequent possibility of transferring a large part of such prisoners back to their country of origin" (p. 2).

In September 2016 the Department for Justice Affairs of the Ministry of Justice issued a circular about the relationship with Romanian authorities that identified a long list of problems in implementing the procedure, giving indications to the judicial authorities on how to proceed to overcome these difficulties (Ministero della Giustizia, 2016a). This circular once again repeated that the transfer of sentenced persons was one of the priorities of the Ministry's international policies, "relying on the coherence of this international cooperation tool with the re-education purposes of the punishment and its positive repercussions in further reducing prison overcrowding" (p. 2). Subsequently, it recalled the initiatives taken to encourage the use of this procedure, acknowledging the preliminary screening carried out by the Prison Administration, the initiatives aimed at raising awareness within Public Prosecutors' offices and finally the Memorandum of Understanding signed on 29 April 2015 by the Italian and Romanian authorities to overcome the procedural obstacles for a smooth cooperation.

Besides underlining some mistakes committed by the judicial authorities in the process of certification and the lack of coordination with the European Arrest Warrant (see Montaldo in this volume; Rosanò, 2020), the Ministry of Justice encouraged public prosecutors to be more proactive in promoting transfer procedures. Moreover, it identified the deportation order imposed by the judge in the sentence as a factor that had positively influenced the transfer procedure. Italian law has several types of deportation orders, including one that can be decided by the judge when the offenders are responsible for serious crimes[10] and are recognised as socially dangerous (the so-called deportation as a security measure).[11]

Reading between the lines, this latter circular animated judges to use the judicial deportation order as a security measure more frequently (ex art. 15 Italian Immigration Law), because it made the FD 909 transfer smoother and faster. From a rule of law point of view, the suggestion is awkward when one considers that it came from the government to directly affect the judicial authorities, raising doubts on the appropriateness of this suggestion from the point of the separation of powers principle. In practice, the role of the deportation order in increasing the effectiveness of the transfer procedures is confirmed by the analysis carried out. All detainees with a judicial deportation order were successfully transferred in a relatively short time (between 1 year and 18 months from the forwarding of the judgement by the Italian authorities to the approval of the transfer).

3. Data on transfer

Having briefly examined the content of both the Framework Decision and the Italian legislation, it is worth analysing, based upon the available data, the number of transfers from Italy to other Member States. The available data (Table 2.1) indicates that, from 2014, the number of files opened did not increase significantly across time; by contrast, the percentage of procedures pending at the end of the year grew continuously. In fact, there were 101 closed files (including successful transfers and archived procedures) and 397 pending files in 2014; 121 closed files and 594 pending files in 2015; with 194 closed files and 793 pending files in 2016;

Table 2.1 Data on FD 909 procedures (open cases and results)

		2014	2015	2016	2017	2018
Detainees in Italian prisons**		53,623	52,164	54,653	57,608	59,655
Non-Italian detainees**		17,462	1,7340	18,621	19,745	20,255
EU detainees		3,779	3,672	3,534	3,374	3,317
Romanian detainees		2,835	2,821	2,720	2,588	2,549
Files pending at the start of the period		n.d.	397	594	793	1,008*
Files opened in the period		498	318	393	324	150*
of which	Romania	424	217	243	216	109*
	Other Member States	74	101	150	108	41*
Authorisation to transfer		48	121	121	107	49*
Archived due to release or negative decision of the foreign State		53	n.d.	73	2	2*
Files pending at the end of the period		397	594	793	1,008	n.d.*

Notes: *data relating to the first six months
** data at 31 December of the year
Source: Our analysis of data from the Ministry of Justice, General Affairs Department Office II

and 109 closed files and 1,008 pending files in 2017. The number of authorisations to transfer was rather stable, thus leading to a situation where the failure to close a high number of cases positively necessarily led to an increase in the number of pending files.

At first sight, the significant number of pending cases could suggest that there was still room for successful transfers. The analysis of the documentation instead revealed that many cases were abandoned due to the absence of a response from the executing Member State and the inaction of the public prosecutor, who, after having sent the certificate, shelved the case. Therefore, the executing Member State did not receive any request to answer promptly or, even worse, when it answered and underlined mistakes in the certificate, the prosecutor replied after a considerable amount of time or did not answer at all. Consequently, these files were de facto closed. The fieldwork also identified some cases where the detention period ended, or the detainees had access to alternatives to imprisonment. Although the analysis did not provide a precise quantification of such cases, the described situation does not appear to be episodic. Among the 289 files analysed in 2016, 103 cases could not have resulted in the enforcement of a transfer because:

- The persons were released (44 cases) or died (3).
- The public prosecutors never replied to the request of the executing Member States (21).
- The procedures were formally closed (4).
- In the remaining cases (31), what happened could not be fully clarified due to the lack of documentation. Still, the detention period had already expired or was too short for any transfer procedure to take place.

Table 2.2 Percentage of EU and Romanian prisoners in Italian prisons (data at 31 December of each year)

	2014	*2015*	*2016*	*2017*	*2018*
% Non-Italian detainees on detainees	32.56	33.24	34.07	34.27	33.95
% EU detainees on detainees	7.05	7.04	6.47	5.86	5.56
% EU detainees on non-Italian	21.64	21.18	18.98	17.09	16.38
% Romanian Nationals of EU detainees	75.02	76.82	76.97	76.70	76.85

Source: Our analysis of data from Ministry of Justice statistics (available at www.giustizia.it/giustizia/it/mg_1_14.page#)

A closer look at the percentage of EU and Romanian nationals in Italian prisons shows that Romanian citizens make up the vast majority of EU national prisoners – a percentage that is stable across time, ca. 75–76 per cent (see Table 2.2). It should also be mentioned that Romanians are the largest non-Italian community living in Italy. Having more than 1 million residents in 2021, Romanians represented more than 20 per cent of the non-Italians living in Italy. Moreover, according to the last available research (Ricci, 2021; Voicu, 2021) the community is widespread across Italy and well-integrated in the country.

The number of FD 909 files relating to Romanian detainees (Table 2.1) is astonishingly high compared to any other nationality, although it has been progressively reduced over time. Indeed, 85 per cent of the cases that opened in 2014 involved Romanian authorities and prisoners. This share declined to 68 per cent in 2015, 62 per cent in 2016, 70 per cent in 2017 and 72 per cent in 2018. Such a significant percentage is undoubtedly due to the first screening carried out by the Prison Administration, which specifically targeted Romanian prisoners. The undeclared strategy of the Italian authorities was to look for potential transferees among the biggest group of detainees, hoping to reach a significant number of successful transfers. A sort of ratchet effect (Harcourt, 2007) is the result: putting so much effort into the transfer of Romanians ended with the most significant number of transfers (Table 2.3) compared to other nationalities. However, the number of effective transfers (324) is not so significant if compared with the number of initiated cases (1109). Moreover, these results occurred at a high cost in terms of procedures that should not have started because the corresponding Romanian nationals lived in Italy with their family, procedures that lasted for years, and procedures that ended because detainees had been already released.

Moving on to examine the data taken from the Ministry of Justice from the entry into force of the FD 909 to 8 June 2018, 1,371 transfer processes were initiated. Of these, 468[12] concluded with a transfer, 819 were in progress, and 84 had no data – therefore, they cannot be considered in the analysis. Looking at the distribution across Italy, 117 judicial authorities opened at least one – either concluded

Table 2.3 Number of transfers from Italy to other MSs (FD 909)

Country	*2014*	*2015*	*2016*	*2017*	*1st semester 2018*	*Total*
Romania	42	100	89	67	26	324
Spain	0	9	19	14	7	49
France	1	3	2	5	0	11
The Netherlands	0	1	1	6	3	11
Belgium	2	3	3	0	0	8
Germany	0	0	0	2	4	6
Slovenia	2	1	2	1	0	6
United Kingdom	1	1	0	1	2	5
Greece	0	0	1	3	1	5
Poland	0	2	0	2	0	4
Hungary	0	0	0	1	3	4
Croatia	0	0	2	1	0	3
Portugal	0	0	0	2	1	3
Latvia	0	1	1	0	0	2
Luxembourg	0	0	1	0	1	2
Austria	0	0	0	0	1	1
Slovakia	0	0	0	1	0	1
Sweden	0	0	0	1	0	1
Total	48	121	121	107	49	446

Source: Our analysis of data from the Ministry of Justice, General Affairs Department Office II

or pending – procedure, but a few presented a number of procedures of some significance. About one-third of the public prosecutor offices opened only one or two files. By contrast, 37 per cent of the procedures concerned just four cities: Rome, Milan, Turin and Genoa. As shown in Table 2.4, only 12 Prosecutors' offices completed more than 10 cases and registered at least 30.

The FD 909 procedure is mainly applied in big urban areas, largely located in the centre-north of Italy – except for the entirely peculiar case of Rome: the public prosecutor office in Rome has a well-structured international cooperation office also because the office deals with several international cooperation mechanisms for the entire country. In addition, many public prosecutors working there have worked at the international cooperation office of the Ministry of Justice and vice versa, with the result of a much deeper knowledge and expertise of the prosecutors working there.

In this regard, therefore, a divide also seems to emerge in the administration of justice which not only is a north-south divide but also concerns the gap between the public prosecutor offices of the big cities and those located in towns or rural areas. Although the data requires further investigation, various hurdles to be faced by the judicial authorities in applying this judicial cooperation mechanism emerge: smaller and decentralised offices need more personnel to pay the required attention to judicial cooperation files. During the days spent at the international cooperation office of the Ministry of Justice, it was clear from several informal conversations that there are difficulties in following these relatively infrequent cases, for which

Table 2.4 Distribution of procedures (offices with at least ten cases concluded)

Public prosecutor office	*Complete procedure*	*Pending procedure*	*Missing data*	*Total*
Rome	73	105	6	184
Milan	61	97	7	165
Turin	39	56	3	98
Genoa	14	45	3	62
Civitavecchia	25	18	3	46
Padua	14	30	2	46
Naples	18	22	3	43
Brescia	15	23	2	40
Florence	10	28	2	40
Venice	12	25	2	39
Bologna	13	16	1	30
Ancona	14	13	2	29

Source: Our analysis of data from the Ministry of Justice, General Affairs Department Office II

there is consequently a lack of time to study the legal rules and procedures properly. In most offices, the judicial cooperation cases are an additional workload with the least priority. The lack of human resources, both judicial authorities and administrative support staff, is such a well-known problem of Italian justice that it is now among the key areas of investment for the Next Generation EU funds.

4. The transfer of EU prisoners: a national and supranational failure

As noted in the 2017 Report on the impact of the FD 909 in Italy, "the use of that important transfer mechanism of foreign prisoners has been very limited" (Camera dei deputati, 2017, p. 17); for this reason, initiatives were promoted to stimulate the use of the instrument, as broadly described in the aforementioned circulars. The research conducted on the Italian implementation of the FD 909 suggests two main considerations, regarding both the failure of the cooperation mechanism as such (see also Brandariz in this volume) and the shortcomings of the Italian justice system.

In 2016, the EU Fundamental Right Agency (FRA, 2016) underlined the limited application of the FD 909. As a matter of fact, the FD was transposed into the national legal systems with two main caveats, namely the lack of the double criminality principle with regard to some crimes, rejected by nine Member States, and the delay in the enactment of the national legislation.[13] In addition to the options exercised upon transposing the Framework Decision, there were differences in the recognition procedures adopted at the national level, which significantly affected the implementation and outcome of the procedure. Each Member State adopted its own procedure of recognition, ranging from a jurisdictional procedure – in some cases also including a right of appeal by the person being transferred (as occurs, for example, in Romania) – to very simple administrative or semi-administrative procedures (an e-mail sent to the Italian International Cooperation office by the executing Member States, a letter of recognition with the opinion of the prison authority or of the liaison magistrate in the country). Furthermore, some Member States (also, in this case, one of the examples is Romania) required, in the case of several judgements, the compilation of a single certificate for each sentence, the absence of which leads to closure of the procedure.

This diversity of implementation makes it particularly difficult for Italian judicial authorities to understand and respond adequately to different operating methods. As we have seen, the judicial cooperation files are not a priority for public prosecutors overloaded of work. The Ministry of Justice's International Cooperation Office is the only office with the proper legal and technical knowledge and expertise, while public prosecutors strive to carry out their duty efficiently, with a few exceptions.

In the files analysed, there were several cases of procedures initiated by prosecutors in circumstances falling outside the scope of the FD 909. There were also many other cases of procedures that were stuck due to errors or omissions in completing the certificate by judicial authorities. This is one of the more problematic elements: the incorrect completion of the certificate leads to the documents being sent back by the executing Member State, requiring correction by the Italian judicial authority and an eventual re-submission. In addition, there are many cases where the procedure had been started with a considerable delay, not only according to the letter of the law but also with respect to the time the detainees manifested – by any possible means – their consent to be transferred.

There are many cases, albeit for different reasons, where procedures are started although they should never have been started, given the detainees' ties in Italy or the very short residual sentence. These cases clearly reveal the unintended consequences of the proactive approach adopted by the prison administration which, in carrying out the screening of prisoners to be transferred, ended with a selection of prisoners based on their citizenship, without any further consideration of the existence of significant bonds in Italy. In other words, the attempt to efficiently map the potentially transferable prisoners was largely useless, also due to the lack of established relationships between prison authorities and the judicial authorities in charge of the transfer procedures.

Another key finding that emerged from the case analysis is the absence of the transferring person and the defence attorney. The transferring person is, by will of the legislator, the silent party in this procedure: the *ratio legis* compels the prisoner to remain silent and to be transferred in all possible cases. The paradox that emerges from the analysed cases is that even when prisoners take an active part in being transferred (e.g. by requesting the issuing and executing authorities and the prison warden to be transferred, and providing all the information on their personal and family situation), they have no certainty that their case will be concluded successfully within a reasonable time frame. Despite being the main actor of the procedure, the prisoner is largely powerless.

One of the reasons for this marginalisation is the absence of the defence attorney. It is no surprise that the right of defence is difficult to exercise fully inside prison. Out of the 362 files analysed, defence attorneys played an active role in only two cases. In most, the prisoners have no legal support (there is no obligation of being legally assisted for the transfers) or the lawyer is incidentally mentioned but there is no evidence of any legal activities in the documentation. This results in an additional obstacle to the transfer. In particular, reading the files, the executing authorities (of some countries more than others) try to hamper the transfer any time there is a minor issue that could lead to denial of recognition in the certification process. In these cases, professional legal support would help. Despite the idea of the EU legislator of a smooth and fast procedure, the research shows that many Member States are not particularly willing to accept their citizens detained in another EU country, except for cases where a judicial deportation measure has been issued. Since the judicial deportation measure ensures the transfer at the end of the detention period, the executing State abandons its reluctant stance, and the transfer procedure becomes much faster. These successful transfers could be considered as an indirect effect of the judicial deportation measure.

The research also led to some reflections on the assessment of the possibilities of social rehabilitation (see also Oancea and Ene in this volume). In general, the judicial authorities do not assess the social rehabilitation of the detainees; only in three cases (out of 362 analysed files) the public prosecutors requested the penitentiary judge to hear the detainees on their situation in the country of origin. In most cases, social rehabilitation is not examined, except for the information provided by the prison administration limited to the place of residence of the prisoner's family. The prison conditions in the executing country are never mentioned or assessed, as if they were irrelevant in offering rehabilitation opportunities (Marguery, 2018). Similarly, the knowledge of the Italian language is not considered as an indicator of integration in Italy. The research confirms all the doubts expressed by the most recent research (Faraldo Cabana, 2019; Martufi, 2018; Montaldo, 2018; Hofmann & Nelen, 2020) on the relevance and ambiguity of social rehabilitation in the transfer procedure.

Conclusion

The Framework Decision on the transfer of prisoners has only recently been receiving interest at the European level. Much more overlooked than the European Arrest Warrant, it is nonetheless the most applied procedure among the legal framework concerning the transfer of foreign offenders (that also includes FD 2008/947/JHA and 2009/829/JHA, see Brandariz in this volume). Having analysed the implementation of FD 909 in Italy, it is clear that the results are below the expectation of the Italian authorities that, completely diverting from the original scope of the FD 909, aimed to use this instrument as a tool to address prison overcrowding.

The research on which this chapter is based revealed that the files on international cooperation, not only those relating to the transfer of foreign offenders, represent in many judicial offices a workload that is added to the ordinary workload. It is, therefore, a marginal activity, which is given little consideration. By looking at the number of transferred persons in Italy (around one hundred per year), we should conclude that the effort made by the prison administration to identify potential candidates for transfer has achieved rather limited results, much lower than expectations, not least due to the great difficulty involved in connecting with the local public prosecutors who are central to the procedure. The prison administration acted entirely autonomously, drawing on its privileged relationship with prisoners but not adequately considering the need to cooperate with other players of the criminal justice system in order to achieve its purposes. The established efficient procedure resulted in ineffective results. There emerges, therefore, a lack of communication between the two key parties in the executive phase, namely those who detain the prisoner and those who have the power to decide on the prisoner's transfer. It is clear that these are not branches of the criminal justice system that are used to working together.

For their part, the foreign offender is relegated to a secondary role and legal assistance is rare. Some files, as stated, highlight that the detainees wishing to be transferred do not achieve their goal, at least not promptly. The inaction of the prosecutor or the obstacles put by the executing Member State cause a denial of justice and an evident frustration of what should be the primary aim of the FD 909, namely the social rehabilitation of foreign offenders. Almost paradoxically, even the purpose of making the FD 909 a tool to counter prison overcrowding did not fulfil the scope, taking into consideration the limited number of the persons transferred compared to the major effort spent by the prison administration and by the Ministry of Justice in general in trying to find detainees to be sent back to the country of origin. The ultimate result is a double failure. The first is the failure of the functioning of the cooperation mechanism and of the mutual trust among EU countries, which still lack a shared vision of criminal justice (Sicurella, 2018). The second is the failure of the national effort to divert the transfer of foreign offenders from its original scope.

Notes

1 The reflections contained in this chapter rework the results of research activity carried out as part of the European project *RePers – Mutual Trust and Social Rehabilitation into Practice*, a comparative study between Italy, Spain and Romania looking into the functioning of the FD 909 and the transposing of laws in those three States, based upon the fact that Romanian detainees constitute the majority of foreign prisoners both in Italy and in Spain.

2 Italy implemented FD 2009/829/JHA and FD 2008/947/JHA by Legislative decree no. 36 of 15 February 2016, in force since 26 March 2016, and Legislative Decree no. 38 of 15 February 2016, in force since 29 March 2016, respectively.

3 *Torreggiani and Others v. Italy*, applications nos. 43517/09, 46882/09, 55400/09, 57875/09, 61535/09, 35315/10 and 37818/10.

4 The files involved the following Member States: Austria (2), Belgium (2), Croatia (3), France (8), Germany (8), United Kingdom (6), Greece (3), Latvia (1), Lithuania (1), Luxembourg (1), The Netherlands (6), Poland (8), Portugal (5), Slovakia (5), Czech Republic (1), Romania (194), Slovenia (3), Spain (28), Sweden (1), and Hungary (1).

5 The files involved the following Member States: Austria (1), Croatia (1), France (1), Germany (4), United Kingdom (2), The Netherlands (2), Poland (4), Romania (42), Slovenia (3), and Spain (11).

6 I would not define it as a proper participant observation because I did not systematically take notes. However, the informal conversations with the working staff and observing their daily work were invaluable.

7 Commission notice – Handbook on the transfer of sentenced persons and custodial sentences in the European Union (2019/C 403/02), p. 14 (at https://eur-lex.europa.eu/legal-content/EN/TXT/PDF/?uri=CELEX:52019XC1129(01)&from=EN).

8 As clarified by the 2019 Handbook, the judgement should not be translated unless the executing Member State has issued a declaration that states the wish to formulate such request.

9 In bold in the original text.

10 The list of crimes is established by the law (Articles 380 and 381 Italian criminal procedure code) but across the years the number of crimes has expanded. Today it includes a long list of offences from sexual violence to drug trafficking and robbery.

11 The security measures are those measures introduced in the Italian criminal law according to the principle of the social defence of the Positivist School. They formed the so-called dual track system (Pifferi, 2020).

12 The numbers of transfers do not coincide with Table 3 because Table 4 also includes pre-2014 transfers.

13 This is the case of Poland that postponed the entry into force of the FD 909 by three years (up to the 5.12.2022), as permitted by Article 28(2) of the FD 909.

References

Aebi, M.F., Berger-Kolopp, L., Burkhardt, C. & Tiago, M.M. (2019) *Prisons in Europe 2005–2015. Vol. I Country Profiles*. Strasbourg: Council of Europe Publishing.

Camera dei Deputati (2017) *Relazione sullo stato di attuazione dell'analisi di impatto della regolamentazione. Trasmessa alla Presidenza il 15 maggio 2017*. http://presidenza.governo.it/DAGL/uff_studi/Relazione_2017.pdf (accessed 28 November 2022).

De Wree, E., Vander Beken, T. & Vermeulen, G. (2009) The transfer of sentenced persons in Europe: Much ado about reintegration. *Punishment &Society* 11(1): 111–128.

European Commission (2004) *Green Paper on the Approximation, Mutual Recognition and Enforcement of Criminal Sanctions in the European Union* (COM (2004) 334 final). Bruxelles: European Union, 39–41.

Faraldo Cabana, P. (2019) One step forwards, two steps back? Social rehabilitation of foreign offenders under Framework Decisions 2008/909/JHA and 2008/947/JHA. *New Journal of European Criminal Law* 10(2): 151–167.

FRA (2016) *Criminal Detention and Alternatives: Fundamental Rights Aspects in EU Cross-Border Transfers*. Wien: FRA. Retrieved from fra.europa.eu/sites/default/files/fra_uploads/fra-2016-criminal-detention-and-alternatives_en.pdf (accessed 28 November 2022).

Froment, J.C. (2002) Les avatars de la Convention sur le transfèrement de détenus en Europe. In: Ceré J. (ed.) *Panorama européen de la prison*. Paris: L'Harmattan, pp. 119–140.

Harcourt, B.E. (2007) *Against Prediction. Profiling, Policing and Punishment in an Actuarial Age*. Chicago, IL: The University of Chicago Press.

Hofmann, R. and Nelen, H. (2020) Cross-border cooperation in the execution of sentences between the Netherlands, Germany and Belgium: an empirical and comparative legal study on the implementation of EU framework decisions 2008/909/JHA and 2008/947/JHA. *Crime, Law and Social Change* 74(4): 381–404.

Marguery, T. (2018) Towards the end of mutual trust? Prison conditions in the context of the European Arrest Warrant and the transfer of prisoners framework decisions. *Maastricht Journal of European and Comparative Law* 25(6): 704–717.

Martufi, A. (2018) Assessing the resilience of 'social rehabilitation' as a rationale for transfer: A commentary on the aims of Framework Decision 2008/909/JHA. *New Journal of European Criminal Law* 9(1): 43–61.

Ministero della Giustizia (2012) *Riconoscimento ed esecuzione delle sentenze penali straniere. D.lgs, 161/2010 recante disposizioni per conformare il diritto interno alla Decisione-quadro 2008/909/GAI. Prime questioni applicative*. Roma, 2 maggio.

Ministero della Giustizia (2014a) *Trasferimento dei detenuti stranieri attuazione della Decisione-quadro 2008/909/GAI*, N. 145680. Roma, 18 aprile.

Ministero della Giustizia (2014b) *Trasferimento dei detenuti stranieri in esecuzione pena verso il loro Paese origine. Decisione-quadro 2008/909/GAI*, N. 54227.U. Roma, 22 aprile.

Ministero della Giustizia (2015) *Trasferimento dei detenuti stranieri in esecuzione pena verso il loro Paese origine. Decisione-quadro 2008/909/GAI*, N. 142825. Roma, 22 aprile.

Ministero della Giustizia, Dipartimento per gli Affari di Giustizia Direzione Generale della Giustizia Penale (2016a) *Circolare in tema di trasferimento dei detenuti ai sensi della DQ 909/2008/GAI. Rapporti con la Repubblica di Romania*. Roma, 19 settembre.

Mitsilegas, V. (2009) The third wave of third pillar law. *European Law Review* 34(4): 523–560.

Montaldo, S. (2018) Offenders' rehabilitation: Towards a new paradigm for EU criminal law? *European Criminal Law Review* 8(2): 223–243.

Pifferi, M. (2020) The theory of social defence and the Italian positive school of criminal law. *Glossae European Journal of Legal History* 17: 23–46.

Ricci, A. (2021) Odi et amo: l'inserimento della collettività romena in Italia. In: Istituto di Studi Politici "S. Pio V" e Centro Studi e Ricerche IDOS (ed.) *Radici a metà. Trent'anni di immigrazione romena in Italia*. Roma: IDOS, pp. 38–64.

Rosanò, A. (2020) Framework Decision 2008/909/JHA in Context: Interplay with the European Arrest Warrant and (EU) Extradition Law. In: Montaldo S (ed.) *The Transfer of Prisoners in the European Union: Challenges and Prospects in the Implementation of Framework Decision 2008/909/JHA*. Den Haag: Eleven/Giappichelli, pp. 79–94.

Sicurella, R. (2018) Fostering a European criminal law culture: In trust we trust. *New Journal of European Criminal Law* 9(3): 308–325.

Vermeulen, G., van Kalmthout, A., Paterson, N., Knapen, M., Verbeke, P. & De Bondt, W. (2011) *Cross-border Execution of Judgements Involving Deprivation of Liberty in the EU*. Antwerpen: Maklu.

Voicu, B. (2021) Sentirsi cittadini europei in Italia. I risultati dell'Indagine sull'inserimento dei cittadini romeni. In Istituto di Studi Politici "S. Pio V" e Centro Studi e Ricerche IDOS (ed.) *Radici a metà. Trent'anni di immigrazione romena in Italia*. Roma: IDOS, pp. 65–81.

3 Transfer for rehabilitation?

Gabriel Oancea and Theodora E.D. Ene

Introduction

On 1 January 2007, Romania joined the European Union. The process started in 1995 when the Romanian Government submitted the official accession request. One of the first advantages of membership was making travel conditions within the EU more flexible for Romanian citizens, a process that started before the actual accession. Since 2002, the visa regime for Romanian citizens was abolished, and they were able to move freely (under certain conditions, before 1 January 2007) within the European Union. This represented a moment of a genuine exodus, mostly for economic reasons. Around 3.6 million Romanians settled in different EU countries (OECD, 2019). It was a phenomenon that occurred in a series of 'phases'. Initially, the preferred destination countries were Spain and Italy, but due to the impact of the 2008 economic crisis, countries such as the UK and Germany became more attractive (Baciu, 2018).

The opening of borders created the potential for migrant Romanians to come into conflict with law enforcement authorities in other countries. Cases such as that of Giovanna Reggiani, the wife of an Italian admiral, who was robbed, raped and then murdered in 2007 by Romulus Mailat, appear in the media from time to time, often as opportunities for political populism.[1] This gives an opportunity to raise issues such as the removal of those in conflict with the law from their country of residence, setting reentry bans, or inducing perceptions of community insecurity. The day Giovanna Reggiani died, the Italian President, Giorgio Napolitano, issued a decree that gave the local prefects the power to expel European citizens of other countries from Italy for being deemed a serious threat against public order (Bird et al., 2016a). A decade later, in 2017, Luigi Di Maio, Vice President of the Italian Chamber of Deputies, sparked controversy when he posted a comment on his Facebook page stating that Italy imports 40% of Romania's criminals while pointing out the need for an improvement in the Italian justice system (Lopapa, 2017, Rai News, 2017).

The figure of 3.6 million Romanians living in EU countries correlates, somewhat naturally, with the number of Romanians serving custodial sentences in these countries. While there are currently no official statistics on the number of Romanian detainees in European Union prisons, there is information from a 2016[2] study

DOI: 10.4324/9781003254584-4

carried out by a team of journalists that put the number of Romanian inmates at 11,511, the second-largest group after those from Morocco (11,706) (Bird et al., 2016b).

The case of Romanian prisoners and the possibility of transferring them to serve their sentences in Romania regularly comes up in bilateral discussions among justice ministers from Romania and other EU countries. It is assumed that the transfer procedure should not raise any special problems in practice. The European Union Framework Decision 2008/909/JHA includes the principle of mutual recognition of judgements in criminal matters imposing custodial sentences or measures involving deprivation of liberty for the purpose of their enforcement in the European Union. This principle has been transposed into national laws by most of the EU Member States. Despite the Framework Decision and the inclusion of the principle in national laws, the transfer of Romanian prisoners presents several peculiarities, especially from the perspective of fulfilling one of the main objectives of the decision, namely, to facilitate the social rehabilitation of the convicted person.

1. Social reintegration as a prerequisite for transfer?

Foreign national prisoners are a vulnerable group in numerous prison systems, facing problems during the execution of their custodial sentence that stem from language and/or cultural barriers. As was pointed out by Brosens et al. (2020), foreign prisoners face three categories of problems: language problems, lack of substantial contact with family members or other persons who can provide moral/material support during detention, and legal problems related to immigration. Regarding language issues, prisoners face multiple difficulties in understanding staff instructions or interacting in an appropriate manner with other detainees (Ugelvik, 2017). Physical contact with family members is difficult, given the distance that often separates prisoners from those families. In addition, it is often difficult for prisoners to maintain a telephone, online or correspondence contact due to the fact that these imply unaffordable costs (Ugelvik & Damsa, 2018). In some cases, the prisoner cannot be visited because his or her relatives do not have documents proving legal residence. In terms of immigration regulations, certain prisoners and/or their family members find themselves facing deportation or removal from the country in which they are incarcerated/residing (Barnoux & Wood, 2013). Foreign national prisoners are more likely to experience mental or psychological health problems, driven or amplified by language barriers or uncertainty about their future (Till et al., 2019). The precariousness of their situation is also highlighted by the fact that they are at greater risk of suicide or other self-harm (Borrill & Taylor, 2009). Given these circumstances, the Committee of Ministers of the Council of Europe has drawn up Recommendation CM/Rec (2012)12 on foreign prisoners, which documented the difficulties faced by foreign prisoners in prison systems and made several recommendations regarding their treatment.

Regarding the percentage of foreign nationals in the European Union's prison systems, there are a number of differences between the countries of the West and East of the Union, that is, the former socialist states that joined the European Union in the first decade of the 2000s. According to the SPACE I report for 2020, foreign prisoners account for 59.1% of the total prison population in Greece, 54.1% in Austria, 44.3% in Belgium, 32.4% in Italy and 23% in France. On the other hand, in the Czech Republic foreign prisoners represent 8.8% of the prison population, in Hungary 5.1%, in Poland 1.7%, and in Romania 1.1% (Aebi & Tiago, 2021).[3]

As stated by Aas (2014) and Stumpf (2006), the use of specific criminal justice means to control migration creates repercussions both for the prison population and the sanctioning system. Several trends can be observed, such as the criminalisation of aspects of migration (Atak & Simeon, 2018) or the approach to deportation as a means of ensuring community security (Turnbull & Hasselberg, 2017). Also, in the case of foreigners, sanctions targeting them are more focused on their removal (*deportation*) and less on their social reintegration (Bosworth et al., 2016). It is no less true that the high proportion of foreign prisoners is exploited for political purposes, especially by representatives of populist political parties. Regarding prison overcrowding, in some cases the over-representation of foreigners is rooted in the way the criminal justice systems in individual countries handle the problem of those in conflict with criminal law. As was highlighted previously (Antonopoulou & Pitsela, 2014; Bosworth, 2011; Hofmann & Nelen, 2020), foreign nationals are more likely to be given harsher sentences or to be subject to pre-trial detention during criminal proceedings. In some cases, foreign prisoners are released on parole at a lower rate, with parole being one of the most important tools to control prison population. There are various reasons for this, but the main reason is related to nationality. For example, foreign national prisoners are often unable to participate in reintegration programs because of language barriers, cannot prove that they have access to a range of internal/external resources after their release which can facilitate social reintegration, or are destined to be removed from the country of imprisonment. For some, there is no reason for them to be sent to their home country since they no longer have any relatives there, and/or no home to return to.

As for the exploitation of the subject of foreign prisoners for political purposes, various narratives focus on a series of issues, including the costs that taxpayers must bear during detention or the insecurity the inmates bring to society after release from prison (Fekete & Webber, 2010; Greer & McLaughlin, 2018; Todd-Kvam, 2019). In some cases, the 'solutions' offered are marked by contradictory demands for harsher punishments for foreigners in conflict with the law, as well as their removal as quickly as possible from the country in question. This is often the case when removal occurs after the sentence had been served. However, one consequence of this populist discourse is that it puts pressure on decision-makers who are asked to show severity in sentencing towards foreigners. In these circumstances, the solution most often discussed is the transfer of foreign prisoners to their *home countries*. The main justification for this option is that their social reintegration process is facilitated by the fact that they no longer face the linguistic or cultural barriers referred to earlier and benefit from increased social capital (Smit & Mulgrew, 2012).

On the European continent, it is possible to notice an intense preoccupation with the issue of prisoner transfer and in this area, judicial cooperation takes place much more intentionally compared to other areas (Conway, 2018). At the institutional level, the Council of Europe initially regulated the framework in which transfers take place. Several documents were subsequently drafted in the European Union related to this issue. Among the instruments drawn up by the Council of Europe, the Convention on the Transfer of Sentenced Persons, adopted in 1983, established a number of prerequisites for transfer: the existence of a court judgement, a period of at least six months remaining to serve the sentence or a life sentence, the express consent of the sentenced person and the consent of the sentencing and the executing States. As stated by Conway (2018), the Convention established the existence of a right of the sentenced person to be transferred, and without her/his consent the procedure could not be carried out.

The consolidation and enlargement of the European Union, which began in the 1990s, required the development of instruments that would have provided a more effective framework for judicial cooperation between Member States, given the free movement of persons in the intra-community space. This led to the Tampere European Council decision in 1999 that the principle of mutual recognition of judgements should underpin judicial cooperation in criminal matters between Member States (Leaf & Marisa, 2004).

However, the enlargement of the European Union to include countries from the former Socialist bloc and the free movement of people within the EU raised many challenges as large number of people from the eastern part of the EU settled in Western European countries. It was a phenomenon that was primarily the result of economic disparities. For example, in 2007 Romania's GDP per capita was USD 8,300, much lower than in countries such as Spain (USD 32,403) or Italy (USD 37,621), the latter two being the main destinations for Romanian citizens at that time (UNSD, 2022). Along with this economically motivated migration, there was also a 'migration' of people in conflict with the criminal law. This represents the context for the adoption of instruments at the EU level that facilitate judicial cooperation. The Framework Decision 2008/909/JHA was clearly based on the desire to create an effective instrument governing the recognition of judgements and the transfer of prisoners within the EU. This is demonstrated by at least two provisions that were lacking in the 1983 Council of Europe's Convention, namely the lack of the requirement of consent of the sentenced person for the transfer procedure and the provision of a 90-day deadline within which the final decision on the recognition of the judgement must be taken and the execution of the sentence ordered. Thus, according to Article 6(2) FD 2008/909/JHA, the consent of the sentenced person is not required when the judgement is transferred to the Member State of which the sentenced person is a national.

Furthermore, the whole procedure is subsumed by the decision to facilitate the rehabilitation process of the convicted person. In this respect, for example, Article 9 of the Framework Decision creates a presumption that enforcement of the sentence in the executing State should enhance the sentenced person's chances of social rehabilitation. Accordingly a few benchmarks are provided to allow the competent authority to assess whether the enforcement of the sentence in the executing State is likely to increase the sentenced person's chances of social rehabilitation, that is, the person's attachment to the executing State, whether he or she considers it the place of family, as well as the linguistic, cultural, social, economic and other links to the executing State.

A shortcoming of the Framework Decision is that it does not define what is meant by the 'rehabilitation' of the sentenced person. As mentioned earlier, the document makes several references to such landmarks as attachment to the executing State or family, linguistic or cultural ties. However, the rehabilitation process is much broader, beginning during the execution of the sentence and continuing after the sentenced person's release from prison. Providing a comprehensive definition of the rehabilitation process at EU level raises many difficulties, given the diversity of penal traditions and different legal definitions of rehabilitation or national practices (Martufi, 2018). Thus, if we refer to the period of serving a sentence in prison, the rehabilitation process is facilitated by: the person's opportunity to participate in reintegration programs, inclusion in services aimed at the treatment of addictions or mental health problems, the climate and conditions in the place of detention, or the quality of relationships between prison staff and inmates (Beijersbergen et al., 2015; Daniel, 2007; Frank & Kolind, 2012; Harding, 2014; Mastrobuoni & Terlizzese, 2014). After his or her release from prison, the successful social reintegration of former prisoners is determined by the existence of a framework to ensure the maintenance of the interventions carried out in prison, of 'buffer' zones to help them adjust to living outside (*half-way house*), a rehabilitation-oriented attitude of government policies, community awareness of the risks of social exclusion of ex-prisoners, and involvement of families in supporting the social reintegration of ex-prisoners (Décarpes & Durnescu, 2014).

In contrast to what has been identified by many authors as elements of the rehabilitation process, the Framework Decision 2008/909/JHA treats the process of social reintegration of prisoners in a simplistic manner, with reintegration being presumed to take place de facto under optimal conditions in the country where the person deprived of liberty is imprisoned, by emphasising the importance of linguistic and cultural factors or the existence of any family relationship with persons who can provide material or moral support. Several relevant aspects which are likely to undermine the social reintegration process are being ignored within the decision-making process, for example, the precarious conditions in the prison system where the prisoner is to be transferred, and the lack of real opportunities at community level to support a prosocial path after release. In some circumstances, it is possible that the prison system where the convicted person is serving his/her sentence prior to transfer offers more prospects of social reintegration compared to the State to which he or she is to be transferred to (Faraldo-Cabana, 2019; Montaldo, 2020).

The Decision does not establish a mechanism to ensure that, in the absence of a structure to facilitate the social reintegration process within the State where the sentenced person lives, the transfer will not take place. It provides for a *possibility* for the competent authority of the executing State to submit a reasoned opinion to the competent authority of the issuing State that the enforcement of the sentence in the executing State would not serve the purpose of facilitating social reintegration (Article 4(4) FD 2008/909/JHA). However, this provision cannot be the sole ground for refusal to transfer based on social rehabilitation. In these circumstances, the lack of a requirement of consent of the sentenced person contributes to undermining of the goal of social reintegration, as prisoners feel excluded from a fundamental decision-making process regarding their future, which is likely to cause feelings of frustration (De Wree et al., 2009). Not less important is the fact that the Framework Decision does not establish a transparent and predictable mechanism as to when a transfer may occur. In practice, a transfer decision can be taken at any time during the entire period of the custodial sentence, which is likely to induce a sense of anxiety for inmates.

To summarise, the factors discussed earlier along with the ambiguity of the approach to social reintegration, the relatively short period of time during which transfer procedures are carried out and the lack of a requirement of consent of the sentenced person led to the Decision serving more as a means of managing the prison population to avoid overcrowding, to remove 'undesirables' and to reduce prison system costs (Montaldo, 2020).

2. Transfer of Romanian inmates from EU countries to Romania – what do we know?

Although theoretical discussions of the problems raised by the application of the Framework Decision are quite numerous, little is known about how sentenced persons perceive the procedures in which they are involved. There are some studies and reports, particularly from those prison systems where there is a significant population of Romanian prisoners (Italy or Spain), and the research referred to in this section is mainly concerned with prisoner's knowledge of the transfer procedure and/or how the prison systems in these countries approached this procedure. There is a lack of research that addresses the full experience of transfer, particularly from the perspective of capturing its effectiveness in terms of social reintegration.

Regarding the Italian prison system, a report on the implementation of the Framework Decision (Ferraris, 2019) found that it was seen mainly as an opportunity to decongest prisons. In this respect, the report refers to a series of documents issued by the Department of Penitentiary Administration that made the transfer process a priority. Particular attention was paid to Romanian prisoners, due to their high ratio in the Italian prison system. In these circumstances, the transfer procedure is described as rather automatic, with no concern for the consequences of the decision relating to the prisoners' social reintegration prospects. However, the transfer procedures were not carried out as quickly as desired by the prison authorities. In addition, the international cooperation activity is described as rather 'marginal' and seen by the Italian judicial authorities as additional workload (see also Ferraris in this volume). Authorities were seen as concerned with carrying out those activities that are strictly related to the mechanism of recognition of judgements, without being concerned with obtaining additional information on the inmates' chances of social reintegration in the executing State.

Research conducted in Italy and Spain (Durnescu et al., 2017) found that most prisoners knew that they could be transferred to serve their sentence in Romania but were not informed about the actual procedure or that the transfer could be carried out without their consent. Although detainees expressed their willingness to serve their sentence in Romania (even if their family was in Spain), the uncertainties about the length of the procedures and the fact that they were unable to 'plan' the execution of their sentence led them to not requesting the transfer. Participants in the study also mentioned that transfer could be relevant for prisoners with long sentences, who have family in Romania and who are at the beginning of their sentence. In the specific case of Romanian prisoners in Italy, an important hindrance to them requesting a transfer was the fact that the parole regulations are much more favourable in Italy.

Although not focused on the transfer procedure per se, research conducted with Romanian prisoners in Spain (Montero & Durnescu, 2016) highlighted information that is highly relevant to social reintegration. This included difficulties prisoners are faced with in obtaining paid employment, the difficulty maintaining contact with their families since some of those may be imprisoned in Romania, and the prisoners' own support network in Spain formed by friends who, according to Spanish law, cannot visit them at their place of detention. Difficulties were also identified, which related to the understanding of legal provisions, as well as perceived discrimination because of their status as foreign detainees. This was sometimes reflected in their difficulty accessing medical services.

Some information about Romanian detainees transferred from EU countries to prisons in Romania (especially when there is a significant number of transfers or when the subject is raised in bilateral meetings at governmental level) can be found in media reporting. Sometimes the procedure is exploited for political purposes, for example, as a proof of the confidence of the authorities of the transferring countries in the capacity of the Romanian penitentiary system to provide adequate detention conditions. The headline "*Italy sends 13 prisoners, including rapists and criminals, back to our country. Toader (former justice minister) says it's proof that we have European standards prisons*"[4] can serve here as an example. This transfer was also exploited for media purposes by the Italian Minister of Justice Matteo Salvini, who in a Twitter post stated, "*A Rome-Bucharest flight transfers to Romania 13 prisoners convicted of sexual assault, murder, human trafficking, robbery, extortion, kidnapping, pimping!*[5] Obviously, the indication of the offences for which the prisoners were convicted is no coincidence, as it is part of a communication policy which emphasises that people who were highly dangerous had been removed from Italy. Sometimes, the media link the high number of detainees transferred to Romania with the costs they represent for the Romanian prison system. Relevant from this perspective is the article *Hundreds of Romanian prisoners from abroad sent to serve their sentences in the country. The upkeep.*[6],[7] However, the media's attention stops strictly at events involving either a high number of transferred prisoners or when the subjects of the transfers are persons who have committed crimes that at some point had an echo in public opinion – see the Mailat case mentioned in the Introduction as an example.

3. Social rehabilitation in the Romanian prison system – a reality?

The reforms that began in Romania after 1989 included a focus on the prison system, which had previously served as a totalitarian power instrument of repression, especially between 1948 and 1964. Reforms were necessary because the prison system was a militarised one and where social reintegration was almost synonymous with forcing prisoners to work for the state. There had also been a series of changes imposed by Nicolae Ceausescu after 1977 that resulted in the closure of prison facilities, following a totally arbitrary decision to lower the number of prisoners to a maximum of 15,000. As the closure of prisons was not accompanied by measures to help reintegrate inmates into society. Since the number of correctional facilities was also decreased, the result was prison overcrowding. Until 1989, overcrowding was being addressed almost exclusively by granting periodic amnesties and pardons to prisoners (Oancea, 2012; Stefan, 2006).

Given that the purpose for which Framework Decision 909/2008/JHA was adopted was to increase the opportunities for social reintegration in the countries of enforcement, the issue that needs to be examined is how the Romanian penitentiary system might contribute to achieving this goal. We will examine this capacity by assessing three dimensions, namely the prison climate, the social reintegration programs run in the penitentiary and the existence of a community context likely to facilitate the social reintegration process following the release of prisoners. When we refer to the prison environment, we consider several material, interpersonal and organisational characteristics of the detention space as well as the interaction between them (Moos, 2018). Different research studies have established a strong correlation between the quality of the prison environment and the success of the rehabilitation process (Bullock & Bunce, 2020; Harding, 2014).

From the perspective of the material characteristics of the detention space, the penitentiary system in Romania faces three major problems represented by the overcrowding of prisons, the inadequate conditions of detention and the lack of newly built detention spaces. These problems have their origin mainly in the underfunding of the penitentiary system. In 1993, Romania became a member of the Council of Europe, and a year later ratified the European Convention on Human Rights, so that conditions in Romanian prisons came under the jurisdiction of the European Court of Human Rights. At the same time, prison conditions became subject of regular monitoring undertaken by the European Committee for the Prevention of Torture (CPT). According to the 2019 report of the National Administration of Penitentiaries of Romania, at the beginning of 2019 there were 7,110 applications to the European Court concerning detention conditions. In two decisions, the European Court found that the precariousness of detention conditions is a *systemic* problem in Romania. The first decision was rendered in 2012 (*Iacov Stanciu v. Romania*[8]) and was considered a 'quasi-pilot' decision, with the Court emphasising that the problems evident in these cases were frequent in the Romanian penitentiary system (overcrowding, inadequate hygiene and lack of adequate medical care in detention facilities) and that, in order to improve the situation, Romania must take new measures including the establishment of an adequate compensation system (damages in line with the Court's usual practice). Furthermore, the Court stressed that the solutions to the problems faced by the penitentiary system were not exclusively the responsibility of the National Administration of Penitentiaries but that it was up to the Romanian government to organise the penitentiary system in such a way as to ensure respect for the dignity of prisoners.

The reforms in the prison system following this decision did not lead to significant changes, and in 2017 the Court handed down a pilot decision against Romania in the case of *Rezmiveş et. al v. Romania*,[9] imposing a six-month deadline for the government to submit a timetable for the implementation of measures to address prison overcrowding and inadequate conditions of detention. In response, the plan drawn up by the Ministry of Justice had five lines of action, namely legislative changes aimed at reducing the prison population; investment in infrastructure; effective functioning of the probation system; implementation of policies for the reintegration of persons deprived of their liberty after release; and legislative measures to ensure effective redress for harm suffered, such as preventive and specific compensatory redress. In the short term, the Ministry of Justice was to identify compensatory appeal as the main solution to the problem of overcrowding in prisons, and Law No 169/2017 was adopted, which established as a compensatory measure that for every 30 days served under inappropriate conditions, even if they are not consecutive, an additional six days of the sentence imposed shall be considered served. However, the law was to be repealed in 2019 due to the compensatory appeal becoming a subject of a dispute between the then-ruling party and the opposition and because the law did not provide for a series of mechanisms to facilitate the social reintegration process following release (Oancea & Neculcea, 2021). Considering this, the strategy to solve the problem of overcrowding had to be revised, with a focus on the modernisation of detention facilities and the construction of new prison facilities. However, in 2020 the National Administration of Prisons noted that overcrowding was still a problem, aggravated by the Covid-19 pandemic[10] as the sole measure that was taken in this context was placing limits on the contact by prisoners with persons outside the penitentiary.

As stated by Marguery (2018), the problems of overcrowding and inadequate conditions of detention are likely to undermine the principle of mutual trust that underpins the recognition of judgements between EU Member States. Relevant from this perspective is the decision of the Court of Justice of the European Union (CJEU) in cases *Aranyosi and Căldăraru*,[11] the Court ruling that when the executing authority of a European Arrest Warrant has evidence of a real risk for detained person to inhuman/degrading treatment in the issuing Member State, this risk must be assessed before making the decision to transfer. The executing authority must consider objective, reliable, accurate and up-to-date information on the conditions of detention in the issuing State, that might demonstrate systemic or generalised deficiencies regarding certain groups of persons or certain penitentiaries. It is also necessary to demonstrate that there are serious and reasonable grounds for believing that the requested person will be exposed to such a risk because of the specific conditions of detention envisaged in his case. The executing authority must request the issuing authority to provide all the necessary information on the actual conditions of detention to which the person concerned will be subjected. If, in the light of the information provided by the issuing authority and all other information, the executing authority finds that there is a real risk of inhuman/degrading treatment in relation to the requested person, the execution of the warrant is to be postponed.

Because overcrowding in prisons is likely to contribute to an increase in violence in the prison environment between prisoners or between prisoners and staff, there is a need to determine the status of prisons with regard to this factor. To address this area of concern, the Committee for the Prevention of Torture (CPT) visited Romanian prisons to investigate specifically the problem of violence in prison facilities following complaints from prisoners. The visit report showed that violence by prison staff or members of intervention groups against inmates is a reality, with several cases of physical, verbal and sexual violence documented. However, there was no adequate response from prison management. Thus, cases of violence were either not recorded or injuries were recorded as the result of altercations between inmates. Also, in some cases the Ministry of Justice investigations were superficial, aiming to discredit the inmates who had complained about the violence. On this occasion, the CPT had to reiterate the need to review the Romanian authorities' approach to self-injury. According to Article 100 of Law 254/2013, self-injury constitutes a disciplinary offence and is sanctioned even though the acts of self-harm often reveal the existence of mental health issues (Favril et al., 2020) requiring psychiatric or psychological intervention.

The National Administration of Penitentiaries highlights the importance of intervention programmes for social reintegration and their importance in the resocialisation process. There are several programmes aimed at adaptation to prison life, preparation for release, development of parenting skills and anger management. The administration also has numerous cooperation protocols with community partners in the field of education or professional training of prisoners and, at the local level, the prisons have a fairly high degree of autonomy in initiating and running programmes aimed at resocialisation. However, the re-offending rate remains high, being estimated in 2019 at 38.4%.[12] This is due to the low number of staff involved in the rehabilitation of inmates, insufficient space dedicated to the implementation of social reintegration programs, limited material resources allocated to them and a high level of bureaucracy (Dâmboeanu, 2011; Ilie et al., 2017). Furthermore, the evaluation of the effectiveness of the programmes implemented in penitentiaries is also carried out by the National Administration of Penitentiaries, and there are no evaluations carried out by external actors (e.g. from academia). As mentioned by Ilie et al. (2017), instead of being conducted in an intensive manner, in relation to the criminogenic needs of the convicted persons, socio-educational activities are more aimed at occupying the time of the prisoner, other than with watching television programmes, playing backgammon, rummy, chess or sports activities. It is also important to consider the impact of the Covid-19 pandemic that contributed to the reduction of prisoners' involvement in rehabilitation programs (Durnescu & Morar, 2020).

Additionally, prisoners face various problems related to stigmatisation post-release, as well as facing a lack of employment opportunities mainly due to criminal records but also due to scarcity of initiatives to facilitate their professional integration. This is compounded by difficulties in accessing the necessary health services, and by housing problems (Durnescu, 2019). There is also a lack of facilities such as shelters or half-way houses to support the prisoners' return to the community. Under these conditions, most people released from prison are exposed to situations of social marginalisation, which is likely to increase their risk of recidivism.

Although people released from prison have numerous specific needs (Jonson & Cullen, 2015; Listwan et al., 2006; Visher et al., 2017), what is noticeable is the lack of targeted approaches. By the time the compensatory appeals law mentioned earlier was adopted, a normative act was drafted that intended to provide for different forms of support to those released from prison: shoes, clothing, medicines, a temporary place in a centre for the homeless, meals provided at the social canteen and free transport. The approach was justified in light of research that noted the importance of immediate release support as a prerequisite for reducing the risk of recidivism (Cid & Ibàñez, 2018; Visher et al., 2011). However, the bill was not adopted as a consequence of the law on compensatory appeals dividing the political class, and the situation of prisoners becoming a focus of political populism (Oancea & Neculcea, 2021).

Given current conditions, some of the former prisoners project their post-release future outside Romania; this approach is seen as a chance to 'start from scratch' in an environment where, at least, no one knows about their past with the criminal law (Durnescu, 2019). It is, however, more of an avoidance strategy, as starting this 'new life' again is not preceded by going through intensive programmes that would have helped, for example, to improve social or problem-solving skills.

4. Transferred for rehabilitation?

The specialised literature in the field of transfer of convicted persons has often focused on theoretical aspects. Sometimes individual experiences have been used through case studies to exemplify how transfer is carried out in judicial practice, without capturing the actual experience of transfer.

In order to capture the experience of transfer, we interviewed ten Romanian prisoners who had been transferred from prisons in Italy (1), Belgium (2), Germany (2), and Austria (5) in January of 2022. The interviews took place in the București – Rahova Penitentiary. The interviews were semi-structured, and the areas evaluated were the consent of the convicted person to initiate the transfer procedure, the identification of those aspects of a decision to transfer that took into consideration the existence of better chances of rehabilitation in Romania, the exploration of the support environment of the prisoner in Romania, the identification of the types of interventions aimed at rehabilitation and the steps that interviewees intended to take after release from prison.

The interviews highlighted the fact that transfer procedure was carried out without their involvement in the decisions that concerned them. Those interviewed did not have the opportunity to express a view on how they would be affected by the transfer decision. Nine of the ten participants stated that they were not asked to give their consent to the initiation of the transfer procedures. Only one participant expressed his wish to be transferred back to Romania to the Austrian authorities. He indicated that he wanted to be close to his family. In very few cases did they use the term 'transfer' in the interviews, instead the terms 'deportation' or 'expulsion' were frequently used. We believe that the use of these terms is not exclusively due to a lack of knowledge of the specialist legal terminology but may be explained by the intention to capture what they perceived was a compulsory transfer.

Apart from the respondent who explicitly expressed his wish to be transferred, the other research participants had no information about when the transfer procedure was initiated. They were not summoned to appear before a judge in the issuing State or by the Romanian court that dealt with the recognition of the judgement. Moreover, the Romanian legal framework transposing the Framework Decision, namely Law No 302/2004 on judicial cooperation in criminal matters, stipulates that the court with jurisdiction to deal with the request for recognition (the court of appeal of the sentenced person's place of residence) adjudicates the case in a single-judge panel, in chambers, without summoning the sentenced person. In these circumstances, since they could not be present before a judge, the interviewees specified that they were unable to express their opposition to a possible transfer.

Not surprisingly, the interviewees brought up issues such as the lack of a supportive environment in Romania, especially if the family members were in the sending state or in other EU countries. In the latter case, the transfer should have been carried out to these countries if the goal of social reintegration was to be achieved.

As for the transfer procedure itself, it was often described as a 'sudden break'. Research participants reported that in most cases they were informed of the fact that they were to be transferred shortly before the transfer (sometimes hours before), which was 'a real shock'. Another point raised by the interviewees was that a consequence of the recognition procedure is the existence of a criminal record in Romania. As mentioned earlier, this is perceived as reducing the possibilities of social reintegration, especially in terms of access to the labour market after release.

Regarding the Framework Decision's requirement that the sentenced person serves his sentence in the executing State to maintain family ties, most respondents reported that this requirement had not been met in their respective cases. For five of the interviewees, the family members who could have provided genuine material or moral support lived in other EU countries (Germany, France, or Belgium). Those interviewees referred to the fact that they should have been transferred to these countries and not to Romania if social reintegration was the aim of transfer procedure. Even in the case of the person who had initiated the transfer procedure, he was not serving his sentence in a prison near the town where his family lived. At the time of the interview, he had been detained for about three months in Rahova Penitentiary in Bucharest, while their family lived in Timişoara (a town about 500 km away). This was due to a combination of factors, which related to the way in which transfers of prisoners are carried out within the Romanian prison system.[13] Four respondents referred to the existence of persons who could provide real material or moral support during the execution of the sentence and after release (i.e., partners and parents) in Romania.

Another aspect that emerged from the interviews was that transfer to Romania for the purpose of serving the sentence was perceived as more of a 'fresh start' (Klaus & Martynowicz, 2021). In this scenario, the detainee went through a series of procedures specific to the initial phases of the period of detention (quarantine, initial assessments, classification within detention regimes, etc.) without considering the developments during the period of imprisonment in the issuing State. Most of these approaches were based on having 'insufficient knowledge' about the detainee, since in many cases the information relevant to the social reintegration process contained in the execution file drawn up in the issuing State (assessments, reference of the programmes which the detainee has been part of) is not officially transmitted to the Romanian authorities. In these circumstances, the prison file of the transferred person contains, at the time of the commencement of enforcement of the sentence pronounced by the issuing State, the recognition decision and the documents relating to the actual implementation of the transfer. Some respondents mentioned that at the time of transfer, the prison authorities of the issuing State gave them copies of various documents relating to the courses they had attended, the programmes in which they had been involved or the work they had done. However, the documents are written in the language of the issuing State, and the burden of translating them into Romanian falls on the transferee. The documents can be used for guidance by the prison's educational staff when drawing up the individualised educational and therapeutic assessment and intervention plan. However, given the fact that translation services entail some expense and that the material resources of detainees are generally limited, they do not always succeed in translating these documents.

Another problem faced by transferred persons is their inclusion in the sentence enforcement regime. According to Law 254/2013 on the execution of sentences and measures of deprivation of liberty ordered by judicial bodies during criminal proceedings, a progressive and regressive regime of execution of sentences has been established in the Romanian penitentiary system, the transition from one regime to another being carried out under the conditions provided by law. There are four such enforcement regimes (maximum security, closed, semi-closed and open), and inclusion in these regimes is made by a commission which considers a series of criteria such as the length of the custodial sentence, the degree of risk, criminal record, age and state of health, criminogenic needs and the conduct of the sentenced person during previous periods of detention (Article 39(2)). However, at the time of the first determination of the enforcement regime, immediately after transfer to Romania, the main criterion considered by the committee is the length of sentence. Some of the research participants referred to the fact that although they were at an advanced stage of serving their sentence, this fact was not taken into account when determining the enforcement regime, the committee being guided by the length of the sentence imposed in the issuing State, and they considered themselves wronged because the way in which they had served their sentence in the issuing State had not been taken into account.

The enforcement regime is also relevant in the consideration of conditional release. The Romanian Criminal Code provides, as a condition for the granting of conditional release, the time spent in the open or semi-open prison regime. Another consequence of the established enforcement regime is the fact that the execution of sentences is carried out in a prison unit specialised in the specific type of regime, which means that the sentence is not always executed in a prison unit close to the sentenced person's place of residence. The situation is much more difficult for women prisoners, given that Romania has only one specialised penitentiary for women (Târgşor).

Three respondents indicated that shortly after their transfer to Romania, their situation was discussed in the parole committee, which decided to postpone their release and set a new deadline for analysis after six months because they were 'insufficiently known' for a decision to be made on their progress.

Regarding the inclusion of the research participants in rehabilitation interventions or work activities, interviewees noted several differences between the prison systems from which they had been transferred and the Romanian one, the opportunities offered by the latter being much more limited. The prisoners transferred from Austria and Germany reported that they had carried out paid work while in prison in these countries, which was no longer possible after their transfer. In terms of social reintegration activities, most interviewees mentioned that they used to watch TV programmes and read. However, given the timing of the interviews, the fact that they were not included in specific rehabilitation programmes could be explained by the impact of the pandemic, which decreased the intensity of psychosocial interventions.

Future plans outlined by the interviewees were mostly oriented (for 8 out of 10) towards leaving Romania and settling in a Western European country. The reasons for this decision were either the fact that their close family/relatives were already living in those countries or because of the much higher integration prospects – professional prospects in these countries compared to Romania. The expressions "*I have no chance*", "*nobody pays any attention to me*" were frequently used to describe the conditions in Romanian society. As mentioned later, another factor that was considered by the respondents as limiting their possibilities of social reintegration in Romania was the fact that they have a criminal record.

Conclusions

The main objective of Framework Decision 909/2008/JHA is to increase the opportunities for social reintegration of sentenced persons in EU Member States by transferring them to serve their sentences in the countries of their nationality. This aim is premised on the assumption that, given family, linguistic, cultural, social, or economic links with the executing State, the sentenced person would benefit from greater opportunities for social reintegration. However, the way in which the Framework Decision is implemented gives the impression that it is a tool used by some countries as a mechanism to reduce prison population and the costs associated with serving sentences by transferring prisoners to their countries of origin.

Rehabilitation of persons in conflict with the law is a complex process, which is not limited to the links mentioned earlier. Factors such as the climate in the prison environment, the intensity of rehabilitation-oriented programmes in which the prisoner is involved during the execution of the sentence, and the opportunities that the transferred person benefits from after release from prison are also relevant. Considering this, the transfer procedure is based more on a presumption of the existence of conditions that contribute to social reintegration in the State of enforcement.

As our findings suggest, the sentenced person is relatively invisible in transfer proceedings. The individuals are not actively involved in decision-making, since their explicit consent is not required for the proceedings to begin, and they cannot appeal the transfer decision. As a result, their views on the appropriateness of the transfer often remain unknown. Another problem is that the transfer of sentenced persons can occur at any time, including towards the end of their sentence, which is likely to increase their anxiety. This is because, as we have shown, the pathway within the prison system of the issuing State is not considered in the State of enforcement.

The application of the Framework Decision has been the subject of studies or evaluations, but most of the time these have concerned either theoretical or practical aspects of relevance to practitioners involved in transfer procedures. However, there are no reliable studies exploring the perspective of transferees and how their transfer to the executing State has contributed to their social reintegration. In the specific case of the persons interviewed in our study, transfer is seen more as a removal procedure from the territory of the sending state, without really considering their social, economic or family contexts in Romania. This aspect is underlined by the fact that our interviewees almost unanimously declared that they would leave Romania again after release, to settle in other EU countries. The reason for this decision is the fact that the persons who represent a material or moral support factor live in these countries, as well as the prisoners' anticipation that by doing so, they will benefit from a more favourable context for their social reintegration.

Notes

1 Quotidiano Nazionale (2007) – *E' morta Giovanna Reggiani Il rom: "Non l'ho violentata" La polizia: "Ha tentato di difendersi" in Quotidiano Nazionale*, November 1st 2007, at www.quotidiano.net/cronaca/2007/11/02/44992-morta_giovanna_reggiani.shtml (accessed 09.01.2022)
2 https://euobserver.com/investigations/135659 (accessed 09.01.2022)
3 https://wp.unil.ch/space/files/2021/04/210330_FinalReport_SPACE_I_2020.pdf (accessed 06.02.2022)
4 Mihalascu, R. (2019). 13 deținuți români din Italia, aduși în țara noastră cu avionul. Sunt condamnați pentru viol, crimă și sclavie. Reacția lui Tudorel Toader. Libertatea available at www.libertatea.ro/stiri/13-romani-detinuti-in-italia-vor-fi-adusi-in-romania-2592892 (accessed 09.01.2022)
5 https://twitter.com/mattcosalviniml/status/1113005947360890880 (accessed 09.01.2022)
6 500 euro.
7 www.digi24.ro/stiri/actualitate/justitie/sute-de-detinuti-romani-din-strainatate-trimisi-sa-si-execute-pedepsele-in-tara-intretinerea-unui-condamnat-costa-2-500-de-lei-lunar-387127 (accessed 09.01.2022)
8 *Iacov Stanciu v. Romania*, no. 35972/05
9 *Rezmiveș et. al v. Romania*, no. 61467/12

10 https://anp.gov.ro/wp-content/uploads/2021/05/Raport-de-activitate-al-Administra%c8%9biei-Na%c8%9bionale-a-Penitenciarelor-pe-anul-2020.pdf (accessed 09.01.2022)
11 Cases C-404/15 and C-659/15 PPU
12 www.statista.com/statistics/1097238/recidivists-in-the-romanian-prisons/ (accessed at 09.01.2022)
13 To transfer a prisoner to another prison unit, an approval from the National Administration of Prisons is necessary, as well as availability of free places of detention to avoid overcrowding, etc.

References

Aas, K. F. (2014). Bordered penality: Precarious membership and abnormal justice. *Punishment & Society, 16*(5), 520–541.

Aebi, M. F., & Tiago, M. M. (2021). S*PACE I – 2020 – Council of Europe Annual Penal Statistics: Prison Populations*. Strasbourg: Council of Europe.

Antonopoulou, A., & Pitsela, A. (2014). Foreign nationals as a minority group in the criminal justice system of Greece: From offending to victimization of non-Greek population. *European Journal on Criminal Policy and Research, 20*(2), 277–294.

Atak, I., & Simeon, J. C. (2018). *The criminalization of migration: Context and consequences* (Vol. 1). Kingston: McGill-Queen's Press-MQUP.

Baciu, I. C. (2018). Analiza statistică a migrației externe după aderarea României la Uniunea Europeană. *Revista Română de Statistică-Supliment nr, 167*.

Barnoux, M., & Wood, J. (2013). The specific needs of foreign national prisoners and the threat to their mental health from being imprisoned in a foreign country. *Aggression and Violent Behavior, 18*(2), 240–246.

Beijersbergen, K. A., Dirkzwager, A. J., Molleman, T., van der Laan, P. H., & Nieuwbeerta, P. (2015). Procedural justice in prison: The importance of staff characteristics. *International Journal of Offender Therapy and Comparative Criminology, 59*(4), 337–358.

Bird, M., Odobescu, V., & Ferrara, C. (2016a). *Expat Romanians: Their worst own enemy*. https://theblacksea.eu/stories/expat-romanians-their-own-worst-enemy/

Bird, M., Odobescu, V., Ferrara, C., & Limontaite, S. (2016b). Romania and Morocco have most expats in EU prisons. *EUobserver*. Retrieved 1 January 2022, from https://euobserver.com/investigations/135659 (accessed 09 January 2022)

Borrill, J., & Taylor, D. A. (2009). Suicides by foreign national prisoners in England and Wales 2007: Mental health and cultural issues. *The Journal of Forensic Psychiatry & Psychology, 20*(6), 886–905.

Bosworth, M. (2011). Deportation, detention and foreign-national prisoners in England and Wales. *Citizenship Studies, 15*(5), 583–595.

Bosworth, M., Hasselberg, I., & Turnbull, S. (2016). *Punishment, citizenship and identity: An introduction* (Vol. 16, pp. 257–266). London: SAGE Publications.

Brosens, D., De Donder, L., Smetcoren, A.-S., & Dury, S. (2020). Exploring educational opportunities for foreign national prisoners in Europe. *Scandinavian Journal of Educational Research, 64*(3), 389–407.

Bullock, K., & Bunce, A. (2020). 'The prison don't talk to you about getting out of prison': On why prisons in England and Wales fail to rehabilitate prisoners. *Criminology & Criminal Justice, 20*(1), 111–127.

Cid, J., & Ibàñez, A. (2018). Prisoner resettlement in Spain: Good practices for early-released prisoners and prisoners lost in transition that fully serve their sentence 1. In *Prisoner resettlement in Europe* (pp. 313–327). Abingdon: Routledge.

Conway, G. (2018). Prospects and problems for European legal cooperation concerning prisoners. *European Journal of Probation*, *10*(2), 136–159.

Dâmboeanu, C. (2011). Fenomenul recidivei în România. *Calitatea vieţii*, *22*(3), 295–312.

Daniel, A. E. (2007). Care of the mentally ill in prisons: Challenges and solutions. *Journal of the American Academy of Psychiatry and the Law*, *35*(4), 406–410.

Décarpes, P., & Durnescu, I. (2014). Where are we in resettlement research. *EuroVista*, *3*(2), 47–67.

De Wree, E., Vander Beken, T., & Vermeulen, G. (2009). The transfer of sentenced persons in Europe: Much ado about reintegration. *Punishment & Society*, *11*(1), 111–128.

Durnescu, I. (2019). Pains of reentry revisited. *International Journal of Offender Therapy and Comparative Criminology*, *63*(8), 1482–1498.

Durnescu, I., & Morar, I. (2020). An examination of the Romanian prison system during the COVID-19 pandemic. Are "zero cases" possible? *Victims & Offenders*, *15*(7–8), 1133–1147.

Durnescu, I., Montero Perez de Tudela, E., & Ravagnani, L. (2017). Prisoner transfer and the importance of the 'release effect'. *Criminology & Criminal Justice*, *17*(4), 450–467.

Faraldo-Cabana, P. (2019). One step forward, two steps back? Social rehabilitation of foreign offenders under Framework Decisions 2008/909/JHA and 2008/947/JHA. *New Journal of European Criminal Law*, *10*(2), 151–167.

Favril, L., Yu, R., Hawton, K., & Fazel, S. (2020). Risk factors for self-harm in prison: A systematic review and meta-analysis. *The Lancet Psychiatry*, *7*(8), 682–691.

Fekete, L., & Webber, F. (2010). Foreign nationals, enemy penology and the criminal justice system. *Race & Class*, *51*(4), 1–25.

Ferraris, V. (2019). Il trasferimento dei detenuti comunitari: l'ennesimo tentativo fallito di riduzione del sovraffollamento, In *Associazione Antigone, Il carcere secondo la Costituzione. XV rapporto sulle condizioni di detenzione* (pp. 299–310). Roma: Antigone.

Frank, V. A., & Kolind, T. (2012). *Prison-based drug treatment and rehabilitation in the Nordic countries* (Vol. 29, pp. 543–546). London: SAGE Publications.

Greer, C., & McLaughlin, E. (2018). Breaking bad news. Penal populism, tabloid adversarialism and Brexit. *The Political Quarterly*, *89*(2), 206–216.

Harding, R. (2014). Rehabilitation and prison social climate: Do 'What Works' rehabilitation programs work better in prisons that have a positive social climate? *Australian & New Zealand Journal of Criminology*, *47*(2), 163–175.

Hofmann, R., & Nelen, H. (2020). Cross-border cooperation in the execution of sentences between the Netherlands, Germany and Belgium: an empirical and comparative legal study on the implementation of EU framework decisions 2008/909/JHA and 2008/947/JHA. *Crime, Law and Social Change*, *74*(4), 381–404.

Ilie, S., Tomescu, C., & Rotariu, L. (2017). Issues regarding the quality of life in the Romanian penitenciaries-a brief research report. *Journal of Community Positive Practices*, (4), 41–64.

Jonson, C. L., & Cullen, F. T. (2015). Prisoner reentry programs. *Crime and Justice*, *44*(1), 517–575.

Klaus, W., & Martynowicz, A. (2021). Introduction: Unwanted citizens of EU Member States and their forced returns within the European Union. *Central and Eastern European Migration Review*, *10*(1).

Leaf, S. A., & Marisa. (2004). Mutual recognition in European judicial cooperation: A step too far too soon? Case study – the European arrest warrant. *European Law Journal*, *10*(2), 200–217.

Listwan, S. J., Cullen, F. T., & Latessa, E. J. (2006). How to prevent prisoners re-entry programs from failing: Insights from evidence-based corrections. *Federal Probation*, *70*, 19.

Lopapa, C. (2017, Aprile 12). Di Maio e il "40% di criminali romeni importati in Italia". La rivolta via web, la protesta di ambasciata e associazioni. *la Repubblica*. Retrieved May 2022, from www.repubblica.it/politica/2017/04/12/news/di_maio_e_il_40_di_criminali_rumeni_importanti_in_italia_la_rivolta_via_web_la_protesta_di_ambasciata_e_associazioni-162799786/

Marguery, T. (2018). Towards the end of mutual trust? Prison conditions in the context of the European Arrest Warrant and the transfer of prisoners framework decisions. *Maastricht Journal of European and Comparative Law*, *25*(6), 704–717.

Martufi, A. (2018). The paths of offender rehabilitation and the European dimension of punishment: New challenges for an old ideal? *Maastricht Journal of European and Comparative Law*, *25*(6), 672–688.

Mastrobuoni, G., & Terlizzese, D. (2014). Rehabilitating rehabilitation: Prison conditions and recidivism. *Einaudi Institute for Economics and Finance EIEF Working Papers Series, 1413*.

Montaldo, S. (2020). Framework Decision 2008/909/JHA on the transfer of prisoners in the EU: Advances and challenges in light of the Italian experience. *New Journal of European Criminal Law*, *11*(1), 69–92.

Montero, E., & Durnescu, I. (2016). The pains of Romanian prisoners in Spanish prisons. *Revista de Asistenta Sociala*, *15*(4), 31–42.

Moos, R. H. (2018). *Evaluating treatment environments: The quality of psychiatric and substance abuse programs*. Abingdon: Routledge.

Oancea, G. (2012). *Probaţiunea în România: Evaluări normative s,i sociologice [Probation in Romania: Normative and sociological evaluation]*. Bucuresti: CH Beck.

Oancea, G., & Neculcea, S. A. (2021). Compensatory remedy against criminal populism: Skargi o odszkodowanie w obliczu populizmu politycznego. *Archiwum Kryminologii*, 1–24.

OECD. (2019). *Talent abroad: A review of Romanian emigrants*. Paris: Talent Abroad, OECD Publishing. https://doi.org/10.1787/bac53150-en

Quotidiano Nazionale. (2007). *E' morta Giovanna Reggiani Il rom: "Non l'ho violentata" La polizia: "Ha tentato di difendersi" in Quotidiano Nazionale*, 1st November 2007, Retrieved from www.quotidiano.net/cronaca/2007/11/02/44992-morta_giovanna_reggiani.shtml (accessed 09 January 2022)

Rai News. (2017). *Di Maio: Importiamo 40% criminali romeni. Scoppia la polemica*. Retrieved May 2022, from www.rainews.it/archivio-rainews/articoli/m5s-di-maio-importiamo-40-per-cento-criminali-romeni-scoppia-polemica-904c47a0-da19–4a6b-b780–3dc0376fbd7b.html

Smit, D. V. Z., & Mulgrew, R. (2012). *Handbook on the international transfer of sentenced persons*. New York: United Nations.

Stefan, B. (2006). Istoria si reforma inchisorilor romanesti (History and Romanian Prison Reform). *Revista Română de Sociologie, anul XVII*(5–6), 485–512.

Stumpf, J. (2006). The crimmigration crisis: Immigrants, crime, and sovereign power. *American University Law Review*, *56*, 367.

Till, A., Sen, P., Chaplin, L., Grange, E., Exworthy, T., & Forrester, A. (2019). The mental health of foreign national prisoners. *Journal of Forensic and Legal Medicine*, *62*, 14–18.

Todd-Kvam, J. (2019). Bordered penal populism: When populism and Scandinavian exceptionalism meet. *Punishment & Society*, *21*(3), 295–314.

Turnbull, S., & Hasselberg, I. (2017). From prison to detention: The carceral trajectories of foreign-national prisoners in the United Kingdom. *Punishment & Society*, *19*(2), 135–154.

Ugelvik, T. (2017). The incarceration of foreigners in European prisons. In *The Routledge handbook on crime and international migration* (pp. 107–120). Abingdon: Routledge.
Ugelvik, T., & Damsa, D. (2018). The pains of crimmigration imprisonment: Perspectives from a Norwegian all-foreign prison. *The British Journal of Criminology*, *58*(5), 1025–1043.
UNSD. (2022) – Per capita GDP at current prices – US dollars. *National Accounts Estimates of Main Aggregates*. http://data.un.org/Data.aspx?q=GDP+per+capita+Romania&d=SNAAMA&f=grID:101;currID:USD;pcFlag:1;crID:642#SNAAMA
Visher, C. A., Debus, S., & Yahner, J. (2011). Employment after prison: A longitudinal study of releasees in three states. *Justice Quarterly*, *28*(5), 698–718.
Visher, C. A., Lattimore, P. K., Barrick, K., & Tueller, S. (2017). Evaluating the long-term effects of prisoner reentry services on recidivism: What types of services matter? *Justice Quarterly*, *34*(1), 136–165.

4 The meaning of 'just punishment' and the role of courts in transnational criminal justice procedures

Witold Klaus

Introduction

One of the most important legal philosophers of the twentieth century, Gustav Radbruch, pointed out while describing the role of philosophy that it confronts people with their decisions and "make[s] life not easy but, on the contrary, problematical" (quoted in Leawoods, 2000, p. 489). Even though I do not have any ambition to make a new contribution to legal philosophy in general, my aim in this chapter is to problematise transnational criminal justice and its procedures by raising questions that are usually asked by philosophers. In doing so, I want to draw attention to the roles of both justice and punishment – the roles which are usually lost in transnational procedures that are ruled rather by bureaucratic and technical principles.

The legal philosophy and the questions that it raises will be my point of departure in this journey. The most important of them include the following: What is justice in modern and mobile societies? What does delivering justice mean and what elements should be included to make it happen? What is the role and purpose of punishment, and what role should the courts play in the process of delivering it? Against this background, I will analyse the practical implementation of some of transnational criminal justice procedures in Poland (mostly connected with application of European Arrest Warrants and other forms of transfer of prisoners, including extradition processes) and their impact on the people subjected to them. This perspective of bringing someone to justice which involves two (or more) jurisdictions, and which focuses on people on the move, is the pivotal element of this chapter.

To evaluate transnational justice procedures, the findings from several studies will be used, including interviews with Polish practitioners who are involved in the implementation of transnational justice instruments, interviews with people who were forced to return to Poland under those procedures, and analyses of court decisions issuing European Arrest Warrants (EAWs).

This chapter comprises five main parts. I begin with some theoretical considerations about justice and punishment, with a special focus on the transnational dimension of those terms. Then I explain the methodology that I used to collect the material on which this chapter is based. In the next three subchapters, I focus on an analysis of the data gathered during the research process. I divide this material into three main topics, starting with a description of the people who are targeted

DOI: 10.4324/9781003254584-5

by EAWs issued by Polish courts – in other words, in which cases and for what deeds people are pursued using this instrument of transnational criminal justice. The next section is focused on the bureaucratisation of such procedures and their influence on people's lives, which leads me to analyse how the idea of 'justice' is understood in transnational justice – how it is perceived and decoded by different actors responsible for its delivery (or those subjected to such practices). Finally, I conclude by bringing together the theoretical dimensions of justice and punishment and the way they are reflected in the practices of Polish authorities when applying transnational criminal justice.

1. Justice, punishment and their delivery – theoretical aspects

Justice is an elusive concept which is exceedingly difficult to grasp and translate to practical actions. What makes it even more complicated is the fact that it refers both to the law (the form it should take to create a society where justice prevails) and its practical application (i.e. how norms should be interpreted and implemented to make justice happen). The latter element includes a certain behaviour of the individual who executes the legal procedures expected of them by the society (even though expectations of different social actors involved in this process could significantly vary between themselves).

Justice is also a highly politicised concept. Various points of referral are used to explain and validate different social practices, including the law, to prove that they are part of this term or serve as a tool to obtain its goals. Those interpretations solely depend on the values and political stances of someone interpreting the term 'justice', and as such they yield a huge variety of concepts and positions, sometimes even contradictory (Dworkin, 1986, p. 425). The Polish philosopher Tadeusz Kotarbiński, while reflecting on the sense of justice, asked:

> What does justice demand? It demands actions according to some equal measure, the fulfilment of what was promised (explicitly or implicitly, clearly or tacitly), the defence of those who have been wronged or are in danger of being wronged in the area available to our interference . . . the important things here are equality, keeping promises and defence.
>
> (Kotarbiński, 1987, p. 182)

This understanding is very much in line with John Rawls' sense of justice, in which it is equal to fairness. "It conveys the idea that the principles of justice are agreed to in an initial situation that is fair" (Rawls, 1999, p. 11). What is 'fair' and thus what is 'just', however, is still based on a social agreement, so it can vary in both time and space. The morality serving as an explanation to what justice is – in other words, what is right and especially what is wrong – is not constant. Law is based on morality, so it is not constant either (Black, 2011, pp. 11–13). One can say that this is an obvious statement, but particularly when we are discussing the implementation of transnational justice it should be recalled, as this concept includes multiple jurisdictions which are translated into different and sometimes distinct models of morality.

Another important (and also quite obvious) reminder is that defining what action constitutes a crime is an element of the sovereign power of a state. The same can be said about imposing a punishment (with only a small exception being made for international criminal tribunals). Even though the process of transnationalisation of criminalisation has been developing recently, it takes time, is based on political interests and requires the agreement of the participating countries. Creating a list of crimes that are common and where criminal acts are understood in the same (or at least a similar) way in different countries also requires an intercultural dialogue between different legal cultures – to define not only what should be penalised but also what the role of punishment should generally be, how it should be enforced and what legal protection (if any) should be offered to an accused person. The concept of human rights and the various ways to (mis)understand them play an important role in this process (Cotterrell, 2018, pp. 140–156).

Justice as a value should be reflected in the law. This concept was developed by Gustav Radbruch, who stated that the "law is the reality whose sense is to serve justice" (quoted in Alexy, 2021, p. 109). In Radbruch's understanding, justice means equality – the same principles apply for all. But it is not enough to draft the statutes in a certain, proper and just way. If justice is to be delivered, it must be accompanied by an expediency and a purpose (which is based on values) since only this allows individualisation, a necessary adjustment of some general norms to the situation of a certain person or a group of people. Both those elements of law are complemented by the third rule: legal certainty. Those three elements refer to the creation of law, but when the law in books reaches a certain threshold of extreme injustice because of its violation of human rights, the law itself is invalidated by its profound unjustness, and thus should not be implemented by a judge, who is obliged to oppose those provisions no matter what personal costs it might bring to them (Alexy, 2021; Leawoods, 2000; Radbruch, 2012). The protection of individual human rights also justifies interference into another country's internal affairs, as stated by the founding father of international law, Hugo Grotius (Nussbaum, 2007, p. 19).

The role of the judge in delivering justice is thus of the greatest importance. The judge is obliged to take into account all elements of the cases they adjudicate on, as well as the law itself (legal provisions) on which the judgement is based. It is not easy to introduce into everyday practice Radbruch's guidance on that matter, as the idea of extreme injustice and violation of human rights is itself quite vague. But even if it were not so difficult to prove an abuse of power of the government and unjust regulations that were introduced into law, courts do not always withstand their role as the protector of justice, the protector of an individual against the state and the law. This especially happens when the idea of national security is introduced into the process of sentencing. The role of the court arises in such cases because it is the only institution designated to protect individual rights and to defend the most vulnerable populations: those who became scapegoats and the focus of a moral panic in a society manipulated into disliking them, being afraid of them and blaming them for their own misfortune (Cohen, 1972). But in a crisis and when the so-called national security is at stake, judges do not necessarily properly fulfil their role of protectors, especially when it comes to shielding individuals from oppressive governmental policies (Cole, 2003).

Human rights are sometimes explicitly evoked as a referral point that should be taken into consideration in the sentencing process in transnational cooperation. The protection of fundamental rights is obligatory while adjudicating on the extradition of a person to another country (Efrat & Newman, 2020; Efrat & Tomasina, 2018) and to some extent in the execution of an EAW (Montaldo, 2016; Ouwerkerk, 2018). In the latter procedure, yet another element is added that requires the deliberation of a judge. A proportionality test should be applied by the judge in the country which is about to issue an arrest warrant against a certain person. This test

> is understood as a check additional to the verification of whether or not the required threshold is met, based on the appropriateness of issuing an EAW in the light of the circumstances of the case.
>
> (Klimek, 2015, p. 134)

In other words, if issuing an EAW violates the individual's rights it should not be imposed. Proportionality was translated into the Polish criminal procedural code as 'the interest of the justice system', and it clearly shows the change of the emphasis – from an individual rights to a state's interest. Theoretically this term includes (or should include) human rights perspective, but it is only one of provisions embedded in it (Jacyna, 2018, pp. 31–33).

All of those provisions were introduced into the law so as to protect the fundamental rights of a perpetrator of a crime. Those measures prevent judges from rubber-stamping decisions taken by other institutions (in one or another country). In practice, though, judges quite often rely on so-called expert opinions or information provided by members of their own administrative staff, and instead of double-checking information presented on paper and hearing a person who is subjected to those procedures, they automatically accept the documents that are provided to them (Fiss, 1983, pp. 1454–1458). This is especially true when it comes to the cases of people from the lower classes. Then the verification of the expert opinions is even more superficial or non-existent, particularly when the judge has a general trust in the expertise of those representing the other institutions, whether the police or probation services (Lipsky, 1980, pp. 129–131). A very similar approach is likely also applied to paperwork from a court of another European country, especially since the rules of mutual recognition of and mutual trust in judicial decisions within the EU have been introduced (Böse, 2015; Klimek, 2015). One can say that this approval comes from bureaucratic reasons and lack of time of the judges receiving EAWs. This is definitely a true assumption but, in my opinion, it is only a part of the whole picture as this rubber-stamping of warrants issued by judges from other countries will not become so easily if it wasn't for the trust in expert's opinions of fellow judges from other EU countries (which is also embedded in the EU law).

The expectation of the court's clientele, as Cyrus Tata (2007) calls them, is also an important element during the process of adjudication – and I do not suggest here by any means any corrupt behaviour but purely a 'smooth' cooperation with other institutions and its representatives. Another reason behind this approach may lie in the fact that judges rely on legal regulations and usually just implement them without giving a second thought to the reasons behind their introduction. On top of that, we should remember that many judges consider their work boring since most of their activities do not pose a challenge to them from a legal point of view (Tata, 2007). One can also argue that due to the accumulation of so many obligations and a significant number of cases to rule on, judges simply do not have the proper time to reflect on every single case (Hester & Eglin, 2017, p. 178), particularly if a case looks easy and obvious, and if a quick approval is expected of them by the bureaucratic judicial system.

Transnational justice usually involves a foreigner as the participant of the judiciary procedure. There is a body of research which shows that foreigners are treated differently and less favourably by courts than citizens (Aliverti, 2018; Brandon & O'Connell, 2018). This begs the question of whether in the opinion of a judge this person "deserves the *same* standards of (normal) justice as the citizen" (Franko, 2020, p. 175; emphasis in the original). It is even more important when one considers that in several jurisdictions and in some procedures the rights of foreigners and legal safeguards have recently been significantly limited by the law – especially when compared to citizens in a similar situation (Ashworth & Zedner, 2015; Dauvergne, 2005; Macías-Rojas, 2016).

In transnational justice – especially when it comes to both imposing and executing a penalty on a certain person, particularly in a prison – an important notion is a different level of what Ben Crewe describes as the depth, weight, tightness and breadth of various penal systems (Crewe, 2015). Again, it seems obvious to assume that different criminal justice systems work differently, thus the conditions inside prisons, the right to apply for an earlier release and any support after serving a sentence vary greatly between jurisdictions. In the process of sentencing, a judge takes those characteristics (but only from their own country) into consideration – more, or likely less, consciously – and bases their verdict on them. Or at least the actual severity of the punishment, the pains and the suffering that the sentence causes to the individual, should be taken into consideration during sentencing. Those characteristics include not only the obvious pains like deprivation of liberty, for instance, but also indirect (oblique) and contextual pains of the punishment, which are related to the execution of the punishment, the condition in which the sentence is served and the social impact that it brings (both during imprisonment and after release) (Hayes, 2016, 2018). But all of those elements are strictly related to a concrete jurisdiction and cannot be easily transferred to another.

This is the perfect segue to bring me to the reflection on the concept of 'just punishment', which is all about adapting the "correct amount" of suffering upon a certain person for their criminal act (van Ginneken & Hayes, 2017, p. 63). In general, the very intention of punishment is "inflicting of pain, intended as pain" (Christie, 1981, p. 1). Obviously, the punishment should be individualised. What makes it difficult, though, is the fact that different people experience what is formally the same punishment differently. This depends on their character, personal situation and previous experience (also with being punished) (van Ginneken & Hayes, 2017). In other words, punishment can only be personalised to a certain extent, and this raises the question of what should be taken into consideration by a judge in the first place. Would it be the personal characteristics of the person being sentenced, followed by their individual experience (which is usually unknown)? Or rather should equality prevail – the notion that the same (or at least similar) punishment should be imposed for each person if they commit the same crime in the same/similar circumstances?

If we go back to the founding father of the contemporary theory of punishment – Cesare Beccaria – we read that according to him "to make the punishment as analogous as possible to the nature of the crime" (Beccaria, 1872, p. 76) is of the greatest importance in the adjudicating process. He also added further recommendations on how to make the punishment just:

> The more immediately, after the commission of a crime, a punishment is inflicted, the more just and useful it will be. . . . The degree of the punishment, and the consequences of a crime, ought to be so contrived, as to have the greatest possible effect on others, with the least possible pain to the delinquent.
>
> (Beccaria, 1872, pp. 73–76)

Those guidelines indicate several points on how to make a punishment just – that is, to impose it rather quickly after the crime was committed, to connect it with that very crime and its severity (the harm that it inflicted on the victim or society) and to make it as mild as possible for the perpetrator. The judge should at the same time take into consideration the preventive element of the punishment – the impact that it has on both the individual and in general (on society). Further on, Beccaria also commented on statutes of limitations and stressed that they should not be too extensive when crimes are of a lesser severity (Beccaria, 1872, pp. 112–116). Recently, the rehabilitation of a sentenced person has been added as an important element of a penalty. In the transnational situation, though, it raises several questions: How should it be implemented? In which country will this aim be better achieved? What elements should be taken into account in the decision of where the sentence will be served – and when, that is, during the sentencing or at the executive stage? Who should be included in this decision-making process? (Wieczorek, 2018)

In this chapter, I would like to reflect on those most important questions – what both justice and just punishment mean in transnational processes and how the latter should be planned and implemented in order to serve justice.

2. Methodology of research

Our research consisted of three basic components.[1] We began the process by interviewing experts: different people who are part of the transnational justice system. They represented a rather broad range of different agencies (both public and private) as there is a big group of institutions involved in this process (see Kalir et al.,

2019, p. 8). We conducted a total of 29 expert interviews with 36 participants (19 women and 17 men). On average, they were between 40 and 55 years old. They were experienced people, with many years of work in their profession, often in managerial positions (especially in law enforcement agencies). The judges had also varied in their experience – from district court[2] judges with just a several years of practice, to highly experienced ones, with more than 30 years in court and a high expertise in international cooperation. Our interviewees included 6 judges, 2 court administration employees, 3 probation officers, 11 NGO social workers from non-profit organisations (including 3 people from Polish organisations helping Poles abroad), 5 police officers, 3 prison officers and 6 border guard officers. The interviews lasted an average of about 1 to 1.5 hours and were carried out according to common guidelines (although they were adapted to the respondents' varying experience with the transnational criminal justice). Seven interviews took the form of dyads. In quoting the following respondents' statements, I provide the interview code and the interviewee's profession.

We conducted the research in the midst of the Covid-19 pandemic, that is, between March 2020 and August 2021. For this reason, most of it took place using remote communication platforms. However, this was not a problem for the experts. In fact, it could be argued that this made it easier for us to contact various people across the country and some of whom we probably would not have been able to reach in the traditional way. As all business meetings at the time were held this way, the remote interview was not an uncommon situation. In fact, it was treated as a normal form of interaction and meeting. In the very beginning, members of the enforcement agencies (police, prison or border guard officers) were rather reluctant to be interviewed online and preferred face-to-face meetings, but as they became more accustomed to remote working during the pandemic, they too agreed to be interviewed remotely (although most of the interviews with this group of interviewees took place in person).

In addition to interviews with experts, we also interviewed individuals who were forcefully transferred to Poland as a result of their contact with the justice system. We carried out these interviews between April 2020 and April 2021. Altogether, 31 people took part, including 4 women. The vast majority had been sent back under the EAW procedure, although a few people were also transferred to Poland following extradition. We were able to reach ten people using contact information we received from social organisations that had worked with them or by posting an add on a Facebook group called 'I live in the UK. Poles in the islands'. However, the latter method of recruitment was not very successful. Another 21 people who spoke with us were in Polish prisons at the time of the interview, where they found themselves after being transferred from another country. All interviews took place remotely (for more on that subject, see Klaus, Włodarczyk-Madejska & Wzorek in this volume). When quoting our respondents subsequently, I use pseudonyms (all names have been changed and all personal information has been anonymised).

The third method of research was to survey the files of individuals against whom Polish courts issued EAWs in 2018 and 2019. We carried out the study in the first half of 2021, by analysing 336 cases, which constituted a statistically representative sample of the total number of court cases pending at that time for the issuance of an EAW (for more on this method, see Włodarczyk-Madejska & Wzorek in this volume). In describing the details of these cases, I give their numbers later in square brackets.

As can be seen earlier, the overwhelming majority of the research material we collected focuses on the use of the EAW. This is the main instrument of transnational justice that is found in Polish practice. However, while the following discussion is based on this research material, it seems that the scope of the topics I address in this text is much broader and can be applied more generally to various forms of transnational collaboration in criminal proceedings.

3. Who is prosecuted by Polish courts under the European arrest warrant?

As I mentioned earlier, justice can be understood and administered differently at different stages of punishment. One of its salient elements is the type of punishment imposed. For years, the most common punishment that Polish courts handed down was a suspended prison sentence. Between 2001 and 2015, it represented between 50% and 60% of all sentences. The percentage began to decline from 2016 in the wake of changes in criminal law, which markedly reduced the courts' ability to impose this type of punishment, and in 2019 it reached 20% of the total penalties (Gruszczyńska et al., 2021, p. 71). Many people who received a suspended prison sentence did not perceive it as a serious and severe punishment, because often in practice it did not entail any additional obligations or inconveniences apart from probation supervision (not always being applied) and refraining from committing further crimes, as this could lead to the suspension being revoked and the person being sent to prison to serve the sentence previously suspended. In fact, the risk of having a suspended sentence revoked was significant, as almost one in four such sentences was eventually carried out and the convict was incarcerated (Klimczak et al., 2020, p. 46). That convicts had a dismissive attitude towards suspended prison sentences was something that judges saw clearly:

> Very often . . . in the eyes of convicts, a suspended prison sentence is not a punishment. Sometimes when defendants stand before the court, . . . the court asks, routinely checking the basic personal data of the accused: 'Do you have a previous criminal record?' Sometimes the answer is 'no'. . . . A suspended sentence is not very memorable to the convicts.
>
> (Judge, ENA_E17)

This judge also noted that convicts often do not register fines as punishment in their minds. It was fines, alongside the sentence of community service, that replaced suspended prison sentences after 2016. On average, the imposition of fines surged from about 10% (2001–2015) to 28% (in 2018), and sentences of community service increased from about 20% to 33%. The adjudication of sentences to immediate custody has also increased, from about 10% to 18% (Gruszczyńska et al., 2021,

p. 71). Both of these non-custodial sentences – in cases when they are not carried out by the offender – can be converted into a prison sentence by the court during the enforcement proceedings. Such a situation was also recorded in our study.

Our research shows that Poland continues to seek extradition for a large number of people for relatively harmless offences. However, the premise behind the establishment of the EAW was just the opposite: the idea was to prosecute perpetrators of the most serious crimes. In fact, for many years Poland has been criticised by the European institutions and other EU countries for excessive use of the EAW procedure and using it to bring minor offenders to justice (HFHR, 2018, p. 17). Our current research reveals that while the crimes being prosecuted are not utterly trivial compared to previous years (Klaus et al., 2021), many are still hardly considered serious enough to set in motion the entire transnational justice machinery to have the offender punished.

These minor crimes, which are the grounds for international searches, were pointed out by the experts we surveyed, when sharing their experiences.

> I also had one such wanted man, who rode [a bicycle] in an inebriated state around a flower bed in front of the municipality office, and suddenly jumped into it and smashed a 300-zloty vase and destroyed some seedlings. And he was a double criminal because of the destruction of property and being intoxicated. And that's what the EAW was for. . . . We had an EAW for stealing flowers from a grave. I had one where a man stole several jars of meatballs and a blanket from a basement.
>
> (Police officer, EAW_E1)

We also met people convicted of such offences during the study. This is what they told us about the criminal act for which they were brought to Poland:

> This is some kind of joke. Stealing a radio from a car, well, you know what I mean. And on top of that, it's a case from 2007 and 2009. Well, but I was guilty, there was a sentence of four years, well, and I had to. . . . I don't know. If it was up to me, I wouldn't prosecute such [cases].
>
> (Jacek)

> I wrote a blank, signed check. Well, and she [a friend] took advantage of it. So it's such a stupid thing, I think. Because this was not so socially harmful to pay it back. Because there was also the possibility of repayment, they could have notified me, because after all, they knew where I was. They all knew. . . . And they knew my address, where I live. I could have been notified or whatever . . . 7,000 zlotys [about 1,500 euros]! And for that I got a sentence of one year and four months.
>
> (Marta)

> The value of what I stole is two and a half thousand zlotys [about 400 euro]. I received a total of two years and two months for this.
>
> (Bartek)

What is striking about Jacek's case is the amount of time that had elapsed since he committed the crimes. We met with him in prison in 2020. Marta did not have a criminal record before and did not know that she was wanted by the justice system in the first place. No one notified her of the verdict itself, under which she received a suspended sentence or the subsequent conversion of that sentence to imprisonment, or that she was under an obligation to return some money, which, incidentally, she had not misappropriated and which she did not even know had been misappropriated. The punishment Bartek was handed down seems very high compared to the deed he committed (provided, of course, that he was telling the truth). This strict penalty may also have been influenced by his previous criminal record.[3]

However, the cases described earlier contradict the opinions of court employees. One court administrative employee argued that "judges do not usually adjudicate draconian punishments for petty theft crimes" (ENA_E29). This was echoed by one judge, who exhorted:

> Let's have some trust in courts, which moderate punishments, and see how a prior criminal record affects the person on trial or how this person is not concerned with it.
>
> (Judge, ENA_E1)

Still, perhaps it is a matter of defining what a draconian punishment is, and whether imprisonment for some minor crimes can be labelled as such. Or what is moderation of punishment. In fact, another of the judges we spoke to admitted that

> the penalty of one year [of imprisonment] is actually a very low penalty in the Polish justice system, but one that is often imposed. Yes, very often.
>
> (Judge, ENA_E12)

Nevertheless, spending a year in prison can hardly be considered a lenient punishment. Moreover, individuals who are not employees of the courts make a much harsher assessment of the activities of the courts and their rulings (as evidenced by the earlier quotes). Furthermore, the concept of punishment should be broad and should include – as Hayes (2016, 2018) proposes – not only the conviction itself but also all the elements of the enforcement proceedings and the consequences of the decisions made in these proceedings. One such consequence is searching for the person who must serve a sentence through an EAW. This broader view sheds light on the punitive nature of the Polish justice system. If we look only at the information on the EAWs issued by Poland to execute sentences, it turns out that only half of the people were sentenced to immediate custody, while the remaining half had other freedom-restricting sentences (see Table 4.1). Thus, it is difficult to find a moderate response in the courts' use of the EAW. Sometimes court personnel see this as well:

> Well, the European Arrest Warrant sounds proud . . ., it is such a serious tool. Admittedly, we issue these European arrest warrants to a large extent for so-called trivialities.
>
> (Judicial administration employee, ENA_E28)

Table 4.1 Penalties imposed on persons wanted under the EAW for enforcement of sentence (N = 269)*

Type of punishment	*Number of persons wanted under an EAW*	*Percentage of persons wanted under an EAW*
Imprisonment (sentences to immediate custody)	143	53%
Suspended imprisonment	134	50%
Community service[4]	13	4%
Fine	23	9%

Notes: * The percentages do not add up to 100% because an offender may have committed more than one crime, and the court may have imposed more than one punishment per person.

> In a sizable, maybe not sizable, but in a certain definite percentage of cases, I see, I see this kind of, not to say pointlessness, but excessive involvement of the judiciary in searching for an offender abroad under the EAW, when compared to the severity of the crime.
>
> (Judge, ENA_E17)

According to a study of cases in which an EAW was issued, fines were most often adjudicated alongside other punishments. In none of the cases was a fine issued as a stand-alone punishment. As for community service, it was imposed alongside another penalty (imprisonment or suspended imprisonment) in three cases; presumably, in these cases the offenders were wanted for more than one conviction. In all 11 cases in which the courts handed down only a custodial sentence against the convict, these sentences were converted to a substitute prison sentence at the stage of enforcement proceedings, most likely for the offenders' failure to meet the obligations that had been placed on them.

Let's look for a moment at the kinds of offences for which custodial sentences were handed down. In many instances, we can definitely speak of trivial matters, such as selling a pawn shop employee an item worth about €40 that did not belong to them [46], driving under the influence of alcohol [54] or other psychoactive substances [174] or after a driving ban [121], or entering someone's home and not leaving it against the owners' wishes [183]. Similarly, minor offences can be found among suspended prison sentences. Some of these include an unsuccessful attempted theft of €460 [205], entering into a contract with a cell phone network and failing to pay phone bills [33], fleeing a gas station without paying €40 for fuel [237], and possessing 0.8 grams of heroin [299].

In this group of cases, there are also many offences of driving while intoxicated. Driving under the influence of alcohol can also lead to a sentence of immediate custody: this occurred in nine cases, including two people who were sentenced to one year of imprisonment [11 and 198]. Prison sentences for this felony are relatively rare, averaging about 3% of such cases nationwide, but there are large differences between different judicial districts on this issue, ranging between 0.7% and 8% of the total cases (Klimczak et al., 2020, pp. 31–32). In general, this crime (or rather, the punishment for it) is relatively common in Poland: In 2018 alone, more than 44,300 people were convicted of this offence, which accounted for 16% of the overall sentenced population (Gruszczyńska et al., 2021, p. 64). In our study, there were a total of 17 people wanted for driving under the influence of psychoactive drugs (mostly alcohol), including nine cases where this was the only offence they committed.

Apart from drink driving, we also have several other crimes in Poland that are quite specific to our country and are clearly visible among all convictions. The first of these is failing to pay child support. In 2018, more than 42,200 people were convicted of this offence (15% of all those convicted), including more than 4,500 sentenced to custodial sentences. This was a record year compared to previous years, as the number of convicted individuals rose almost fivefold, due to a change in the sentencing policy for this crime and a subsequent amendment to the criminal law. Even in earlier years, however, the number of convictions for this offence was considerable, averaging thousands per year, with about 1,000–1,200 people being sentenced to mandatory imprisonment (Gruszczyńska et al., 2021, p. 88; Ostaszewski, 2020). The problem of how to deal with (mostly) men refusing to support their children is an important social policy issue. However, solving it using criminal justice measures is certainly not the best way to address it. Polish studies have long shown that a large proportion of child support offenders are alcohol abusers or addicts (about one-quarter of those convicted), and that most of the offenders are poor, financially distressed, unemployed or even homeless. Over 10% have serious health problems (physical or mental) (Ostaszewski, 2020, pp. 199–202). In the EAW cases we studied, there were 11 people sentenced for not paying child support. Paweł Ostaszewski's research shows that, in general, about 1% of those convicted of this crime live outside Poland (Ostaszewski, 2020, p. 202).

Another law that has a strong presence in Polish practice is a severe punishment for drug possession. It is true that since 2011 it has been possible to waive punishment for a person who possesses a small amount of drugs for personal use, but this is only an option, not an obligation for law enforcement agencies or courts (in 2014, more than 40% of prosecutors' offices did not use this option even once [Jankowski & Momot, 2015, p. 1]). Additionally, different courts interpret this provision differently. As for the internationally prosecuted persons we studied, there were also cases of people convicted of possessing small amounts of drugs, such as 0.7 or 2.7 grams of amphetamines [115, 80], 0.75 or 8.3 grams of marijuana [224, 320] and 0.8 grams of heroin [299]. Another convicted person was growing seven cannabis plants in his flat [248].

The prosecution of these specifically Polish, rather petty offences was criticised by some of the experts in our research. This is because, having worked with people who were brought to Poland for these offences, they saw little point in involving the entire machinery of the transnational justice system in these matters. They also saw the people behind these criminal acts and the interruption to their lives – they saw them on their own eyes and met them; they didn't have just a small note about them in their files. They were much more than just someone described on paper. One example is the following statement by a police officer, who nonetheless caveated that, of course, the decision to issue an EAW is the sole competence of the courts.[5]

> It is the role of the judge to assess the gravity of the crime. If I were a judge, I wouldn't, for example, issue an EAW for failing to pay child support, or for drink driving on a bicycle. On the other hand, it's the sovereign decision of the court and the prosecutor's office whether they want to prosecute someone on the basis of the European Arrest Warrant, and we just carry it out.
>
> (Police officer, EAW_E1)

> I've come across an EAW for failure to pay child support, which I think is kind of, well, it's a bit odd. Because the guy is abroad and working to earn money for his children, and he ends up in a Polish prison, where he's going to do time. I don't understand it. Well, but I don't have to understand everything.
>
> (Prison officer, ENA_E14)

The low number of EAWs issued in the types of cases described earlier, however, was due not so much to the realisation that these are petty offences and the response to them should be different (or that, in general, a criminal law response to offences resulting from alcohol or drug abuse and solving social problems in this way is not a good idea), but to the pragmatism of judges. This is because at some point they came to the realisation that there was no chance of prosecuting these people through the EAW, because in many European countries these kinds of actions are simply not recognised as crimes, and thus one of the fundamental conditions for issuing a warrant, that is, the obligation of double criminality, does not apply.

> I was no longer issuing European arrest warrants at that time, for example, for all those cases of unpaid child support. Because it was clear, I was aware, that generally in many European countries this does not constitute a crime. It is only prosecuted as a civil violation in general, and there's no chance of it being issued at all. But this was [also] a category of offences that I thought it would be disproportionate to prosecute. Another thing was also such famous cases as . . . detection of marijuana in urine, [. . . that is] possession of drugs.
>
> (Judge, ENA_E19)

> When we were dealing with the crime of driving under the influence of alcohol, on the other hand, there was the problem that in some countries this threshold is set lower, in others [it's] higher. So, with this [alcohol level] between 0.2 and 0.5 [per mile of alcohol in the blood] we also rather did not [issue the EAW].
>
> (Judge, EAW_E18)

The previous discussion shows that when judges decide whether to use transnational measures they are most often guided by pragmatism, that is, the knowledge that the offender will not be transferred anyway for certain crimes. However, two elements are important here. First, they don't always have this reflection (the study included judges who were more committed and more reflective, while others declined to be interviewed) and EAWs are issued in such cases anyway. Second, this reflection does not extend to a general approach to the imposition of punishments or to decision-making in enforcement proceedings, such as those involving commutation of non-custodial sentences to imprisonment.

4. The bureaucratisation of transnational justice – is the person lost between the papers?

The problem of bringing back to Poland people who have committed relatively minor crimes and have been given various types of non-custodial sentences lies in the excessive bureaucracy and formalism of the Polish justice system connected with punitive criminal law and sentencing practices (Krajewski, 2016). Indeed, the entire justice process is fragmented: One court (or judge) decides on the punishment for the offence, another on the question of commuting a non-custodial sentence to imprisonment, another motions for an EAW and yet another decides whether to issue it. Throughout this process and at its various stages, the person and the crime they committed are lost, because judicial proceedings from the executive stage onward are based mainly on documents. Judges do not get to see the convicted person or hear about their situation. Next, our experts give examples of such cases:

> Well, these are different kinds of fraud; the vast majority of them are where the convicted person . . . showed up at the bank, took out a loan and did not pay the instalments. And it turned out that their ability [to repay] was non-existent. Often there was also a false certificate of employment, so it is obviously fraud. . . . the bank has long since got rid of this debt, because it sold it. So then there is the question: Whom would they [the convicted person] have to compensate for this damage, so to speak. But [the court] doesn't have the resources to check this. There is no time for that. And punishment is also sometimes ordered against such people.
>
> (Judge, ENA_E17)

> [It was a case for] burglary and [there was] an obligation imposed on the convict to compensate for the damages. He did not fulfil this obligation. It was a liquor store in that village where he lives, you know, a broken window, some goods stolen, high-alcohol-content products. He didn't remedy that either.
>
> (Probation officer, EAW_E24)

In the latter case, the suspended prison sentence was revoked for failure to fulfil the court-imposed obligation. As in the bank cases, suspended sentences are sometimes revoked because, as the judge pointed out, the court does not have time to get to the bottom of the case and investigate whether it makes sense to carry out the ruling – makes sense from any point of view when it comes to the goals of punishment, as stated in the Polish Criminal Code: individual prevention and rehabilitation, reparation of damage, the interests of justice or even deterrence. None of these goals will be achieved, and the convicted person will only suffer further unnecessary hardship, which may negatively affect their future life.

Another problem that judges face is the lack of time and a large caseload, including executive proceedings. One judge spoke explicitly about this: "We can't cope with the number of [cases]" (Judge, ENA_E17). On the other hand, executive proceedings are not thought of as important or a priority by judges. Here, guilt is not being adjudicated, so they are – as one of the interviewed judges said – dead boring.

> During all those years of my work [as a judge]. . . . I dealt with this second stage, i.e. the execution of punishment, literally by accident. . . . I never liked doing it. Somehow it seemed to me that it was such, such, I don't know, well dead proceedings. . . . Actually, boring. But in fact, this is the essence of this principle of inevitability of punishment and of such a justice approach.
>
> (Judge, ENA_E12)

Reflection on the significance of the decisions she was taking and how crucial they were to administering and experiencing justice only came years later, when our interviewee was no longer involved in these types of proceedings. While working on these cases, the judge was overcome by a sense of boredom. It may also have been because executive proceedings take place in the silence of the office and are based only on documents, with no contact with people. Additionally, the ruling in the case has already been made, and the punishment has been 'administered'. The technicalities involved in how it is executed are of little interest.

This adherence of judges to legalism, to following first and foremost the letter of the law, the literal formulation of a certain provision without any deeper thought about the effect of these actions and their impact on the lives of those subjected to them, is problematic. Such thoughts rarely enter the judges' minds, and they most often give way to pragmatism or habit. This is what one judge said during an interview:

> After this conversation with you I will probably think about it even more often, because in such minor, let's say trivial, matters.
>
> (Judge, ENA_E17)

Because judges are not in the habit of going beyond the strictly literal letter of the law and thinking about the principles of applying the law or the guidelines on what the punishment is supposed to achieve, they rarely resort to the discretionary instruments contained in the regulations, even when it is possible to do so. And it is the EAW procedure that creates such opportunities, for example, of using the proportionality check when issuing EAWs (Carrera et al., 2013, pp. 16–18). This principle is interpreted from the Council Framework Decision of 13 June 2002 on the European arrest warrant and the surrender procedures between Member States (2002/584/JHA) and recommended by the European Commission (EC, 2017), but in practice it has not been applied in Polish courts for many years, as it was not explicitly introduced into national legislation. Instead, it was used only by way of exception and required judges to have a good understanding of European law, which was rare. Finally, it was included in the Polish Code of Criminal Procedure. This is how one judge assessed the step:

> I was very happy when the rules changed from 1 July 2015, and when principle of proportionality gave way to 'the interests of justice'. It's a pity that it had to come to this. After all, we are bound by EU law, the principle of proportionality too. And there was no need at all to write it directly in the Code. [But] it is important that it is there. Perhaps it is easier now.
>
> (Judge, ENA_E16)

In the interviews, we asked judges how they understood the concept of 'the interest of justice'. The answers depended on the judges' experience. Some of them, who have been dealing with the subject of transnational collaboration for a long time, had this to say:

> The interest of justice must be understood more broadly than just the interest of the Polish judiciary. I guess it should be defined as the interest of European justice in the sense that this international instrument should work efficiently and be executed, so that the system is not overloaded with unnecessary searches for people.
>
> (Judge, ENA_E18)

> I assess [it] from two sides: it must be the interest of the victim and . . . of the accused, also construed from the perspective of a fair trial to the very end: a certain loyalty and fairness of the judicial bodies, which then carry out the verdict. . . . And this is how I try to evaluate this interest of justice, that is, a little bit through the fairness of the proceedings and a little bit through the attitude of the courts.
>
> (Judge, ENA_E19)

However, these are model approaches, and probably rarely seen in practice (judging by a survey of EAW case rulings). Lower-level judges with less seniority treat the principle of the interest of justice in a utilitarian way. For them, the interest of justice is their own interest. As one judge put it:

> There was a problem with these pending cases, where we couldn't track down a person. And there were constantly inspections of these cases, and they went on and on. And in fact, the European warrant was a salutary measure . . .

> from my point of view as a judge who is supposed to execute a sentence and keeps running into problems, because the case is pending. And because of the audits of pending cases and the inability to execute the sentence, I evaluate this interest of justice differently. And that's why, as I say, I think I would still apply for the European Arrest Warrant, with wilful persistence.
>
> (Judge, EAW_E12)

The justice system is a huge hierarchical, bureaucratic machine. This affects the actions of individuals who must keep their 'paperwork in order'. With many cases to handle, it turns out that this bureaucratic duty comes before the values and principles involved in the administration of justice. This is because order in documents is a very tangible thing that can be subjected to scrutiny. It is important, for example, in the promotion proceedings of judges, when they are evaluated by senior judges; this assessment is formalised, specifically based on an analysis of the files of the cases they handle (Guarnieri, 2003). Thus, these files must be in order, and more ephemeral things like fairness or equity become less of a priority. This is why judges take such care with documents. And they use a variety of legal instruments precisely to make sure that the documents are complete and correct and that the authorities overseeing their work have no grounds for objection. They do this not only for pragmatic reasons but also out of routine, perfunctorily. In the interviews, they were very straightforward about this:

> [The EAW] is an institution that we are keen to use. I think it's mostly to keep our files in order. And so it goes – we use it sort of mechanically.
>
> (Judge, EAW_E17)

> From the perspective of a district judge [the EAW is] the only, the last resort, to execute a punishment, just to apprehend the defendant . . . then this poor court applies . . . for the European Arrest Warrant . . . it is a comfortable situation insofar as the district court filed for a warrant, did everything it could and has this record in the documents. But the regional court refused to issue it. And everyone is happy, you can say, because [a convicted person] is also safe where he is staying, his life has not crumbled to pieces. And as I said everyone is happy. It is also a little bit of a conformist approach, well maybe, but sadly that's the way it is.
>
> (Judge, ENA_E12)

Let's take a closer look at these statements: It's the court that is 'poor' here, and applying for the EAW is its 'last resort' to 'get the files in order'. And, after all, the higher court can ultimately refuse to issue the order and ensure the safety of the convict, preventing his life 'crumbling to pieces'. Then, 'everyone is happy'. It is the separation of this part of the criminal procedure into different stages, as I described earlier, that makes it easy to avoid responsibility for the application of its various elements and to shift it onto another person. Because it is this other person who – sooner or later – should do something, check or consider. And the person who is currently 'handling' the issue wants to get rid of it as soon as possible just to get the documents in order.

Sometimes this responsibility for the case is even shifted onto the convict, who supposedly should have done something to change their situation. This is illustrated well in the following statement: The initial deliberation of our respondent on whether to hastily commute the sentence is quickly superseded by other arguments, that, after all, it is not the judge, but the convict who should remember about many things, because it is, in the end, their punishment. Moreover, even the court's failures – such as 'overlooking in a flurry of cases' to revoke some prohibitions incumbent on the convict – are also shifted to the convict. The court may have forgotten, but the convict must remember. Because it is their case. As if it was not also the case of the judge who adjudicates it and who is responsible for it. Not the state (that the judge represents) who is and should be responsible for it (Carlen, 1994).

> One can sometimes conclude that someone was rash in executing this punishment. And on the other hand, one can take a closer look at it and wonder why it is the convict not contacting [the court]? . . . And as I think about it here, I regret a little bit, here I recognise that this is a minor crime. But then the thought still comes back: all right, but what have you, man, done for yourself to have this punishment revoked? Do you even have any idea that it will happen someday? Do you even want it to happen? Do you care about it? Do you even care about paying off all those debts that you owe? . . . So, on the one hand, it's the convicts' lack of responsibility and remembering that there's still some kind of a ban – for example, a ban on leaving the country – and there's this failure to make such a request. The court will sometimes, with a flood of these cases, overlook the measure altogether and not lift it. Well, on the other hand, if the punishment is not yet fully executed, there are some obligations. If no-one has applied for it to be waived, the ban is there. It must not be violated!
>
> (Judge, ENA_E17)

In many of the interviews, the judges mentioned the obligations of convicts. In doing so, they assumed that the convicted persons were similar to them: well versed in the regulations and all their intricacies. They assumed that these people have an excellent understanding of instructions about their rights and obligations, which are written in difficult legal language. Thus, what is required of the convicted persons is exceptional agency, which they often do not possess. And the judges who meet them in the courtroom should know this and see it. They should understand that they are dealing with poorly educated people, some of whom have a problem with various kinds of substances, who have an unstable living situation, and that remembering to inform the court even of changes in their address is a requirement that is definitely beyond their capabilities. Besides, even if they informed the court of their foreign address, it is customary for Polish courts not to send correspondence abroad anyway, because this is their practice. One of the judges confirmed this herself:

> If we have two addresses of the accused person, sometimes an overseas address and a Polish address, there's the question: Should we go out of our way and try to serve at this foreign address or not?
>
> (Judge, ENA_E17)

And the answer to this question is usually 'not'. This means that even fulfilling these expectations of the court and informing them of an address change would not accomplish much in practice. And these individuals may simply not have a permanent address in Poland. Specifically, people with prior criminal records often have nowhere to go after leaving prison (Klaus, 2023). But instead of seeing all this and trying to understand them, it is more convenient for judges to maintain the fiction of convicts' full responsibility for 'their' proceedings – in which, at the executive stage, they do not actually participate in after all, and about which they often know nothing at all.

5. What does justice mean in transnational criminal justice cooperation?

If we think and talk about justice in terms of its transnational cooperation, two – seemingly contradictory – elements most often come into conflict. On the one hand, there is the inevitability of punishment and the equality of all people who have been convicted, equality being defined as the necessity for each person to serve the sentence they have been ordered to serve, regardless of whether they remain in or have left the country. On the other hand, there is the fulfilment of other goals of punishment besides retribution understood as inflicting direct pains of it, as the point is to reflect on whether (especially in the case of petty cases), it makes sense to prosecute someone years later and to execute a punishment against them. In this chapter, I would like to focus on this dichotomy.

The basis underlying Polish criminal procedure is the principle of legality (Daniluk & Leciak, 2016, p. 154). Thus, in principle, there is no room for discretion, that is, for saying that prosecuting certain cases or perpetrators simply does not make sense from a financial or pragmatic point of view. As one judge put it:

> we have the principle of legalism in our system. The principle of prosecuting a convict for the rest of their life and one day longer.
>
> (Judge, ENA_E19)

A police officer added:

> in Poland, there is the so-called inevitability of punishment. And it doesn't matter whether it's for stealing a bicycle for 500 zlotys [120 euro] or for

fraud involving millions. In Poland, there is an inevitability of punishment, and the courts act according to this principle.

(Police officer, ENA_E2)

Basically, the principle of legalism applies at all stages of criminal proceedings: from the pre-trial stage to the executive stage. It shapes the Polish idea of what justice is by often equating it with the inevitability of punishment. However, it should be remembered that the purpose of introducing the EAW was specifically to deter offenders from hiding abroad and to ensure that the punishment is enforced. This aspect of counteracting impunity, which is made possible by transnational instruments, was noted by our experts (as well as convicts like Katarzyna) when they spoke about the goals of their application:

> So that people who commit a criminal act do not feel that they will go unpunished in the territory of another member state or in the territory of another country, if we are talking globally. And so they don't feel that they can go unpunished, and so they feel that they can't hide or continue to carry out certain actions that would result in them breaking the law again.
>
> (Border guard officer, ENA_E15)

> We are all equal under the law, and any of those people being supervised or convicts who knowingly or unknowingly stay abroad should be brought back to the country and serve their sentence here.
>
> (Probation officer, ENA_E23)

> Penalties are necessary and they serve a purpose. In fact, I think that if it [getting caught] hadn't happened, well, I and probably everyone who was on that [returned] flight would have continued to avoid [punishment], right? And we would have continued to live in our world, kind of like we avoided serving this punishment. . . . Well, because if there is a crime, there must be a punishment too. Yes! That's my opinion.
>
> (Katarzyna)

However, one element is missing from the statements made earlier. The interviewees assume that the only way to serve a punishment is to be sent back to Poland for this purpose. This inconsistency, however, was noted very accurately in the context of the EAW by one of the judges:

> The inevitability of punishment does not at all mean that one has to deploy god knows what resources. . . . And if we don't want to do something like that, to issue this European Arrest Warrant, well then let's make a little more effort and apply for this punishment to be served there. Come on, this is the

way to make sure the punishment is honoured, and the convict doesn't necessarily have to serve it in Poland.

(Judge, ENA_E27)

The judge's view was echoed by a probation officer, who stressed that serving a sentence is often necessary, especially when it comes to more serious crimes in which someone has suffered. In such cases, waiving enforcement of the sentence would violate the victims' sense of justice, or society's. But at the same time, he pointed out that serving one's sentence abroad, in another EU country, would both satisfy the sense of justice and not be overly burdensome and harsh for the convicts themselves (for more on the consequences of the forced transfer of convicts to Poland for themselves and their families, see Klaus, Wlodarczyk-Madejska & Wzorek in this volume).

Someone lives [abroad], has a family there, has a life there. Why drag them all the way to Poland? Let them serve their sentence there, right? . . . Because there are also serious crimes, which, well, can't be forgiven, . . . where someone has suffered. There is always this other party who must feel that justice has been done. But I think it's not always the case that we need to bring them to Poland.

(Probation officer, ENA_E24)

It is also worth remembering that transnational justice cannot always be applied, hence in practice the principle of legalism and the related principle of the inevitability of punishment will not be applied anyway. This divergence may occur especially in two circumstances. First, we may be dealing with an offence against which the principle of dual criminality in another EU country does not hold, as in the aforementioned cases of drink driving, failing to pay child support or drug possession. In these instances, for formal reasons, there will be no transfer of the offender to Poland, and therefore no serving of the sentence. The second circumstance is the application of the principle of proportionality. This occurs of course when the judge issuing the order takes a closer look at the case in question, instead of simply approving it without going deeper into it, as I wrote earlier. In transnational proceedings, there is a better chance for this to happen, because it is one of the few executive proceedings in which a case is analysed by two different judges. Sometimes even three judges are involved, because a judge from the other Member State also takes part in the proceedings, and decides whether to approve an EAW against a particular person by drawing precisely on the principle of proportionality or referring to fundamental rights (Böse, 2015; Ouwerkerk, 2018; Schallmoser, 2014).

In this type of a situation [drink driving] in the UK, this person would get a fine and probably a [driving] ban. In Poland, on the other hand, the most severe penalty in the catalogue of punishments was ordered. . . . The court imposed a suspended prison sentence of 5 years plus a fine in connection

> with the suspended sentence – not a small one either. . . . [The convict] paid this fine. . . . Meanwhile, there was an order for the execution of this [suspended] sentence. I don't know for what reasons. . . . And the British court writes that according to British law this was too harsh a repercussion. And because of this, it took the position that, as it were, these interests of justice weigh against upholding this European Arrest Warrant.
>
> (Judge, ENA_E12)

This is how the same judge went on to deliberate on the principle of legalism vis-à-vis the principle of proportionality:

> for example, there was a man who drove drunk, colloquially speaking . . . and fortunately did not kill anyone. He just simply drove under the influence of alcohol. Of course, in no way am I trying to commend this act, but [looking] from the perspective of these mechanisms, well, there should not be motions [for the EAW] in these types of cases. There really shouldn't! In spite of the fact that the inevitability of punishment will actually amount to nothing, this idea of a trial and conviction of a person who has, let's say, violated traffic rules will amount to nothing. But well, tough. It seems that the rule of proportionality is screaming to be heard here. Is screaming to be heard and should be taken into account.
>
> (Judge, ENA_E12)

Other people involved in transnational justice also referred to exactly this type of minor cases in condemning the overly strict and formalistic approach of the law (and therefore the judge who applies the law) to the person. A border guard officer called the procedure a 'machine' and said that using it in such cases is like 'using a hammer to crack a nut'. He further added:

> If these people were offered, I don't know, to pay back the debt, to work, 90% of them would pay it back. Bags of money would stay in our country in the pockets of taxpayers, and the whole procedure would not have to be triggered.
>
> (Border guard officer, EAW_E15)

This pointlessness, especially from a financial point of view, of launching the whole transnational procedure, was also evident to others, both convicted persons and judges:

> I think that this European warrant is being abused for sure. . . . Because I think that a man who has to serve 3 months in jail because he didn't pay 800 zlotys [180 euro] . . ., he automatically gets the European warrant, and this is totally unreasonable . . . from the point of view of not even justice, but finances. Well, because the whole procedure is very expensive, it's very costly, because to bring someone . . . from Bulgaria, from England, on a

special plane sent by Poland, we are talking about hundreds of thousands of zlotys. And this person actually owes the Polish state or society – let's call it that – 800 zlotys. So, where is the sense, where is the logic?

(Marcin)

We order this punishment, and we see it is 6 months, and sometimes 5 months, and sometimes even 4 months [of imprisonment]. Such a short-term punishment because of 3,000 zlotys that someone did not pay and the court must get involved again. . . . Then we have the whole international machinery . . . because we have to fly not only the convict, but also their guards. I then put these numbers together and say: really? 3,000?!!! 4,000 [zloty]?! Is it worth it?!!! . . . And that's something to think about: To what extent is this very sense of justice, the obligation to serve the sentence, more important to us than the costs we pay for it?

(Judge, ENA_E17)

Departing from the principle of legalism and moving towards a different understanding of justice should also be done when it is justified by the circumstances of the convicted person. We should consider the individual with the warrant, against whom there is no point in carrying out the punishment at a given point in their life, because not only would the punishment not bring the expected results (such as rehabilitation and the cessation of their crimes), but its effects could be counterproductive and could even cause the person to return to crime. I am referring to cases where enforcing the punishment by means of bringing the convict to Poland and incarcerating them would lead to a loss of a job or the end of a life built abroad. Thus, the goals of punishment as indicated in the Polish Criminal Code would certainly not be achieved (see Klaus, Włodarczyk-Madejska & Wzorek, in this volume). But these problems are mainly perceived by those who work with convicts. And from the point of view of the judge and the documents that they analyse, this problem is unfortunately invisible because, to reiterate, the judge does not see the particular person whose case they are deciding, and relies basically only on documents in these proceedings.

The fact is that it often happens, that they actually leave [Poland and] work, cut themselves off from their peers . . . alcohol and drugs and so on . . . this man works diligently, hard and honestly [abroad], and this is a good reason to think that he will not commit these crimes again. And at this point, taking him away from this place to serve some outstanding few months of suspended probation, well that is a bit pointless.

(Prison officer, EAW_E14)

The isolation of such people, separation from their loved ones or loss of work, can negatively affect their family and social relations. And I think that the courts should take into account exactly these sorts of aspects. But this is my personal opinion. So that families don't suffer.

(Border guard officer, ENA_E25)

> Another problem with our judicial system is that cases last for years, that someone who committed a crime on Polish territory 10 years ago, managed to leave, start a family, become a respectable person, a businessman and so on, . . . well, and then he just has to . . . serve the sentence, although . . . he is a completely different person. Well, but that doesn't exempt him from facing the consequences for it. . . . It's completely pointless. I mean, completely pointless!
>
> (NGO social worker, ENA_E11)

The last interviewee pointed out another important thing, namely the criminal proceedings that often last for years. Our research has shown that in the case of those prosecuted to serve their sentences (i.e. almost 80% of all EAW prosecutions), in one out of four cases more than ten years have passed from the crime itself to the issuance of the warrant, and in one out of three cases at least five years have passed from the issuance of the sentence (see Wlodarczyk-Madejska & Wzorek in this volume). This is an inordinately long time, during which a lot can change in a person's life. The paradox of this situation with regard to the sense of justice was something that one of our respondents commented on:

> Punishment should be inevitable. But also, from what I remember, it should be immediate. So this is where I think we are a bit inconsistent.
>
> (Prison Officer, ENA_E14)

The convicts mentioned this problem as well. It was well captured by Karol, who did not question his guilt or his sentence. Rather, he spoke generally about his expectations of the entire justice system:

> Maybe I'll start by saying that I would like the justice system to be fair, just. It sounds so strange: for the justice system to be just. I'm not allowed to judge . . ., but I can express an opinion that some sentences are really unjust. On the other hand, when it comes to the question of whether we should bring people to Poland, I'm absolutely for it. Only that it should be done in the normal way: that is, quick extradition and not detention of people. . . . A quick guilty verdict, and that these sentences are really appropriate to those, to the offences committed.
>
> (Karol)

This is an excellent summary of the previous discussion. Everything is captured in this quote: an appeal to justice that comes quickly and is proportional to the deed.

Participation in transnational justice brings another important change from the perspective of justice. Judges begin to see the differences in how courts function in other countries and what punishments they hand out. In theory, it is fairly obvious to say that such differences exist, but it is one thing to know something in a general theoretical sense, and quite another to come across it in one's own practice. This is especially true when a ruling issued by a Polish court is subject to some kind of evaluation by a judge in another EU country, and this court, for example, reprimands Poland's repressive justice system. These differences in how punitive the judiciary is, and how stringent the Polish courts are, are also seen by other people who participate in international cooperation, including people who work with convicts and the convicts themselves.

> Our clients serve sentences [in Poland] which are . . . really out there. In England, they would get a suspended sentence for this offence or just get out after a short while. And here they serve 6 years, for example.
>
> (NGO social worker, ENA_E11)

> In other countries, the justice systems are more liberal. They're not as harsh as in Poland, where they lock you up and punish you for any crime. You can do – I don't know – substitute punishments, and not immediately [go to prison].
>
> (Wojciech)

> In the UK it's like this: A sentence is pronounced, you serve half the sentence and you don't write any letters to the court, requests – nothing. You just automatically get out of half your sentence right away. And here I am long past half my sentence and I still have a little more than 6 months to go and still nothing. I'm still locked up here for no purpose. I don't have a job, or anything gainful to do. What am I doing here?
>
> (Marek)

These quotes show that differences in the functioning of the justice system occur at the level of criminalisation for certain offences (or the lack thereof), the length of the sentence, the rate of mandatory imprisonment and the operation of the imprisonment system. These differences demonstrate once again that justice and the concept of justice are fluid, or perhaps differently understood by different people and by the justice systems in different countries. This leads to the great difficulty of trying to standardise these practices and develop some sort of common platform and ground on how to respond to criminal acts (or to even create a common list of such acts). And this difficulty occurs even among countries as ostensibly similar as the EU states.

Conclusions

The interpretation of the concepts of 'justice' and 'just punishment' within transnational proceedings is quite complicated. There are a number of reasons for this: these terms are decoded differently in national justice systems; each country has different degrees of punitiveness and a general approach to sentencing and punishment. The problem is the very definition of a common catalogue of criminal acts, not to mention the severity of punishments for particular ones (combining both what is contained in the laws and their application in practice) or the manner and form of executing punishments (e.g. resulting from the design and operation of prisons), which has a massive impact on the severity of the punishment that is imposed and executed (Hayes, 2016, 2018).

When we think about just punishment, we basically go back to Beccaria's guidelines, which focus on how fast the punitive response is and how appropriate it is to the crime committed. However, he makes an important addition to this theory, namely the need for statutes of limitations:

> in less considerable and more obscure crimes, a time should be fixed, after which the delinquent should be no longer uncertain of his fate. For in the latter case, the length of time, in which the crime is almost forgotten, prevents the example of impunity, and allows the criminal to amend, and become a better member of society.
>
> (Beccaria, 1872, pp. 112–113)

It seems that this premise is especially relevant for the research we have conducted and people who were prosecuted transnationally many years after they committed a criminal act, especially if it was not a serious one.

Another important element emerges from Beccaria's discussion, in my opinion: seeing beyond a rigid understanding of the law and paying attention to its objective and social function. This is where the role of judges in interpreting the law in accordance with the purpose it is intended to fulfil is especially important. Unfortunately, the formalism that Polish judges exercise in applying the law distorts its purpose. They choose formalism because it is easier to apply in practice, as it requires only a simple, almost literal understanding and application of a provision to an event, without the need for deeper inquiry into it. This way of looking at the application of the law is fundamentally bureaucratic. Proponents of this approach insist that such easy-to-apply regulations, which limit the judge's discretionary power, lead to standardised practice and more uniform sentences. This, however, does not seem to be true (if only considering the far-reaching discrepancies in the rulings of Polish judges [Klimczak et al., 2020]). This is because in the sentencing process it is necessary to have recourse to legal principles, and thus it is indispensable to leave some discretionary power to the judge. The role of judges' discretion is to prevent the law from being unjust (Thomas, 2003). As a matter of fact, the judge should be, as it were, forced to refer to these principles (or at least to consider them) when making any rulings. After all, this is what gives them the opportunity to implement the principle of justice and the rule of law (Matczak, 2018).

Radbruch takes a similar view, noting the necessity of applying the law of clemency to some people in order to be able to alter the punishment that has already been imposed. The purpose is precisely to restore justice.

> The purpose of clemency, then, is to ensure the triumph of justice over positive law, so that the purposiveness of law, which mandates that a person be treated as an individual, overrides the impersonal proceduralism of compensatory justice (*schematische Gerechichkeit*).
>
> (Radbruch, 2012, pp. 186–187)

Radbruch's claim can be extended beyond the formal right of clemency to an injunction for judges to use various types of instruments (including, for example, the principle of proportionality) in executive proceedings so as to see the human being and adjust the criminal response to their situation, especially if a certain amount of time has passed since the verdict. This is by no means to say that the punishment should be completely waived in every instance. However, another form of its execution should be contemplated, such as serving it abroad or giving one more chance for the convict to fulfil the obligations that were previously imposed on them. But for this, it is necessary to end bureaucratism and see the individual behind the documents (Fiss, 1983, p. 1443). This is very difficult in the Polish system of sentence enforcement, although it is possible when issuing EAWs, if only by applying the principle of proportionality. However, this principle is very rarely used by judges.

Although this study deals with the Polish practice of applying the transnational justice system, it says a lot in general about the criminal justice system in Poland and the Polish system of sentence execution. And sadly, it reflects very poorly on this system. The excessive formalism, legalism and bureaucracy of this system often lead to a negation of justice. This can be clearly seen in international proceedings, as I have tried to show in this chapter. However, the same rules apply to all executive proceedings in Poland when suspended sentences are revoked without any contact with the people convicted, and people are sent to prison many years after committing a crime – sometimes even when they are on the right track of desisting. This system makes the desistance more and more difficult, but afterwards the convicted person is blamed for its failure. And no one recognises (or takes responsibility for) the contribution of the justice system to the situation in which the convict finds themselves (Carlen, 1994; Klaus, 2023).

The findings I outlined earlier show another highly interesting point, which is a typically Polish issue. For many years, studies of forced migration and the expulsion of people from one country to another have paid attention to the role of criminal law and the justice system in this process. Most often, however, it is the justice system of the receiving state that makes considerable efforts to first criminalise unwanted migrants and then have them expelled from its territory, which is sometimes a form of punishment, but more often a convenient excuse to get rid of these people (Franko, 2020). Increasingly, these actions also affect EU citizens, especially those from Central Europe, including Poles (Brandariz, 2021; Klaus et al., 2021). But our research shows a very different context for these migratory movements. It is the Polish courts bringing back such large numbers of their citizens to the country (on a scale of more than 20,000 in the past few years) that contribute immensely to their forced mobility. It is the Polish courts which, as a result of their actions, can shut down the path for these people to return to other European countries (which do not want to 'host' criminals or ex-criminals). This contribution of the judiciary of the country of origin to the forced migration of its citizens is a unique phenomenon worldwide. The question of the purpose and meaning of these actions remain open in the vast majority of cases.

Notes

1 The research team for the project, besides the author of the text, included Justyna Włodarczyk-Madejska and Dominik Wzorek. The research presented in this chapter is part of the project 'Experiences of Poles Deported from the UK in the Context of the Criminal Justice System Involvement', funded by the National Science Centre, Poland, under Grant No. UMO-2018/30/M/HS5/00816.
2 Polish justice system consists of three types of courts: district courts (318), regional courts (46), appeal courts (11), ultimately overseen by the Supreme Court (GUS, 2022, p. 83).
3 A separate issue is how much a previous criminal record should influence the increase in sentence (as mentioned by the interviewee) and how this practice affects the desistance from crime (Klaus, 2023; Schinkel et al., 2019). The result of these measures is that quite serious punishment is being imposed for petty offences.
4 The official Polish name of this penalty is 'a penalty of restrictions of liberty', but it mirrors to a large extent a community service in other jurisdictions.
5 In general, in our research, officers from various enforcement agencies were eager to talk about their work and its challenges but avoided making general assessments of the system or judging the performance of other institutions, particularly the courts. One person put it bluntly: "I will tell you this: I am the last person who will evaluate the functioning of the judiciary. . . . Because it is not within the scope of my duties" (Police officer, EAW_E2).

References

Alexy, R. (2021). *The Ideal Dimension of Law*. Oxford University Press.
Aliverti, A. (2018). Strangers in Our Midst. The Construction of Difference through Cultural Appeals in Criminal Justice Litigation. In M. Bosworth, A. Parmar, & Y. Vazquez (Eds.), *Race, Criminal Justice, and Migration Control: Enforcing the Boundaries of Belonging* (pp. 127–141). Oxford University Press.
Ashworth, A., & Zedner, L. (2015). *Preventive Justice*. Oxford University Press.
Beccaria, C. (1872). *An Essay on Crimes and Punishments. By the Marquis Beccaria of Milan. With a Commentary by M. de Voltaire. A New Edition Corrected*. W.C. Little & Co.
Black, D. (2011). *Moral Time*. Oxford University Press.
Böse, M. (2015). Human Rights Violations and Mutual Trust: Recent Case Law on the European Arrest Warrant. In S. Ruggeri (Ed.), *Human Rights in European Criminal Law* (pp. 135–145). Springer International Publishing.
Brandariz, J. A. (2021). The Removal of EU Nationals: An Unaccounted Dimension of the European Deportation Apparatus. *Central and Eastern European Migration Review, 10*(1), 13–33. https://doi.org/10.17467/ceemr.2021.06
Brandon, A. M., & O'Connell, M. (2018). Same Crime: Different Punishment? Investigating Sentencing Disparities between Irish and Non-Irish Nationals in the Irish Criminal Justice System. *The British Journal of Criminology, 58*(5), 1127–1146. https://doi.org/10.1093/bjc/azx080
Carlen, P. (1994). Crime, Inequality, and Sentencing. In A. Duff & D. Garland (Eds.), *A Reader on Punishment* (pp. 306–332). Oxford University Press.
Carrera, S., Guild, E., & Hernanz, N. (2013). *Europe's Most Wanted? Recalibrating Trust in the European Arrest Warrant System*. CEPS.
Christie, N. (1981). *Limits to Pain: The Role of Punishment in Penal Policy*. M. Robertson.
Cohen, S. (1972). *Folk Devils and Moral Panics*. Routledge.

Cole, D. (2003). Judging the Next Emergency: Judicial Review and Individual Rights in Times of Crisis. *Michigan Law Review*, *101*(8), 2565–2595.

Cotterrell, R. (2018). *Sociological Jurisprudence: Juristic Thought and Social Inquiry*. Routledge.

Crewe, B. (2015). Inside the Belly of the Penal Beast: Understanding the Experience of Imprisonment. *International Journal for Crime, Justice and Social Democracy*, *4*(1), Article 1. https://doi.org/10.5204/ijcjsd.v4i1.201

Daniluk, P., & Leciak, M. (2016). Statute of Limitations in the Polish Criminal Law. *Journal of Eastern-European Criminal Law*, *2016*(2), 150–161.

Dauvergne, C. (2005). *Making People Illegal: What Globalization Means for Migration and Law*. Cambridge University Press.

Dworkin, R. (1986). *Law's Empire*. Harvard University Press.

EC. (2017). Commission Notice – Handbook on How to Issue and Execute a European Arrest Warrant. *European Commission*. https://eur-lex.europa.eu/legal-content/EN/TXT/PDF/?uri=CELEX:52017XC1006(02)&from=PL

Efrat, A., & Newman, A. L. (2020). Defending Core Values: Human Rights and the Extradition of Fugitives. *Journal of Peace Research*, *57*(4), 581–596. https://doi.org/10.1177/0022343319898231

Efrat, A., & Tomasina, M. (2018). Value-free Extradition? Human Rights and the Dilemma of Surrendering Wanted Persons to China. *Journal of Human Rights*, *17*(5), 605–621. https://doi.org/10.1080/14754835.2018.1533454

Fiss, O. M. (1983). The Bureaucratization of the Judiciary. *The Yale Law Journal*, *92*(8), 1442–1468. https://doi.org/10.2307/796182

Franko, K. (2020). *The Crimmigrant Other: Migration and Penal Power*. Routledge.

Gruszczyńska, B., Marczewski, M., Siemaszko, A., Ostaszewski, P., Włodarczyk-Madejska, J., & Klimczak, J. (2021). *Atlas przestępczości w Polsce 6*. Wydawnictwo Instytutu Wymiaru Sprawiedliwości.

Guarnieri, C. (2003). Courts as an Instrument of Horizontal Accountability: The Case of Latin Europe. In J. M. Maravall & A. Przeworski (Eds.), *Democracy and the Rule of Law* (pp. 223–241). Cambridge University Press.

GUS. (2022). *Concise Statistical Yearbook of Poland*. Statistics Poland.

Hayes, D. (2016). Penal Impact: Towards a More Intersubjective Measurement of Penal Severity. *Oxford Journal of Legal Studies*, *36*(4), 724–750. https://doi.org/10.1093/ojls/gqv042

Hayes, D. (2018). Proximity, Pain, and State Punishment. *Punishment & Society*, *20*(2), 235–254. https://doi.org/10.1177/1462474517701303

Hester, S., & Eglin, P. (2017). *A Sociology of Crime* (2nd edition). Routledge.

HFHR. (2018). The Practice of the European Arrest Warrant in Poland as an Issuing Country. Country Report. *Helsinki Foundation for Human Rights*. www.hfhr.pl/wp-content/uploads/2018/07/European-Arrest-Warrant-EN.pdf

Jacyna, M. (2018). *Country Report on the European Arrest Warrant. The Republic of Poland*. www.inabsentieaw.eu/wp-content/uploads/2018/10/Background-Report_in-absentia-EAW-in-the-Republic-of-Poland.pdf

Jankowski, M., & Momot, S. (2015). *Stosowanie przepisu art. 62a ustawy o przeciwdziałaniu narkomanii*. Instytut Wymiaru Sprawiedliwości.

Kalir, B., Achermann, C., & Rosset, D. (2019). Re-searching Access: What do Attempts at Studying Migration Control Tell Us About the State? *Social Anthropology*, *27*(S1), 5–16. https://doi.org/10.1111/1469-8676.12675

Klaus, W. (2023). Snares and Pains, or What Stands in the Path to Desistance from Crime. In W. Klaus, I. Rzeplińska, & D. Woźniakowska-Fajst (Eds.), *Life and Crime Trajectories of Former Juvenile Offenders in Adulthood. A Criminal Career*. Routledge.

Klaus, W., Włodarczyk-Madejska, J., & Wzorek, D. (2021). In the Pursuit of Justice: (Ab)Use of the European Arrest Warrant in the Polish Criminal Justice System. *Central and Eastern European Migration Review, 10*(1), 95–117. https://doi.org/10.17467/ceemr.2021.02
Klimczak, J., Marczewski, M., Ostaszewski, P., Sidor, P., & Włodarczyk-Madejska, J. (2020). *Geografia karania. Obraz statystyczny spójności stosowania sankcji karnych.* Instytut Wymiaru Sprawiedliwości
Klimek, L. (2015). *European Arrest Warrant.* Springer International Publishing. https://doi.org/10.1007/978-3-319-07338-5
Kotarbiński, T. (1987). *Pisma etyczne.* Wydawnictwo Ossolineum.
Krajewski, K. (2016). Sentencing in Poland: Failed Attempts to Reduce Punitiveness. *Crime and Justice, 45*, 175–219. https://doi.org/10.1086/685539
Leawoods, H. (2000). Gustav Radbruch: An Extraordinary Legal Philosopher. *Washington University Journal of Law & Policy, 2*(1), Article 1.
Lipsky, M. (1980). *Street-Level Bureaucracy. Dilemmas of the Individuals in Public Service.* Russell Sage Foundation.
Macías-Rojas, P. (2016). *From Deportation to Prison: The Politics of Immigration Enforcement in Post-Civil Rights America.* New York University Press.
Matczak, M. (2018). Why Judicial Formalism is Incompatible with the Rule of Law. *Canadian Journal of Law & Jurisprudence, 31*(1), 61–85. https://doi.org/10.1017/cjlj.2018.3
Montaldo, S. (2016). On a Collision Course! Mutual Recognition, Mutual Trust and the Protection of Fundamental Rights in the Recent Case-law of the Court of Justice. *European Papers – A Journal on Law and Integration, 1*(3), 965–996. https://doi.org/10.15166/2499-8249/113
Nussbaum, M. C. (2007). *Frontiers of Justice. Disability, Nationality, Species Membership.* Harvard University Press.
Ostaszewski, P. (2020). Transition in Offences of Not Paying Maintenance in Poland. *Archiwum Kryminologii, XLII*(1), 185–206. https://doi.org/10.7420/AK2020C
Ouwerkerk, J. (2018). Balancing Mutual Trust and Fundamental Rights Protection in the Context of the European Arrest Warrant What Role for the Gravity of the Underlying Offence in cjeu Case Law? *European Journal of Crime, Criminal Law and Criminal Justice, 26*(2), 103–109.
Radbruch, G. (2012). *Filozofia Prawa.* Wydawnictwo Naukowe PWN.
Rawls, J. (1999). *A Theory of Justice* (Revised edition). Harvard University Press.
Schallmoser, N. M. (2014). The European Arrest Warrant and Fundamental Rights. *European Journal of Crime, Criminal Law and Criminal Justice, 22*, 135–165.
Schinkel, M., Atkinson, C., & Anderson, S. (2019). 'Well-kent Faces': Policing Persistent Offenders and the Possibilities for Desistance. *The British Journal of Criminology, 59*(3), 634–652.
Tata, C. (2007). Sentencing as Craftwork and the Binary Epistemologies of the Discretionary Decision Process: *Social & Legal Studies, 16*(3), 425–447. https://doi.org/10.1177/0964663907079767
Thomas, D. (2003). Judicial Discretion in Sentencing. In L. Gelsthorpe & N. Padfield (Eds.), *Exercising Discretion. Decision-making in the Criminal Justice System and Beyond* (pp. 50–73). Willan.
van Ginneken, E. F., & Hayes, D. (2017). 'Just' Punishment? Offenders' Views on the Meaning and Severity of Punishment. *Criminology & Criminal Justice, 17*(1), 62–78. https://doi.org/10.1177/1748895816654204
Wieczorek, I. (2018). EU Constitutional Limits to the Europeanization of Punishment: A Case Study on Offenders' Rehabilitation. *Maastricht Journal of European and Comparative Law, 25*(6), 655–671. https://doi.org/10.1177/1023263X18820692

5 Judicial cooperation versus migration control. Critical reflections on the implementation of grounds for refusing the execution of a European arrest warrant for residents and stayers

European trends and insights from Italy

Stefano Montaldo[1]

Introduction: judicial cooperation, mutual recognition and the role of transposition choices at national level

As the European Arrest Warrant celebrates its 20th anniversary,[2] it is now surrounded by a vast body of EU secondary acts devoted to the implementation of mutual recognition and contributing to the EU goal of establishing an area of freedom, security and justice. Over the years, the European model of judicial cooperation in criminal matters has developed from an embryonic and fragmented series of acts to a consolidated system of closely intertwined and complementary mechanisms (Ouwerkerk, 2021, p. 87), unparalleled around the globe. This evolution has brought with it pressing considerations on the nature of this EU policy, on the interests that are worthy of protection in a cross-border scenario and on the delicate relationship with national criminal systems (Weyembergh & Wieczorek, 2016, p. 29). In fact, notwithstanding the recurring – and factually correct – narrative on the inherently technical and judicially driven nature of judicial cooperation mechanisms, the departure from traditional intergovernmental patterns of mutual legal assistance does not obliterate the political implications of the adoption of common rules in the domain of criminal justice. Every EU initiative requires the normativisation of a balance between structurally competing interests, such as individual rights and collective security, or nationality ties and the *vis expansiva* of Union citizenship and free movement.

These underlying choices made by the European legislator are further amplified by the vertical divide of competences between the EU and the Member States, which requires careful transposition decisions to avoid normative and practical discrepancies with domestic substantive and procedural criminal laws. In this context, the duty to implement Framework Decisions (FDs) and Directives echoes the objectives underpinning EU secondary legislation but, at the same time, offers

DOI: 10.4324/9781003254584-6

remarkable opportunities for what has been termed the domestification of EU patterns (Knill & Tosun, 2012, p. 309). Leaving aside any consideration on the difficult multilevel interplay between the Union and the Member States, the premise of this chapter is that, notwithstanding the efforts for effective EU law enforcement, transposition offers leeway to national legislators and governments to apply their own policy priority, not necessarily in plain contrast with the EU footprint (Thoman & Sager, 2017, p. 1253).

These dynamics are particularly evident in relation to the acts allowing for the – consensual or forced – movement of offenders, such as the European Arrest Warrant and the FD 2008/909/JHA on the transfer of prisoners.[3] The practical outcome of these mechanisms is the identification of the place in Europe where a person charged with an offence or sentenced in a Member State will be tried or will serve the prison term. These acts then have implications which are likely to provide a varied set of incentives and disincentives to the national authorities, such as the possibility of exercising criminal jurisdiction, the protection of the offenders' family ties, the allocation of the practical and financial burden connected to prosecution or detention, the opportunity to allocate responsibility for potentially dangerous persons and the related public order risks to the authorities of other States. The implementation phase is not immune from these and other factors, which ultimately influence the policy choices at the basis of the domestic transposition laws, often focused on the primary goal of minimising the role and responsibilities of national authorities with regard to unwanted offenders.

The European trend on the implementation of Article 4, no. 6 of FD 2002/584/JHA on the European Arrest Warrant (EAW FD) is a particularly interesting example. While this provision enables the executing judicial authorities to refuse surrender if the offender is a national of that State or is residing or staying in its territory, an overview of the clauses implementing this optional ground for refusal across Europe reveals a generally cautious – if not plainly restrictive – approach at an earlier stage, namely the normative choices delimiting the room for manoeuvre of judicial authorities faced with EAW certificates.

The Italian case study provides clear and recent evidence of this approach. A long-awaited reform of the national implementation law entered into force in February 2021[4] and was expressly designed to delimit the scope of application of grounds allowing the judicial authorities to deny execution, to comply more fully with the principle of mutual recognition. A key element of the reform was precisely the minimisation of the role played by the offender's nationality, residence and stay in a Member State with regard to the possibility of resisting surrender to the issuing State. The practical implications of the new limits on the possibility of invoking Article 4, no. 6 of the EAW FD are twofold. On the one hand, considerations on the chances of the offender's social rehabilitation and on the preservation of his or her personal and societal ties in the host State, to the benefit of the right to private and family life, are largely neglected. On the other hand, and conversely, the reform maximises the room for automatic and swift surrenders to the States issuing EAWs, thereby demonstrating formal adherence to the purposes of the systems established by FD 2002/584/JHA.

The chapter focuses on the roots and discusses the underlying rationale of the recent amendments to the Italian EAW law. It addresses its controversial consequences and presents possible elements of friction with EU law. In particular, Section 2 outlines the relevant normative framework and the main interpretative clarifications established by the Court of Justice (CJEU). The following section recalls the history of the EAW in Italy and the developments that the national transposition law has undergone from the original version to the freshly reformed text. Section 4 discusses the reform in greater detail and critically addresses its practical implications and inherent drivers. It is argued that, by restricting the personal scope of application of the grounds for refusal in question, the Italian authorities are aiming to use the EAW as an indirect means of disposing of unwanted offenders. Section 5 builds on this premise to focus on the consequences of the reform in question on the interplay between the EAW system and the FD on the transfer of prisoners, with specific attention to the Italian normative approach to the implementation of the latter EU act.

1. Citizenship, residence and stay as an optional ground for refusing the execution of a European arrest warrant

The regulation of the grounds for refusal of surrender represents one of the most important aspects of FD 2002/584/JHA. In fact, these provisions expressly predetermine, by virtue of a legislative choice, the scope of mutual recognition and its boundaries in the EAW system. While mutual trust allows for the establishment of a quasi-absolute and automatic model of horizontal cooperation between national judicial authorities, the grounds for refusal require a balancing exercise with competing (and, in some cases, compelling) interests that are worthy of protection.

As is well known, FD 2002/584/JHA distinguishes between mandatory and optional limits to surrender,[5] a difference abandoned by the subsequent EU legislation on judicial cooperation in criminal matters, which instead focuses only on discretionary clauses.[6] The latter category is regulated by Article 4 and includes a heterogeneous series of impediments to surrender, encompassing inter alia the existence of ongoing proceedings in idem in the executing State; the expiry of the limitation period for prosecution or punishment; and the violation of the right to participate in the trial. Article 4, no. 6 establishes one of the most debated and commonly used grounds for refusal, which applies only to EAWs issued for the purpose of enforcing a custodial sentence or detention order. Pursuant to this provision, surrender can be refused "where the requested person is staying in, or is a national or a resident of the executing Member State". In addition, refusal is conditioned upon the executing State undertaking to enforce the sentence or detention order itself, in accordance with its national law. This provision must be interpreted in conjunction with Article 5(3), which enshrines the so-called guarantee of return: where the same situations referred to earlier occur in the context of EAWs issued for prosecution purposes, surrender "may be subject to the condition that the person, after being heard, is returned to the executing Member State in order to serve there the custodial sentence or detention order passed against him in the issuing Member State".

Both Article 4, no. 6, and Article 5(3) constitute the evolution of the nationality exception barring surrender in traditional intergovernmental extradition cases, with the foundational limit of the *aut dedere aut iudicare* – either surrender or prosecute and determine the criminal liability – principle.[7] However, while this exception merely presupposes the existence of an interest – in many cases of constitutional nature – in protecting one's own citizens with regard to coercive measures issued abroad,[8] a more fine-grained rationale underpins FD 2002/584/JHA. As the Court of Justice has clarified, Article 4, no. 6 – and therefore, indirectly, also Article 5(3) – aims to prevent any disruption of the connections that a person may have established with a Member State, regardless of his or her nationality.

As such, this provision is firstly functional to the fully fledged freedom of movement in a borderless European space, as foreign nationals settled in another Member State can seek protection of their personal, family, cultural, societal and work links in the host society. Second – and consequently – the preservation of a person's stable environment is regarded as a powerful means of engaging the offender in successful social rehabilitation, to the benefit of the host Member State and the whole European judicial space. Lastly, the clause at issue can shield the right to family life codified in Article 7 of the Charter of Fundamental Rights of the European Union (the Charter), insofar as the refusal of execution facilitates the maintenance of family ties while the sentence is being enforced.

Building on these premises, the Court of Justice has acknowledged that offenders' social rehabilitation is an interest shared by the Member States and the EU itself,[9] such that it is worthy of appropriate protection by the relevant EU legislation. At the same time, its individual dimension must be carefully balanced with the collective expectations of the effective combating of crime and sound management of criminal justice. This consideration led the EU judiciary to rule that States must take the execution clause enshrined in Article 4, no. 6 seriously, to the extent that a mere declaration of will to take over enforcement of the sentence does not comply with the EAW FD and the executing authorities are themselves required to ensure that the sentence pronounced against that person is actually served.[10] Over the years, various preliminary references from national courts have offered the Court of Justice the opportunity to provide some guidance on settling the clash between the quest for an effective system of surrender and the achievement of the complex set of interests at the basis of this provision.

In *Kozlowski*, the first preliminary ruling addressing Article 4, no. 6, the Court clarified the substance of the concept of stay, which must be regarded as an autonomous notion of EU law and applies to situations where a person has established connections with a Member State, without acquiring formal residence. Therefore, the notion of stay requires an overall assessment of objective factors characterising the situation of a person, "which include, in particular, the length, nature and conditions of his presence and the family and economic connections which he has with the executing Member State".[11] It follows that the scope of Article 4, no. 6 is, in principle, wide, as it enables the executing authority to pay due consideration to the concrete circumstances of an individual case. At the same time, shortly afterwards, in *Wolzenburg*,[12] the Court of Justice took the opportunity provided by the referral of a second case to clarify that the optional nature of the grounds for refusal does not only refer to the assessment conducted by the executing judicial authorities. Instead, it also allows national legislators to decide either not to implement the relevant EU provisions or to adopt national rules restricting their scope of application, thus minimising the opportunities for departures from the golden rule of 'recognise and execute'. This stance led the Court to consider that the Dutch implementation law, which subjected the ground for refusal in question to the demonstration of a previous period of residence or stay of five years, was compatible with the EAW FD. According to the Court, such a normative choice codified a proportionate balance between the need to protect individuals, the preservation of public order and the objective of reserving greater chances of social rehabilitation in the country only to offenders whose connections with the host Member State are particularly stable, solid and reliable. It is actually no coincidence that the five-year threshold reflects the quantitative criterion to be fulfilled by EU nationals and their family members in order to enjoy the qualified status of permanent residence, pursuant to Directive 2004/38/EC,[13] the highest expression of the 'long-term' perspective of the freedom of movement of persons in the EU.

At the same time, crucially, the room for manoeuvre entrusted to national legislators is restricted by a compelling limit inherent to the essence of the integration process, namely compliance with the general principles of the EU legal order. Therefore, any decision to limit the scope of optional grounds for refusal must be respectful of the principles of proportionality and non-discrimination. On this premise, in *Lopes da Silva* the Court of Justice denied the compatibility of the French implementation law of the EAW FD, as its original wording reserved the possibility of invoking Article 4, no. 6 only for its own nationals, to the detriment of all other Union citizens.[14]

As demonstrated by this brief overview of the relevant case law, the implementation of optional grounds for denying surrender is highly strategic for the advanced system of cooperation established by FD 2002/584/JHA. This is true *a fortiori* for Article 4, no. 6, which implies significant policy choices, especially in terms of who is entitled to invoke it in order to resist surrender. The normative solutions enacted at domestic level can strongly influence the balance between mutual recognition and its limits, in light of national political priorities or perceptions on how judicial cooperation instruments allowing for forced cross-border movement should be managed in practice. In this respect, the Italian approach to the transposition of the EAW FD and its Article 4, no. 6, and Article 5(3) is particularly illustrative of these hidden driving forces. Therefore, the next paragraph outlines the context of the implementation of this EU act by the Italian legislator and its evolution up until a recent reform which entered into force in February 2021.

2. The history of the European arrest warrant in Italy: from its controversial implementation to the 2021 reform

The implementation of the EAW FD in Italy was the outcome of a serious original sin. On various occasions during the negotiations of this instrument within the Council, Italian representatives had resisted the adoption of some of the most significant departures from the traditional extradition system, such as the lifting of the double criminality requirement and the minimisation of the grounds for refusing execution (Impalà, 2005, p. 56). This attitude also crucially affected the implementation process. On the one hand, Italy was the last EU Member State to transpose the FD[15]; on the other hand, the quality of this implementation effort turned out to be extremely poor from an EU law perspective, as the parliamentary majority filled the text with a varied set of obstacles to the surrender mechanism.

As far as the grounds for refusal are concerned, the original text of Law 69 of 2005 marked a threefold departure from FD 2002/584/JHA. First, Article 18 included various new grounds for refusal, which had not been envisaged by the European legislator (Montaldo & Lipani, 2017, p. 1). Some of them were intended to protect certain situations of vulnerability of the person concerned, such as the state of pregnancy or being a mother of children under three years of age.[16] Others were intended to give the national authorities the power to prioritise certain aspects of the domestic penal system. Thus, for example, surrender was precluded in the case of offences committed with the consent of the victim, in the exercise of a right or performance of a duty or as a result of unforeseeable circumstances or force majeure. Overall, these limitations were in total dissonance with the canons of mutual recognition, as they allowed the Italian authorities to conduct a substantive assessment on the appropriateness of executing the EAW, in light of factual circumstances already assessed in the issuing State or of a different legal framework. Second, the Italian implementation law qualified all the grounds for refusal as mandatory. Notwithstanding various adjustments made by the Court of Cassation over the years (Montaldo & Lipani, 2017, p. 15), this choice clashed strongly with the obligation to recognise and enforce foreign judicial decisions.

Lastly, the substance of some grounds for refusal had been altered significantly. The implementation of Article 4, no. 6 of the EAW FD was a clear illustration, since the original text of Article 18(r) of Italian Law 69/2005 allowed only own nationals to benefit from the denial of surrender. No provisions were made for citizens of other Member States residing or staying in Italy, in plain contrast with the principle of non-discrimination on grounds of nationality, as the Court of Justice would acknowledge years later in *Lopes da Silva*. The justification for this normative choice was twofold. On the one hand, formally, the legislator had been influenced by the intergovernmental extradition model. On the other hand, *in concreto*, the trajectory of the reform had been influenced by the public and political arena, which was filled with widespread concerns regarding threats to public order breaking out as a side effect of the free movement of persons. In particular, this debate was strongly influenced by the broader context of the EU enlargement to ten new Member States, some of which were seen across Europe as likely to be a source of security challenges, particularly due to the increased possibilities for their nationals to move freely in a borderless area. Some consolation can be taken from the fact that the same discriminatory approach characterised several other national implementation laws at the time,[17] but a European overview of this situation sadly revealed how far national trends and perceptions had grown apart from the founding pillars of judicial cooperation.

However, even before the clarifications provided by the CJEU, this major gap between Italian and EU law was bridged by the Constitutional Court. In its landmark judgement no. 227 of 2010,[18] for the first time in its history, the Constitutional Court addressed its duties as domestic guardian of the correct implementation of EU law and declared the illegitimacy of Article 18, l. r) due to its incompatibility with some constitutional provisions and, ultimately, with the EU principle on non-discrimination. Therefore, the Court stated that this provision was to be interpreted as including all EU citizens legally and effectively residing or staying in Italy. Notwithstanding the improvements upheld by case law, the Italian legislator's approach demonstrated a certain degree of misinterpretation – if not a plain betrayal – of the underlying rationale of the European Arrest Warrant. This distortion was made even clearer by the case law of the Court of Justice over time and was unsurprisingly and repeatedly highlighted with particular emphasis in the periodic reports of the European Commission on the implementation status of FD 2002/584/JHA.[19]

The increasingly pressing calls for greater alignment to the relevant EU law eventually brought about a comprehensive reform process, conducted by the Government upon parliamentary delegation. The reform was ignited by Article 6(5) of the European Delegation Act 2018, no. 117 of 2019,[20] which codified the distinction between mandatory and optional grounds for refusal, the latter being listed in the newly introduced Article 18 *bis* of Law no. 69 of 2005. In addition, this provision mandated the Executive to align these articles to the FD. Legislative Decree 10 of 2021, implementing this delegation, eventually completed the process. The reform followed two main guidelines: on the one hand, it considerably reduced the list of grounds for refusal, by repealing those having no connections with the FD; on the other hand, the delegating legislature allowed the government to exercise some discretion in modelling the optional grounds for refusal, according to its political priorities. More specifically, the rules implementing Article 4, no. 6 of the EAW FD were rephrased and moved to Article 18 *bis*, l. b). This provision underwent a seemingly limited intervention, but one capable of profoundly affecting its scope of application, especially in relation to Union citizens. In fact, the new wording conditions the possibility of this category of persons successfully invoking the ground for refusal in question upon the fulfilment of a chronological requirement, namely a previous five-year period of legal and effective residence or stay in Italy.

3. The Italian (and Dutch) approach to the EAW: restricting the scope of grounds for refusal as a way for disposing of unwanted EU citizens

As expressly highlighted in the report accompanying the text of the reform, Article 18 *bis*, letter b) follows the Dutch legislation verbatim, which the *Wolzenburg* preliminary ruling, cited earlier, confirmed to be in line with the FD. The Italian legislator and the government built on the Court's statement according to which the national authorities can legitimately decide to pursue the objective of enhancing the individual chances of social integration "only in respect of persons who have demonstrated a certain degree of integration into society".[21] It follows that, compared with the pre-existing regime, the margin of discretion for an executing judicial authority to consider the degree of integration of a Union national subject to an EAW is now considerably reduced. If the quantitative threshold in question is not met or is impossible to demonstrate, the case simply does not fall under the umbrella of this ground for refusal and – unless there are other reasons to deny execution – surrender is the only option.

It could be argued that such a backward step for the protection of individuals is a sacrifice worth making to the benefit of the greater effectiveness of the EAW mechanism. Such a stance is perfectly understandable from a systemic perspective, as it follows the rationale of mutual trust and mutual recognition. However, the aspiration for fully fledged compliance with the pillars of judicial cooperation appears to be a façade driver of the reform in question. A closer look at the preparatory texts reveals that the European attitude of the Italian legislator and government was – at least – reinforced by the converging political priority of more easily disposing of unwanted EU nationals embodying possible threats to public order and public security. This underlying concern is illustrated by the fact that the justification in support of the new legislation in question has been focused solely on the presentation of the Dutch regulatory archetype and its declared compatibility with the FD as the only available model.[22] Notwithstanding the serious implications of these amendments, equally compelling considerations, such as the analysis of transposition choices made in other Member States and a retrospective discussion on the state of affairs of this ground for refusal and its daily application in Italy, were completely ignored.

Crucially, the approach codified in Dutch legislation was – at least until the Italian reform – an isolated example across Europe. All other Member States, including many which joined the European Union after the launch of the EAW system, had opted for more flexible normative solutions, which can be positioned in two main categories. In many national legal orders, the implementation of Article 4, no. 6 simply refers to residence in the executing State without adding further limits or criteria;[23] in others (fewer), it must be demonstrated that residence is habitual or that refusal to surrender is the most appropriate decision in terms of the offender's social rehabilitation needs.[24] In any event, no other examples of a regulatory approach like the one embraced by Italy can be found. The argumentative mantra urging strong reliance on the Dutch footprint is ultimately deprived of its alleged conclusiveness.

From the second point of view, a more careful analysis of Italian practice on the original version of this ground for refusal would have revealed a significant body of case law, reasonably not univocal, but certainly enriched by consolidated and largely satisfactory evaluation paths. As various studies confirm, both the Courts of Appeal and the Supreme Court were generally able to balance the individual situation of each surrenderer, the identification of the best place to complete the execution of the sentence and the collective quest for public order and public security.[25] The original wording had the advantage of reserving a reasonable margin of appreciation to the executing authorities, in order to assess the relevant circumstances of a case, such as the duration and continuity of the stay in Italy and the quality and solidity of family, social, cultural and work ties in the host State and in the State of origin. On its part, the Court of Cassation itself had accordingly developed a holistic approach, by virtue of which the existence of real and not extemporaneous roots in Italy was key to "demonstrating the fact that [the subject] has established there, with temporal continuity and sufficient territorial stability, the main, even if not exclusive, seat of his affective, professional or economic interests".[26]

From a broader perspective – and in line with this approach – the essence of the social rehabilitation purpose of punishment is generally regarded as requiring the comprehensive consideration for the individual situation in question, not only in its constitutional dimension but also in light of its legal conceptualisation – admittedly still embryonic – by the Court of Justice and the European Court of Human Rights. In fact, the EU judiciary has acknowledged that the enhancement of an offender's chances for successful re-socialisation in a post-execution phase is an interest of the Union itself, requiring any public coercive measure – in terms of adoption and subsequent implementation – to be carefully crafted also considering the varied set of factors characterising the individual's situation. This stance acquires further significance in the European Union, where free movement maximises the number and variety of situations displaying a cross-border element, for instance, in connection to the *locus commissi delicti* or to the offender's or victim's nationality or residence. In this complex scenario, the determination of the best place for serving a sentence amounts to a key choice for the individual, but also for the fully fledged implementation of free movement in the long run, regardless of nationality ties. On its part, the European Court of Human Rights has repeatedly contended that social rehabilitation entails a positive obligation of means, whereby national authorities are expected to enact all necessary measures – whether they are normative, organisational or of another nature – to allow a person to follow a path towards a successful return to society, while also preventing reoffending (Montaldo, 2018, p. 223).[27]

Against this background, the predetermination of a fixed – and, in effect, considerably high – quantitative limit clearly moves in the opposite direction. This choice runs the serious risk of frustrating the interest in question and some of the rights enshrined in the Charter, such as the right to family life and the rights of minors and of elderly people, especially in situations where the five-year residence or stay requirement is not formally fulfilled, but a stable establishment in Italy can be demonstrated. In this regard, it is worth noting that the need to reserve the refusal of surrender only to offenders who can prove they have appropriate connections to Italian society and have loose – if not entirely absent – ties to the State of origin was already ensured by the text amended by the Constitutional Court in 2010, which established the double requirement of a legal and effective residence or stay. Therefore, the tools available to the executing judicial authorities already included an array of instruments to avoid an excessive expansion of the operational scope of the ground for refusal in question.

A further fallacy of the arguments in support of the reformed ground for refusal is worthy of careful consideration, as it may lead to further restrictive interpretative solutions in the application of the amended text. Building on the Court's legal reasoning in *Wolzenburg*, the preparatory works of the reform highlight that the five-year period coincides with the duration of the legal and uninterrupted residence on which the acquisition of the right of permanent residence in the host Member State is conditional. As is well known, this institution is governed by Article 16 of Directive 2004/38 and is aimed at facilitating the stability of the Union citizen's permanence in the host State, after the exercise of the freedom of movement. In light of this consideration, the Court of Justice has taken a rigorous stance, since it has clarified that meeting the aforementioned quantitative criterion is not sufficient for acquiring the right in question, as the person concerned is also under a duty to demonstrate an appropriate level of integration within the host society.[28] In the years following the *Wolzenburg* preliminary ruling, the Court of Justice considered that this additional qualitative requirement can be regarded as not being fulfilled when the European citizen in question has committed one or more offences. In fact, the violation of interests covered by criminalisation choices affects the core values of the host society and, in the end, can provide evidence of an incomplete or unsuccessful integration process.[29] Therefore, provided that the principle of proportionality is met, the commission of an offence can undermine the legality of the presence in the national territory, thereby leading to the denial of permanent residence. Building on these premises, the Court of Justice has also held that periods of imprisonment, in principle, interrupt the continuity of residence, such that the duration accrued up to that point is reset and the calculation of the five-year period must start from zero (Coutts, 2018, p. 761).

The new wording of Article 18 *bis*, letter b) still includes the double and additional qualitative requirement of a lawful and effective residence or stay. Although these additional features, compared to the five-year time requirement, do not coincide verbatim with the conditions of legality and continuity of residence envisaged by Article 16 of Directive 2004/38, they still require an assessment of the merits of the individual circumstances. In essence, the formal fulfilment of the quantitative criterion alone is not sufficient to trigger the ground for refusal, for instance, if the executing authority finds that the offender's stay in Italy is not legal or effective or has not been such for a given period. If the Italian courts were to link the restrictive interpretation of the qualitative criteria governing the acquisition of the right of permanent residence to the similar – though not entirely coinciding – parameters established by Article 18 *bis*, letter b), the consequences of such an interpretative osmosis would be detrimental, particularly for an offender who has committed one or more offences during the period of residence or stay.

4. The automatic exclusion of third country nationals from the possibility to invoke Article 4, no. 6, framework decision 2002/584/JHA

Another aspect of the Italian approach to the implementation of the EAW FD worthy of consideration is that the original text of Law 69/2005 contained a discrepancy between the transposition of Article 4, no. 6 and the implementation of Article 5, no. 3. As outlined earlier, the latter provision regulates the guarantee of return in relation to EAWs issued for prosecution purposes. While the text implementing the ground for refusal did not cover cases involving third-country nationals, the transposition of Article 5 made a general reference to the wanted person, with no delimitation whatsoever based on citizenship or other connecting factors. Consequently, the legislator's silence was interpreted as allowing the guarantee of return to be extended to third-country nationals.

This inconsistency was striking, as the provisions in question are clearly complementary in nature and pursue the same objectives. Moreover, both Article 4, no. 6 and Article 5, no. 3 are nationality-neutral, as they refer broadly to the person who is the subject of an EAW. Over time, this situation gave rise to a growing debate, aimed at invoking the extension of the possibility to deny execution of EAWs to third-country nationals.[30] However, the February 2021 reform moved in the opposite direction, as the provision on the guarantee of return was aligned to the restrictive choice made for the new version of the optional ground for refusal. This means that the possibility of being returned to the executing State following surrender with a view to prosecution is reserved only to Italian nationals and to EU citizens who have been residing or staying in Italy legally and effectively for at least five years.[31]

The choice made by the Italian legislator once again reflects a restrictive approach to allegedly 'external' threats to public order and public security. On the one hand, it does not appear *icto oculi* contrary to the provisions of FD 2002/584/JHA: the fact that the EU act makes a neutral reference to the residence of the requested person does not remove the power of States to limit the scope of application of the ground for refusal in question, nor does it justify the extension of the protection ensured by the principle of non-discrimination on the basis of nationality under Article 18 TFEU to third-country nationals.[32] On the other hand, it is open to criticism, due to its underlying rationale and practical implications. While it is true that the amended text reflects a widespread trend in the implementation laws of the Member States,[33] the European demography has vastly changed since the entry into force of the FD and the wave of domestic transposition laws. The number of third-country nationals residing in Italy and more generally in the EU has increased exponentially, as has the rate of long-term residents who have settled in the territory of a Member State and established roots there.[34] In view of this scenario, the reform is outdated and represents a missed opportunity, as it allows judicial cooperation mechanisms to be moulded to the – legitimate but questionable – quest by national authorities for new tools to manage migration phenomena.[35]

These considerations *de iure condendo* are reflected in the evolution of EU law over the past two decades, which demonstrates the Union legislator's attention to regular migration. Directive 2003/109/EC on long-term resident status[36] and Directive 2003/86/EC on family reunification[37] are emblems of this regulatory season. Still today, these two acts are the main grounds for the entry and subsequent stay of third-country nationals in the EU and reveal how the EU legislator intended to facilitate the stabilisation of those who have established growing roots in the host Member States. That being said, the current configuration of Italian EAW law reveals some criticalities, at least with regard to certain categories of third-country nationals.

First, these criticalities affect EU citizens' family members, to whom Directive 2004/38/EC extends the regime of free movement and residence provided for Union nationals. In the plausible case of an offender who is a family member of an EU citizen residing in Italy, he/she would not be able to oppose the surrender, nor could he/she benefit from the guarantee of return. In addition to issues related to the right to family life and to the rehabilitation purpose of a sentence, already discussed earlier, this approach poses an obstacle to the full effectiveness of the freedom of movement. In fact, the Union citizen could be discouraged from exercising this freedom or urged to return to his/her Member State of origin in order to avoid the subsequent break-up of the family unit. This consideration is not only in line with what the Court of Justice has ruled on several occasions in the case of undue obstacles to the enjoyment of this fundamental freedom, but, above all, it is not new to the complex intertwining of prerogatives linked to European citizenship and the coordination of national criminal jurisdictions. In fact, the foundations of the European *ne bis in idem*, today enshrined in Article 50 of the Charter, lie precisely in the attempt to prevent the citizen of a Member State from being held back when exercising his/her freedom of movement, in the face of the risk – no matter how minimal – of being subjected to a second criminal proceeding or to a duplication of sanctions in the host State.[38] Similar arguments provide substance to the Court's case law on the extradition of EU citizens to third countries: it follows from *Petruhhin* that the duty incumbent upon national authorities to consult the Member State of origin and to check its intention to issue an EAW to prosecute its national or make him/her serve the sentence there stems also from Article 21 TFEU of free movement of Union citizens.[39]

In addition, this approach to the implementation of the EAW system is at odds with the rules granting protection against deportation of EU citizens and their family members, pursuant to Article 28 of Directive 2004/38. Under that branch of EU law, in fact, the third-country national who qualifies as a family member enjoys enhanced protection against expulsion, so that the establishment in the territory of the host State and the preservation of family ties require an appropriate balance with concerns about public order and public security. In conclusion, the impossibility of invoking the ground of refusal and the guarantee of return by the EU national's family member appears to be in contrast with the prerogatives attached to the status of Union citizenship. This contrast could have been avoided, with no detriment to the underlying policy choices, by a simple and explicit reference in Article 18 *bis*, letter b) of Law 69/2005 to the category of EU citizens' family members, as defined by Directive 2004/38, without necessarily removing the strict approach regarding the duration of the period of residence in Italy.

Long-term residents are the second category of third-country nationals requiring some reflections. This status is governed by Directive 2003/109/EC and presupposes legal and continuous residence in the host State for five years. These parameters materialise the purpose of the legislation in question, namely the completion of the integration process of those who have demonstrated their will to establish their centre of interests in a Member State of the Union. The Directive itself and the case law – also in relation to disputes arising in Italy – underline that third-country nationals who are long-term residents must be able to enjoy equal treatment with EU citizens in many areas, such as the enjoyment of social assistance or social protection benefits "which contribute to enabling the individual to satisfy his basic needs, such as food, housing and health",[40] the exercise of employed or self-employed activity, education and vocational training. The result is a so-called "*quasi-citizenship*" (Arcarazo, 2011) or "*denizenship*" (Hammar, 1990), whereby the third-country nationals and the family members wishing to join them are provided with a qualified regime, because of the quantity and quality of ties established in a Member State.

Given these premises, it must be noted that the length of the period of stay required to acquire the condition of long-term resident is the same as that imposed by the reform of the Italian EAW law for activating the ground for refusal and the guarantee of return, in the shared belief that the respective regimes should be reserved only for those who demonstrate a suitable degree of integration in the host State. Although, in abstract terms, the situation of a third-country national cannot be equated with that of an EU citizen, in practice, a stable residence facilitates the establishment of stronger personal and social ties, regardless of the nationality of origin. However, the intertwining of the EAW and the regime of long-term residents demonstrate some structural discrepancies. First, the same ties which the EU legal system considers worthy of protection under Directive 2003/109/EC, on the assumption of the high level of integration of the third-country nationals involved, are entirely neglected within the realm of the EAW. While the former act urges enhanced protection for the migrants' family ties, also by virtue of Article 7 of the Charter on the right to family life, the automaticity and inevitability of surrender leave no margin for manoeuvre other than frustrating the right at issue.

Second, this blanket rule causes friction with the individual need for re-socialisation and collective security concerns, as it removes from any long-term resident the benefit of the re-educational paradigm of the sentence, regardless of the individual circumstances of a case. Such an implication is particularly critical in the frequent circumstances where the EAW concerns very old crimes, committed even prior to the start of the five-year period of residence (Klaus, Włodarczyk-Madejska & Wzorek, 2021, p. 95). Third, it is no coincidence that Directive 2003/109/EC itself regulates the removal of long-term residents with caution, to the extent that this can only take place in the event of a current and sufficiently serious threat to public order or public security and, in any case, after careful consideration of the length of stay in Italy, the family and emotional ties and the employment situation.[41]

Automatic surrender, in short, repudiates the purpose of Directive 2003/109/EC, in that it causes, without exception or possibility of individual assessment, the interruption of the ties created over time in the host society. Such considerations become even more pressing when considering the strict national rules on the acquisition of Italian – and therefore European – citizenship, which considerably prolong the status of third-country nationals, even for the descendants of parents who are third-country nationals, thereby maximising the implications of the reform at issue. It is therefore reasonable to regard the exclusion of third-country nationals from the ground for refusal under Article 4, no. 6 of the EAW FD and the complementary guarantee of return as a legacy of the past, neglecting a more forward-looking approach. Accordingly, it should be noted that, following a complaint of constitutionality from the Court of Cassation precisely dealing with the exclusion of all third-country nationals from the personal scope of these provisions, the Italian Constitutional Court has recently referred to the Court of Justice for a preliminary ruling of interpretation, with a view to allowing the EU judiciary to take a clear stance on the compatibility of this normative choice with the FD and with Article 7 of the Charter of Fundamental Rights.[42]

5. Converging mobility and migration management ambitions? The implications of the reform on the interplay between the EAW system and the transfer of prisoners in the Italian legal order

Some further critical considerations relate to how the reform in question impacts the wider spectrum of judicial cooperation mechanisms available in the toolbox of national judicial authorities.

Under the previous regime, the absence of an anchorage to predetermined quantitative criteria constituted a powerful incentive to defensive strategies aimed at invoking the ground for refusal under Article 4, no. 6 of the EAW FD, with substantial chances of success. The reform makes it reasonable to foresee a lower incidence of cases of denial of execution, even – as already noted – in circumstances where the offender demonstrates family ties or other connections to Italy. As discussed earlier, such concerns are exacerbated by the exclusion of all third-country nationals from the personal scope of application of this provision and of the guarantee of return. The question is, then, whether there are any alternatives capable of ensuring the preservation of personal ties, even in a post-surrender phase. In this respect, for both Union citizens and third-country nationals, the main reference point is FD 2008/909/JHA on the cross-border transfer of prisoners between Member States (Montaldo, 2020a). Indeed, this former Third Pillar act shares the same rationale as Article 4, no. 6 and Article 5 EAW FD, insofar as it allows the enforcement of a custodial sentence definitively imposed in the State of conviction to be transferred to another Member State, where the person involved demonstrates that he/she has greater chances of rehabilitation, due to his/her predominant family, social, cultural or work-related ties.[43]

For the purposes of this analysis, the distinctive element of FD 2008/909/JHA is that, in principle, a transfer does not necessarily depend upon formal factors, such as citizenship, residence or length of stay. In fact, while the transfer to the Member State of origin is the main option pursuant to Article 6(1), the same provision allows for the allocation of the execution phase to any of the Member States, provided that the relevant authorities consent to the transfer. Therefore, while, in the EAW system, States can restrict the scope of the grounds for refusal, to the benefit of the duty to recognise and execute foreign decisions, the perspective of cross-border transfers is reversed: any additional criterion or limitation which does not feature in this EU act risks undermining its effectiveness and, ultimately, being incompatible with it. Accordingly, the Italian implementation law of this FD generically outlines the evaluation to be carried out by both the issuing and the executing authorities in order to identify the best place for the sentence to be enforced, with a view to maximising its rehabilitation potential.[44] The *fulcrum* for activating the procedure is the situation of the person involved.[45] This implies that – almost paradoxically – a person surrendered as a result of an EAW could subsequently request and obtain, before the authorities of the State that issued the EAW, the transmission to Italy on a request under FD 2008/909/JHA. For third-country nationals, this would be the sole opportunity to obtain a judicial assessment of their individual situation, since surrender is the only available option under the EAW regime. In the case of EU citizens, the authority tasked with recognition and execution would have to evaluate such a request on the basis of different legal parameters, as it would not be bound by the five-year term introduced by Article 18 *bis*, letter b) of the Italian EAW law and due to the different teleological pivot of the transfer mechanism of detainees. Therefore, a period of presence in the host State of less than five years may prove to be sufficient for the successful completion of the judicial cooperation procedure.

In relation to this aspect, the normative coordination of the two FDs in question is far from swift and leaves room for gaps and inconsistencies, which have been reflected thus far in Italian domestic practice, including in cases similar to those described earlier. In any event, the reform in question has the immediate effect of exacerbating these problems: it significantly reduces the scope of application of the ground for refusal concerning residence and stay, while also broadening the spectrum of cases in which a convict would be entitled to request – and obtain – (re)transfer to Italy, unless interpretative solutions contrary to the spirit of FD 2008/909/JHA occur. Aside from the lack of systemic consistency and the scant consideration for rehabilitation aspects, the reform may ultimately lead to a serious risk of duplication of procedures, work and costs, mainly for the Italian authorities.

One way out of this clash calls into play the role of the Ministry of Justice, to which the Italian Legislative Decree implementing FD 2008/909/JHA grants a power to veto transfer requests involving any prisoner who is not an Italian national. In these situations, in principle, the certificate can be forwarded to the competent judicial authority only with prior ministerial consensus. While this preliminary institutional step may, in theory, contribute to overcoming the operational overlaps between the EAW system and the transfer of prisoners, in practice, it is extremely critical, for two main reasons. First, the passage in question is far from transparent and can block the judicial cooperation procedure in the absence of any available judicial scrutiny. Second, even though the Ministry of Justice is the Italian central authority and mainly performs various coordination tasks, this specific phase of the passive mechanism of transfer is highly discretionary, providing leeway for political considerations on whether the national prison system should bear the burden of a foreign offender. Here, a closer look at the history of FD 2008/909/JHA in Italy reveals the real risk of a constant rejection of transfer requests. In fact, the *mise en place* of this FD in the Italian legal order provides an illustration of the real driving forces behind its transposition (Montaldo, 2020b, p. 69).

Italy was the first Member State to implement this FD, by the transposition deadline, back in 2010. This was quite surprising for this particular Member State, especially in the context of the former Third Pillar measures, to which Italy generally reacted with inaction and astonishing delays. The whys and wherefores of this unique virtuous (formal) compliance were compelling questions which went far beyond the enthusiastic incorporation of the mutual recognition paradigm. A clear answer to these underlying questions can be found in some of the many circular letters issued by the Italian Ministry of Justice to clarify the scope of the implementation law and to address some of the challenges arising from its initial years of application. For instance, on 28 April 2014, a circular letter issued by the Department of Justice Affairs openly framed transfer procedures within the articulated set of measures enacted by the Italian Government to cope with the prison overcrowding emergency, in the aftermath of the *Torreggiani* pilot judgement[46] in which the European Court of Human Rights had highlighted the generalised structural flaws of the Italian prison system (see also Ferraris in this volume). The Ministry of Justice stressed the need for a more effective use of this mechanism to redistribute foreign inmates detained in Italy to the 'sending' States.

Whereas circular letters represent soft-law instruments, usually merely listing guidelines and disseminating useful information and best practices among the relevant stakeholders, this and other similar documents provide an illustrative overview of the actual aims underpinning the Italian performance, as they repeatedly refer to the need to reduce the pressure on the domestic prison system and to cope with more pressing public order concerns, providing no indications on the assessment of the rehabilitation chances of the persons concerned. Against this background, domestic judicial authorities tend to take the core purpose of the FD more seriously, whereas the Italian experience reveals the strong governmental commitment to using this mechanism as an indirect way of coping with mobility and migration. Indeed, some incentives make the increase in successful transfers appealing, such as the allocation of the responsibility for problematic citizens to their countries of origin or residence, the perception of greater security that can be generated in the public audience through ad hoc news campaigns, the avoidance of possible public order threats once the sentence has been served or, more practically, the saving of public resources. The Italian practice demonstrates that this is particularly true in relation to some Member States, such as Romania and Spain, which regularly rank first and second respectively in the scoreboard of the Member States of destination of transferred prisoners (Montaldo, 2020b, p. 75).

In conclusion, the interplay of the freshly reformed Italian provisions on the EAW and the mechanism for the transfer of prisoners displays various discrepancies, which offer significant opportunities for political use of these judicial cooperation procedures and affect the protection granted to the persons concerned.

Conclusions

Following its 30-year evolution, judicial cooperation in criminal matters is now a key component of the broader EU objective of establishing an Area of Freedom, Security and Justice. One of the prominent explanations for the success of EU initiatives in this domain is their design as a mainly technical and judicially focused mechanism, relying on judicial oversight on the basis of predetermined parameters rather than the exercise of political discretion on the part of the executive branch.

However, judicial cooperation tools encroach upon important domestic policies, which are still immune from EU competence and which reflect key societal perceptions and choices on interests worthy of protection by the domestic legal order. Consequently, when implementing FDs and Directives, national legislators and governments often see the two-phase nature of these acts as an opportunity to inject their own political priorities into the judicial cooperation system.

As demonstrated by the analysis conducted thus far, the domestic approach to the EU acts allowing for the surrender or transfer of (alleged) offenders provides an interesting illustration of these dynamics. The Italian case study – which, to some extent, reflects a broader European trend – shows that the paradigm of mutual recognition can be used to justify restrictive approaches to the presence of foreigners in the national territory. The *vis expansiva* of European citizenship and of EU policy on regular migration from third countries and the freedom of movement of persons give way to normative solutions aimed at transferring, to the greatest possible extent, the responsibility for unwanted citizens to the Member States of origin or elsewhere. While formally in line with the EAW FD due to the *Wolzenburg* case law, the newly reworded provision implementing the ground for refusal under Article 4, no. 6 is, in substance, out of time and constitutes a missed opportunity for a truly European attitude towards crime and offenders' rehabilitation in a borderless space. Moreover, it obliterates years of consolidated and successful judicial practices, whereby any attempt to resist surrender on the basis of this provision entailed a careful assessment of the individual circumstances of each case.

As far as third-country nationals are concerned, the Italian reform of 2021 echoes the normative choices upheld in the vast majority of the Member States, with the exception of Germany. Once more, a blanket rule excluding *in toto* any third-country national from the possibility of preserving their family and social ties established in the host Member States is in plain contradiction with the normative efforts – both at EU and at national levels – to facilitate the integration pathway of long-term residents and is even more critical in relation to Union citizens' family members. The preliminary reference raised by the Italian Constitutional Court will clarify whether or not and to what extent this discrepancy is acceptable from the viewpoint of the compatibility of national legislation with EU law, including the Charter of Fundamental Rights. In this respect, even if the answer is yes – for instance, because the Member States are, in principle, allowed to restrict the scope of the grounds for refusal and because the principle of non-discrimination on grounds of nationality does not apply to third-country nationals – political forces will continue to urge greater consistency within the Area of Freedom, Security and Justice and more forward-looking choices, the responsibility for which can be assigned to both European and national legislators.

Notes

1 This Chapter was drafted with the support of the Erasmus+ Programme of the European Union, in the framework of the Jean Monnet Module 'EU Mobility and Migration Law' (2019–2022), www.eumomi.unito.it. The European Commission support for the production of this publication does not constitute an endorsement of the contents, which

reflects the views only of the Author, and the Commission cannot be held responsible for any use which may be made of the information contained therein.

2 Council Framework Decision 2002/584/JHA of 13 June 2002 on the European arrest warrant and the surrender procedures between Member States – Statements made by certain Member States on the adoption of the Framework Decision, OJ L 190, 18.7.2002, 1.

3 Council Framework Decision 2008/909/JHA of 27 November 2008 on the application of the principle of mutual recognition to judgements in criminal matters imposing custodial sentences or measures involving deprivation of liberty for the purpose of their enforcement in the European Union OJ L 327, 5.12.2008, 27.

4 Legislative Decree no. 10 of 2 February 2021.

5 The analysis refers only to the provisions of the EAW FD, which are formally labelled as grounds for refusal. Therefore, it leaves aside further aspects of the EU acts at issue – such as the failure to pass the double criminality test or to meet the pre-determined punishment thresholds – which in the end can amount to blocking surrender.

6 See, for instance, Directive 2014/41/EU of the European Parliament and of the Council of 3 April 2014 regarding the European Investigation Order in criminal matters OJ L 130, 1.5.2014, 1.

7 The principle at issue requires a State to avoid offenders' impunity in cross-border cases. In the event of a decision not to extradite a person, the domestic authorities must take the responsibility to prosecute the person involved and to decide on his or her criminal liability. In the aftermath of the expiry of the implementation deadline of the FD, disposing of the nationality exception led to various constitutional struggles.

8 Including considerations for a sound management of justice in a cross-border scenario, urged by the mentioned *aut dedere aut iudicare* principle.

9 See, inter alia, Court of Justice, case C-171/16, *Beshkov*.

10 Court of Justice, case C-579/15, *Poplawski*, 18–24. The enforcement clause plays a particularly pressing role in the Court's case law. In *Sut*, the Court stressed that considerations for social rehabilitation can justify refusal of surrender despite the fact that the offence which provides the basis for that warrant is, under that national law of the executing Member State, punishable by fine only, under the condition that, in accordance with its national law, that fact does not prevent the custodial sentence imposed on the person requested from actually being enforced in that Member State. See Court of Justice, case C-514/17, *Sut*.

11 Court of Justice, case C-66/08, *Kozlowski*, 48.

12 Court of Justice, case C-123/08, *Wolzenburg*.

13 Article 16 Directive 2004/38/EC of the European Parliament and of the Council of 29 April 2004 on the right of citizens of the Union and their family members to move and reside freely within the territory of the Member States, OJ L 158, 30.4.2004, 77.

14 Court of Justice, case C-42/11, *Lopes Da Silva Jorge*

15 Law no. 69 of 22 April 2005.

16 As the case law of the Italian Supreme Court has confirmed, this ground for refusal – controversially enough – did not apply to fathers.

17 The texts of the national laws of implementation are available – in most cases with translations in English – on the website of the European Judicial Network: www.ejn-crimjust.europa.eu.

18 Italian Constitutional Court, judgement no. 227 of 21 June 2010.

19 See, for instance, Report of 2 July 2020 from the Commission to the European Parliament and the Council on the implementation of Council Framework Decision of 13 June 2002 on the European arrest warrant and the surrender procedures between Member States COM(2020)270 final.

20 Law no. 117 of 4 October 2019 (legge di delegazione europea 2018).

21 *Wolzenburg*, cit., 67.

22 Ministero della Giustizia, Relazione illustrative allo schema di decreto legislativo recante disposizioni per I compiuto adeguamento della normative nazionale alle

disposizioni della decisione Quadro 2002/584/GAI, available at www.giustizia.it/giustizia/it/mg_1_2_1.page?facetNode_1=1_6_5&facetNode_2=0_0&contentId=SAN305201&previsiousPage=mg_1_2#rel.

23 In this category, for instance, Belgium, Greece, Hungary, Ireland and Germany.

24 See the laws of Czech Republic, Finland and Luxembourg.

25 Empirical studies have been conducted as well. See, for instance, the analysis on the execution of EAWs by the Bononia Court of Appeal between 2006 and 2019, available at www.camerapenale-bologna.org/2021/09/02/m-a-e-ed-estradizione-indagine-statistica-sulla-giurisprudenza-della-c-d-a-di-bologna-2006–2019/.

26 Italian Court of Cassation, order of 4.2.2020, no. 10371. The translation in English of the original text is not official.

27 European Court of Human Rights: *Vinter and others v. United Kingdom*, applications nos. 66069/09, 130/10 and 3896/10; *Khoroshenko v. Russia*, application no. 41418/04; *Murray v. The Netherlands*, application no. 10511/10.

28 Court of Justice, case C-325/09, *Dias*.

29 Court of Justice, case C-378/12, *Onuekwere*.

30 See *inter alia* Amalfitano, Chiara and Aranci, Matteo. 2021. "Mandato d'arresto europeo ed extracomunitario residente o dimorante in Italia: ancora nessuna tutela da parte della Corte costituzionale (né del legislatore)." *Sistema penale* 5–34, www.sistemapenale.it/it/sentenza/corte-costituzionale-2021-60-amalfitano-aranci-mae-extracomunitario.

31 The Court of Justice also clarified that the guarantee of return applies as soon as the sentencing decision becomes final. Court of Justice, case C-314/18, *SF*.

32 Court of Justice, case C-897/19, *Ruska Federacija*.

33 Only the German law of implementation provides for a specific clause on third-country nationals.

34 See to this respect the statistics developed by Eurostat: https://ec.europa.eu/eurostat/statistics-explained/index.php?title=Migration_and_migrant_population_statistics.

35 On the managerial ambitions of the States, see Jesse, Moritz. 2020. *European Societies, Migration and the Law*. Cambridge: Cambridge University Press.

36 Council Directive 2003/109/EC of 25 November 2003 concerning the status of third-country nationals who are long-term residents, *OJ L 16, 23.1.2004, 44–53.*

37 Council Directive 2003/86/EC of 22 September 2003 on the right to family reunification, *OJ L 251, 3.10.2003, 12–18.*

38 Court of Justice, case C-436/04, *van Esbroeck*, 33–34.

39 Court of Justice, case C-182/15, *Petruhhin*.

40 Court of Justice, case C-571/10, *Kamberaj*, 91.

41 Article 12 Directive 2003/109/EC, cit.

42 Italian Constitutional Court, order no. 217 of 18 November 2021.

43 The formal coordination between these two instruments is provided by Article 25 FD 2008/909/JHA.

44 Legislative decree no. 161 of 7 September 2010.

45 Article 6 FD 2008/909/JHA.

46 European Court of Human Rights, *Torreggiani and Others v. Italy*, applications nos. 43517/09, 46882/09, 55400/09, 57875/09, 61535/09, 35315/10 and 37818/10.

References

Arcarazo, D. (2011). *The long-term residence status as a subsidiary form of EU citizenship*. Den Haag: Brill.

Coutts, S. (2018). "The absence of integration and the responsibilisation of Union citizenship." *European Papers* 3 (2): 761–80.

Hammar, T. (1990). *Democracy and the nation state: Aliens, denizens, and citizens in a world of international migration*. Aldershot: Avebury.

Impalà, F. (2005). "The European arrest warrant in the Italian legal system. Between mutual recognition and mutual fear in the area of freedom, security and justice." *Utrecht Law Review* 1 (2): 56–78.

Klaus, W., Włodarczyk-Madejska, J. & Wzorek, D. (2021). "In the pursuit of justice: Ab(use) of the European arrest warrant in the polish criminal justice system." *Central and Eastern European Migration Review* 10 (1): 95–117.

Knill, C. & Tosun, J. (2012). "Governance institutions and policy implementation in the European Union." In *Constructing a Policy-Making State? Policy Dynamics in the EU*, edited by Jeremy Richardson, 309–21. Oxford: Oxford University Press.

Montaldo, S. (2018). "Offenders' rehabilitation: Towards a new paradigm for EU criminal law?" *European Criminal Law Review* 8 (2): 223–43.

Montaldo, S. (2020a). *The transfer of prisoners in the European Union. Challenges and prospects in the implementation of Framework Decision 2008/909/JHA*. Den Haag-Torino: Eleven-Giappichelli.

Montaldo, S. (2020b). "Framework Decision 2008/909/JHA on the transfer of prisoners in the EU: Advances and challenges in light of the Italian experience." *New Journal of European Criminal Law* 11 (1): 69–92.

Montaldo, S. & Lipani, M. (2017). "I motivi ostativi all'esecuzione del mandato d'arresto europeo nella legge italiana di recepimento e la Corte di Cassazione: uno sguardo di insieme, alla luce dei principi generali dell'ordinamento UE e della giurisprudenza della Corte di giustizia." *La legislazione penale* 1–23 (at: www.lalegislazionepenale.eu/i-motivi-ostativi-allesecuzione-del-mandato-darresto-europeo-nella-legge-italiana-di-recepimento-e-la-corte-di-cassazione-uno-sguardo-di-insieme-alla-luce-dei-principi-generali-dellordinamento/.)

Ouwerkerk, J. (2021). "Are alternatives to the European arrest warrant underused? The case for an integrative approach to judicial cooperation mechanisms in the EU criminal justice area." *European Journal of Crime, Criminal Law and Criminal Justice* 29 (2): 87–101.

Thoman, E. & Sager, F. (2017). "Moving beyond legal compliance: Innovative approaches to EU multilevel implementation." *Journal of European Public Policy* 24(9): 1253–68.

Weyembergh, A. & Wieczorek, I. (2016). "Is there an EU criminal policy?" In *EU Criminal Justice and the Challenges of Legal Diversity*, edited by Robert Colson and Stewart Field, 29–47. Cambridge: Cambridge University Press.

6 Is the EAW efficient?

Assessment of the European arrest warrant procedure based on opinions of Polish criminal justice practitioners

Justyna Włodarczyk-Madejska and Dominik Wzorek

Introduction

The Council Framework Decision on the European Arrest Warrant (EAW) of 2002[1] introduced a measure that simplified the extradition procedures based on international conventions which were previously in force in the EU. The Framework Decision is often referred to as the 'cornerstone' of judicial collaboration in the EU because it implements two fundamental principles: of mutual recognition and mutual trust (Hofmański et al., 2008, p. 2007; Królak et al., 2006, p. 400). The first principle means that the judicial authorities of one EU Member State are tasked with enforcing a judgement or sentence issued by a judicial authority of another Member State (Klimek, 2015, p. 19). These judgements are treated as if they had been issued by a domestic court. In order to guarantee smooth enforcement of rulings, Member States are obliged to mutually recognise their legal orders and the accuracy of judgements (Hofmański et al., 2008, p. 27; Klimek, 2015, p. 19). In other words, the judicial authorities of a Member State are obliged to trust in the legitimacy of legal decisions taken by the authorities of another Member State (see Aranyosi and Căldăraru, C-404/V5 and C-659/15, para. 79; Lanigan, C-237/15 PPU, para. 36).

The EAW procedure shifted the competence to make extradition decisions from the political to the legal arena. The previous conventional mechanism required, in addition to a court order for extradition, the political will of the Ministries of Justice of both States to issue an extradition warrant and carry out the extradition. This step is omitted in the Directive.

The Framework Decision allows for:

- the surrender of persons who have been sentenced to imprisonment but who have not served their sentence, having fled from justice to the territory of another Member State, and
- the surrender of persons suspected of having committed an offence and who are being prosecuted for offences punishable by a custodial sentence of at least 12 months.

DOI: 10.4324/9781003254584-7

The introduction of legal instruments of European judicial cooperation in criminal matters was in principle designed to enable rigorous, efficient and expeditious cross-border proceedings in criminal matters. Polish courts quickly adopted all the tools foreseen by the Framework Decision and incorporated them into the Polish criminal procedure legislation as part of their measures for searching for offenders.

As statistics show, Poland is the undisputed 'leader' in issuing European Arrest Warrants (EAWs). Between 2005 and 2013, every third EAW was issued by a Polish court. Data from 2014 onwards show a significant decrease in number of EAW issued by Polish courts. In 2019 there were 2338 EAW issued by Polish courts – 12% of all EAW issued in 2019 (European Commission, 2021, pp. 40–41). It seems Germany overtook Poland in the number of EAWs issued that year (Klaus et al., 2021, p. 103). The statistics suggest that EAWs are not particularly efficient. Only 26.3% of the EAWs issued between 2005 and 2013 were executed by handing over the wanted person. This percentage varies between Member States and over time (Klaus et al., 2021, pp. 103–104), and recently we can observe an increase in the efficiency of this measure. Data for 2019 alone show that of the 9217 EAWs issued that year, 62% were successfully enforced (in 5665 cases) (European Commission, 2021, p. 11). However, it should be borne in mind that an EAW can be executed a year or years after it is issued, so these statistics should be interpreted with caution. A much more precise source of such data are the records of court cases, which allow a detailed analysis of an EAW issued in a particular case, including the manner in which the case was resolved. Since Poland was the leader in issuing EAWs until recently, it is worth examining the reasons for such a large number of EAWs issued by Polish courts. It seems justified to look at the processing of EAW in the broader context of the structure and operation of the Polish justice system.

In Poland, EAW cases are dealt with by first-instance regional courts, of which there are 46. Approximately 2.5 million criminal cases are filed in Polish courts annually. Nearly three-quarters of them are heard in district courts (there are 318 of them) and nearly one in four go to regional courts (Siemaszko et al., 2020, pp. 88, 90, 130). In 2020, the volume of criminal cases submitted to regional courts was 347,793 (Ministry of Justice, 2020b), and the number of EAWs issued that year was 1,795 (Ministry of Justice, 2020a). EAW proceedings therefore make up a negligible proportion of the cases heard by Polish regional courts. In some courts they are handled by dedicated and therefore specialised judges (e.g. in specially established international proceedings departments), while in others they are adjudicated by all judges. These rules not only vary from court to court but also change over time, as one expert (judge) pointed out in an interview for research on which this chapter is based:

> Until last year it was also customary in our country that [international cooperation] cases were not distributed among all the Department Judges, but there were two Department Judges who specialised in this area.
>
> (ENA_E18_C)

The question we would like to answer in this chapter is whether the EAW is an efficient instrument of European judicial cooperation in criminal matters in the Polish context. In order to answer this question, we used two different sets of data: information from a survey of court files of cases in which EAWs were issued by Polish courts, and in-depth expert interviews with individuals implementing EAWs in Poland. Although, as the title of the chapter suggests, it is mainly based on expert statements, we also found it necessary to show quantitative data from court case files in order to analyse the efficiency of EAWs. Before we outline the full research methodology, we explain what we mean by 'efficiency'.

1. Efficiency – what is it and how to measure it?

Without doubt, it is necessary to first clarify what we mean by 'efficiency' in this analysis. Efficiency is most often defined in economic terms. The concept is commonly used in the economic analysis of law to weigh the costs and benefits of legal action (Mathis, 2009, pp. 31–32). In the procedural context, efficiency is regarded as part of the principle of due process of law. The European Convention on Human Rights states in Article 6 that everyone has the right to a fair and public hearing within a reasonable time. This means that one of the fundamental elements of the right to a fair trial is the time aspect. Procedures should be structured in such a way that everyone can be heard by the court within a reasonable period of time. The European Commission for the Efficiency of Justice has introduced the term 'optimal and foreseeable time', meaning that "the time frame is not a deadline or a maximum time limit, but an operational and inter-departmental instrument that can be used to set a measurable 'target' for the length of proceedings" (Roghină, 2012, p. 51).

The operationalisation of the concept of efficiency in the context of the functioning of the judiciary seems extremely difficult, hence efficiency is most often defined with the use of indicators. The Polish Ministry of Justice names at least a dozen of such measures, including the duration of proceedings, the management of the receipt of cases to the court, the number of cases that have not been resolved by the end of the year in which they were received by the court, the number of assistant jobs per full-time judge, the average duration of court proceedings, and the percentage of cases dealt with by the courts in which the duration of proceedings exceeds 12 months or 3 years (Ministry of Justice, 2017). Most commonly, however, efficiency is viewed as the efficient and accurate adjudication of a case (Dandurand, 2014, p. 388; Easton, 2018). Yvon Dandurand writes that the symptoms of an inefficient justice system are significant court backlogs, drawn-out criminal trials, unnecessary delays or failed prosecutions and collapsed trials resulting from poor cooperation between institutions and the many uncertainties that emerge during the proceedings (Dandurand, 2014, p. 391).

When analysing the work of judges, Kamil Joński made the economic assumption that efficiency refers to the use of available resources to achieve certain results. An efficient judicial system, therefore, is one that is able to ensure that the right to a trial is properly exercised (i.e. where judgements are accurate and proceedings are efficiently run) (Joński, 2016, p. 3). The accuracy of rulings can be assessed by the percentage of rulings that were appealed and, as a consequence, amended or overturned (Zielińska, 2017, p. 6). The efficiency of proceedings, on the other hand, can be measured by defining the judge's working time as a resource and recognising the case as a result. Higher efficiency therefore means the ability of a judge to competently adjudicate more cases in the same amount of time (Joński, 2017, pp. 13–14).

In the interviews, the supervising judges (judges who assess work of others judges) highlighted the same two key elements. They stressed the inherent elements of efficiency such as: examining a case in a competent manner in terms of content and procedure so that the ruling is fair and the parties are satisfied enough not to appeal, and also examining the case in a timely manner so as to avoid protraction (Włodarczyk-Madejska et al., 2020, p. 298). They also stressed that the court is only efficient if there is adequate cooperation between the judge and the registry or assistant. When any of these links is weakened, the whole system is weakened (Włodarczyk-Madejska et al., 2020, pp. 301, 305). The aforementioned statistical indicators have been assessed as helpful for a very concise numerical description of different aspects of the functioning of the courts, as well as the best tool to date for assessing the performance of a judge (Włodarczyk-Madejska et al., 2020, pp. 339–340), but they are only meaningful if the staffing of the court is proper (Włodarczyk-Madejska et al., 2020, p. 345).

Some measures are also used in international benchmarking, for example, to analyse the efficiency of court proceedings in individual countries. The most important of them include disposition time (which is used to estimate how many days a court takes to resolve pending cases) and the clearance rate (which can be used to analyse the ability to manage the volume of cases of a given type in a court) (Council of Europe, 2018, p. 238). The financial aspect is also often considered when analysing the efficiency of the justice system, for example, the income of the courts, the costs of court operations per judge or per litigation case settled, and the average monthly salaries of judges, clerks and support staff (Klimczak, 2020, pp. 286–290; Siemaszko & Ostaszewski, 2013, pp. 3–6).

Efficiency indicators therefore depend largely on the issue we are trying to measure. We used three indicators to measure the efficiency of the EAW: (1) the speed of the judgements issued, (2) the accuracy of the judgements issued, and (3) the costs of issuing and executing the EAW. We have also analysed the problem of cooperation of various services and institutions when issuing and executing EAW.

2. Research methods

We conducted the research using two methods. The first one was the examination of court case files. We were interested only in finalised cases in which the EAW was issued between 2018 and 2019. The sample frame for the study was a list of references of such cases obtained from all regional courts in the first half of 2020, following written requests from the Institute of Law Studies Polish Academy of Sciences. This list consisted of 4,306 cases. We increased the minimum sample size of 326 cases by 25%.[2] We applied random stratified sampling, taking into account the difference in the number of cases heard in individual courts. In total, we requested 408 cases, of which we received and examined 336, or 82%. We conducted this survey in the first half of 2021.

The second method was in-depth interviews. We interviewed two groups: experts and people with transfer experience. The experts included police officers, judges, probation officers, prison and border guard staff, court staff, and representatives of community organisations involved in providing support and assistance to individuals who have served a custodial sentence. The second group included (1) persons who were sentenced by British courts for committing a crime in the UK, and then deported to Poland after serving a prison sentence as a result of an order from a British court or a decision from the Secretary of State, and (2) persons who were wanted by the Polish authorities under the European Arrest Warrant, that is, those who were returned from the UK or an EU country to Poland under the EAW procedure as a result of a previous criminal offence committed in Poland. In total, we conducted 60 interviews, including 29 with experts and 31 with people with surrender experience.

The aim of the overall project[3] was to explore the post-deportation and post-extradition experiences (including post-surrender experiences) of Poles who had been expelled from the UK and EU countries as a result of their previous contact with the justice system. We were primarily interested in the transfer procedure. The material we collected from various sources and using various methods allowed for a detailed analysis of the efficiency of the EAW. The file survey provided us with statistical data on, for example, the time which elapsed from committing the crime to issuing the EAW or from issuing the sentence to issuing the EAW, as well as the manner of resolving the EAW cases: on how many wanted persons were detained, transferred or refused transfer and for what reason. The respondents' statements, in turn, helped us to analyse in more detail the measures of efficiency of the EAW that we identified. For the sake of clarity, we assigned special codes to the quoted statements, consisting of three elements: (1) the type of study (EAW), (2) the order of the expert interview (E1, E2, etc.) and (3) the institution that the expert worked for (P – police, F – foundation, C – court, PS – prison service, BG – border guard and PO – probation officers). The project was approved by the Research Ethics Committee of the Institute of Law Studies of the Polish Academy of Sciences.

3. Speed of issuing warrants

As we mentioned earlier, one of the elements of efficiency of procedural measures is time. This is because, as the literature suggests, the right to a fair trial is linked to the right to have a case heard within a reasonable time. This not only includes the duration of the court proceedings but should also extend to the enforcement proceedings, that is, the ordering of the execution of the sentence. Therefore, we were interested to see how much time elapsed from the moment the offence was committed and, in the case of searching for persons to be sentenced, from the issuance of a judgement in a particular case, to the moment the EAW was issued by Polish courts between 2018 and 2019.

Table 6.1 Time from commission of the act to surrender in years (N = 333)

From the commission of the act to issuing the EAW								
Stage of proceedings	*up to 2 years*	*up to 5 years*	*up to 8 years*	*up to 10 years*	*up to 16 years*	*up to 20 years*	*over 20 years*	*Total*
preparatory (66)	23%	40%	20%	6%	6%	3%	2%	100%
judicial (3)	0%	33%	67%	0%	0%	0%	0%	100%
executive (266)	7%	30%	35%	4%	18%	5%	1%	100%

Source: Based on the survey of files. It is possible that the EAW concerned different proceedings, at different stages; thus, the values do not add up to 333.

Table 6.2 Time from the court sentence to EAW in years (N = 266)

From the court judgement to issuing the EAW								
Stage of the procedure	*up to 2 years*	*up to 5 years*	*up to 8 years*	*up to 10 years*	*up to 16 years*	*up to 20 years*	*over 20 years*	*Total*
executive (266)	23%	43%	22%	4%	7%	1%	0%	100%
an order for execution of a conditionally suspended sentence (133)	6%	49%	31%	5%	8%	1%	0%	100%

Source: Based on the survey of files. The table concerns only EAWs issued at the stage of executive proceedings.

The data collected in the course of the file survey show that, depending on the stage of criminal proceedings at which the EAW was issued, the time which elapsed from the commission of the act to the issuance of the EAW may vary. The majority of EAWs were issued in order to execute a sentence (266, i.e. 79.3%), whereas the lowest number of warrants were issued in judicial proceedings (3). As for EAWs issued by Polish courts in pre-trial proceedings (there were 66 such EAWs in the sample, i.e. 19.8%), not more than five years passed since the act was committed in two-thirds of the cases. When it comes to judicial proceedings, all EAWs were issued more than two but no later than eight years after the act was committed, while the EAW issued in order to execute a sentence three-quarters of the warrants were issued up to eight years after the act was committed, but nearly one-fifth of them were issued more than 10 to 16 years after the act was committed. The average duration of judicial proceedings in 2019 was 8.7 months (Ministry of Justice, 2020c).

The efficiency of EAWs should also be measured by the time that elapses between the issuance of an EAW by a court in one EU state and the arrest of a wanted person in another EU state. In one-quarter of the cases, apprehension took place within a month or less, and it is worth noting that some wanted persons may already have been in custody in another Member State at the time the EAW was issued. Within six months after the EAW was issued, almost three-quarters of the wanted persons were detained. This clearly demonstrates that the EAW is a very fast instrument, because information on the issuing of an EAW is sent immediately to all Member States which participate in the EAW procedure. Of course, we are referring to the most recent years that we have studied. Compared to the total statistical data presented earlier, it can thus be seen that this instrument is being used with increasing efficiency over time; this is certainly true in Polish cases. We should point out that more than a half of perpetrators wanted for execution of sentence are those with suspended imprisonment sentences and where due to violations of the conditions under which the sentence was suspended, the courts order the execution of their prison sentence.

It is worth considering whether, in every case, especially if many years have passed since the act was committed and the crime was not serious, people should be sought by means of an EAW. One of the points of reference that Polish judges refer to when issuing EAWs for perpetrators of less serious crimes is the principle of legalism that is binding in the Polish Code of Criminal Procedure and that requires unconditional pursuit of offenders by all lawful means. As one of the judges said:

> In the course of proceedings before a first-instance district court, when we at last have a final judgment and sentence . . . it turns out that the convicted person is not in the country, because he or she is somewhere abroad, then the poor district court applies to the regional court for a European Arrest Warrant. In reality, . . . from the perspective of the district judge, this is a last resort in order to carry out this sentence.
>
> (EAW_E12_C)

This quotation implies not only legalism but also a desire to fulfil the bureaucratic requirements imposed on judges, that is, to ensure that the sentence is carried out even in a minor case and after many years. The imperative of searching for the perpetrator is also reinforced by the belief in the preventive function of punishment that is, deterring the perpetrator from committing further crimes. However, as our respondents say, this is not the case. There are situations, in fact, when the same persons are sought repeatedly.

> Some people have already been wanted many times because one search ends and the person comes back to us after some time. Because, for example, they have served their sentence, their imprisonment, and then they start committing crimes again and are wanted again.
>
> (ENA_E1_P)

Several measures are taken to increase the efficiency of the EAW. In order to accelerate the work of judges and to provide substantive support when issuing the

EAW, judges rely on assistants who prepare the preliminary ruling and fill in the EAW form.

> Fortunately, we also have the support of assistants . . . the assistant examines whether there are grounds for granting the request for issuing the EAW or not and drafts a ruling and presents it to the court clerk. And I, after reading the files of the case and the draft, actually . . . make a decision. So it is a very quick procedure.
>
> (EAW_E12_C)

Regional court judges also try to influence indirectly the number of EAW requests submitted to their courts. In the justifications for refusing to issue an EAW, they specify what exactly motivated the refusal to issue the EAW so as to teach the district court judges in which cases it is not even worth submitting a motion. One such case of refusal to issue an EAW might include unusually dilatory conduct of preparatory or executive proceedings (e.g. when there is a long delay between the steps in the proceedings). Some judges also try to encourage the use of other instruments, for example, transferring the sentence for execution to another EU state, if there are grounds for doing so. In such cases, when refusing to issue the EAW, they justify their decision by suggesting to the court that a more adequate and less burdensome measure of cooperation in criminal matters should be used. Some remedy for the vast number of applications for EAWs, according to our experts, is to provide informal guidelines and training for district court judges on which cases should be subject to EAWs and which should not. Another method of reducing the number of applications from district courts is to keep a record – for example, in the form of an order – of a judge's decision not to apply for an EAW, with a brief statement of reasons. The directive under the principle of legalism to use all means to prosecute the offender is then satisfied, as the judge can explain in the reasons for such a decision and report that the EAW is not an adequate means of prosecution in the particular case.

4. Accuracy of rulings

An indicator of the accuracy of rulings is the degree of their execution, including information on the number of cases in which a wanted person was detained, in which foreign courts refused to execute the EAW and for what reason. In 2020, courts in Poland issued 1795 EAWs, 153 of them, that is, 8.5%, concluded with a ruling on refusal of surrender by judicial authorities of another Member State. If we compare only 2020 with the previous year, we can see more than 20% decrease in the number of EAWs issued and more than 15% increase in refusals (Ministry of Justice, 2019, 2020b). The increase in refusals may be due to the political situation in Poland and the concerns of EU Member States about the rule of law in our country, as well as doubts about the autonomy of Polish judges adjudicating in criminal cases as a result of the changes in the structure of the judiciary that have been taking place since 2015 and the launch of disciplinary proceedings against judges who adjudicate contrary to the official position of the Polish Ministry of Justice (Bober et al., 2020). This is one of the reasons for refusals to execute EAWs, as well as one of the issues that foreign courts are asking more and more about. As one judge noted:

> at the moment we are receiving refusals to surrender our citizens under the European Arrest Warrant. This concerns situations which are related to the fact, of which we are all aware, that the rule of law is being questioned in Poland.
>
> (ENA_E27_C)

The change that we observed in 2020 may also be a consequence of the Covid-19 pandemic, as statistical data show that both the overall volume of cases submitted to Polish courts and the number of cases processed fell in that year (Ostaszewski et al., 2021, pp. 111–115). The percentage of EAW refusals recorded in the file survey reflects the nationwide trend. Out of 336 examined court files, arrests were made in almost 80% of the cases, out of which detainees were transferred to Poland in almost 70% of the cases. On the other hand, 6% of the cases involved refusals to execute an EAW. Most refusals came from Germany, the Netherlands and the United Kingdom, that is the countries to which Poland sends or has sent most EAWs (Ministry of Justice, 2020a). Concerns about the rule of law are only one of the motives for refusals. These are governed by, inter alia, Article 9 of the Framework Decision and include, in particular, the issuance of a judgement referring to acts which did not constitute an offence under the law of the executing State, the statute of limitations for the enforcement of the sentence under the law of the executing State, a period of less than six months remaining to be served by the wanted person, and the issuance of a judgement in absentia.

Research shows that the most common reasons for refusals are in absentia proceedings (Brodersen et al., 2020, pp. 3, 65 et seq.). This reason was found in one-third of the examined cases in which transfer was refused. One of the court staff handling international cases and therefore all EAWs in a given court estimated that, together with joint sentences, this reason accounts for the majority of refusals:

> First and foremost, there are refusals for judgments in absentia and summary judgments. This is 80% of all refusals. . . . These are mainly situations where a person claims before a foreign authority that they did not know about the proceedings against them, that they are wanted . . . it happens that someone from their family receives a notification of sentence enforcement or collects a copy of the judgment.
>
> (EAW_E28_C)

Equally often, as the analysis of the files shows, it was the convicted person who refused transfer as he or she was a national of the executing state or should be treated as such (he or she lived there for many years, is a spouse of a national of that state, his or her children are nationals of the executing state) and did not consent to the transfer to Poland. In one in ten cases, refusal was due to the petty nature of the act committed, disproportionality (e.g. the court found that the defendant was not evading justice, so surrender would not be proportionate, or that it would be incompatible with his/her rights under the European Convention on Human Rights) or lack of assimilation with the requesting state (the person being prosecuted has socially assimilated, but into the state to which he or she has travelled).

If the EAW was issued in a petty case, the executing authority may proceed in two ways: (1) refuse to execute the order on the grounds of a breach of fundamental rights or (2) conduct a proportionality review and then decide whether the circumstances of the case justify meeting the threshold conditions for issuing the order, which should ensure that this instrument is not abused by Member States (Mitsilegas, 2020, p. 20). Acts considered trivial in our file survey included defrauding a bank to extort a loan of nearly €1125 and driving under the influence of drugs. However, the files we studied contained far more acts that might be qualified as minor. In 16% of the cases, the EAW was issued for minor drug offences, and in every fifth case in this category it was possession of narcotic drugs or psychotropic substances. Seven per cent were offences against family and guardianship, and half of these were offences of failure to pay child support, while 7% were offences against road safety, 80% of which were drunk-driving offences. Teresa Gardocka's earlier research drew similar conclusions. She found that in 80% of the studied cases in which a warrant was issued, the perpetrators had failed to pay child support, or committed acts against property, offences against safety of transport, offences against documents or drug-related offences (Gardocka, 2011, pp. 23–24, 28). The EAW was also requested for offenders who, for example, had stolen a case of beer or 10 pens worth €275, had been in possession of cannabis or ridden a bicycle under the influence of alcohol (Gardocka, 2011, pp. 34–39; HFHR, 2018, pp. 28–32). The most serious acts, for which the EAW was issued, account for a negligible proportion of cases. A similar trend is also evident in other EU countries (Fair Trials, 2018, pp. 10–11).

Experts also understood a petty offence as one punished by the court with light penalties. In the cases we studied, EAWs were most often issued against persons who had been sentenced to a mandatory prison sentence (53%) or a suspended prison sentence (50%). A fine was imposed in 9% of the cases, and a restriction of liberty in 4%. It should be explained that a court may have pronounced more than one penalty on a single person, hence the percentages do not add up to 100. In the case of a conditionally suspended penalty or a penalty other than incarceration, the basis for issuing the EAW was the ordering of the execution of the conditionally suspended penalty or the conversion of the penalty into a substitute penalty of imprisonment. Some of the experts said that courts do not issue EAWs when the sentence does not exceed one year. This is seen as pragmatic as such cases are often considered trivial abroad:

> We still have such a . . . practice that . . . we try [to issue EAWs in the case of custodial sentences] only after a year, . . . because they do not want us [other states] to surrender [wanted persons] for less than a year. This is one of the reasons [for refusal].
>
> (EAW_E29_C)

However, this is the practice of one particular court. The file study shows that the lowest mandatory term of imprisonment in which a warrant was issued was six months, and in 22% of cases it did not exceed a year. As far as suspended sentences are concerned, the lowest term of imprisonment was only 4 months, while sentences not exceeding 12 months constituted more than 40% of the cases with that type of penalty. It is worth noting that since the court pronounced suspended imprisonment at the outset, the act committed by the offender could not have been serious. It is all the more surprising that so many applications for the EAW were submitted in these cases.

There are also instances of refusals to execute the order due to inappropriate conditions in prisons, and also because the person wanted under the EAW has been staying for several years in the territory of a foreign state, where he or she has built a life (they work, have a family), and the act for which they are wanted was committed a long time before. This is how one judge explained this, by citing one of his cases:

> The person wanted in the European Arrest Warrant resided in the UK . . . and was sentenced by a Polish court to around a year and eight months of imprisonment. . . . The British court refused to release the Polish citizen, arguing that he had been sentenced five years earlier and had settled in the United Kingdom about four years earlier. He has a permanent job, a partner with whom he had a two-year-old child, he was the sole breadwinner, and he had been convicted of drink-driving by a Polish court. . . . Anyway, the British court decided that, yes, the offence was criminal, but it was not so serious that it was worth ruining the life of this man and his family by honouring the European Arrest Warrant.
>
> (EAW_E12_C)

In one in 20 cases, the refusal to execute the EAW was motivated by the statute of limitations on the execution of the sentence in the country where the perpetrator was arrested. However, as the experts indicated, the statute of limitations as well as the fact that the act in question is not a criminal offence in the territory of a foreign state are sporadically the reason.

> Sometimes there are refusals . . . if the offence is not [an offence] on the territory of the foreign State or . . . the sentence is time-barred in the executing State, . . . but these are rare situations.
>
> (EAW_E28_C)

One offence for which enforcement is typically refused is failure to pay child support. In many countries, such refusal does not constitute a criminal offence and the debt is recovered in civil proceedings. Although the file survey shows that there are a number of cases where this is the ground for issuing an EAW (they accounted for about 3% of the cases we examined), interviews with experts suggest that in some courts no EAW is issued for failure to pay child support, precisely because Member States refuse to enforce it.

> they do not hand [people] over to us for child support at all, I mean no country does. . . . We have also adopted the practice over the last few years that . . . we do not issue European Arrest Warrants for failure to pay child support because it is not worth generating costs.
>
> (EAW_E29_C)

The experts also said that it is not always clear for what reason a court in another country refuses to enforce a warrant. Usually very precise explanations are sent by German courts. However, the respondents expressed most concern about refusals on the grounds of Poland's violation of the rule of law, an issue that they cannot really control or influence, and which calls into question whether Poland should be a party to EAW decisions and to what extent Member States can assume that standards of judicial independence in Poland are similar to those in other EU states. Experienced judges often spoke about this bitterly:

> in general, in my opinion, our situation now is such that . . . it is difficult to assume a mutual trust towards us, and I believe that, in practical terms, we should not be treated as a state which is a party to the decision on the European Arrest Warrant, but as a regular extradition state in which the admissibility of surrender is examined, for example, on the basis of reports from international organisations, NGOs and so on. In my opinion, this offensive to bring the courts under political control has already gone so far that it is difficult for us to apply without reservation a mechanism based on mutual recognition of judgments, that is to say, executing them as our own, on the assumption that we represent a similar standard of judicial independence. . . . However, the mechanism proposed by the CJEU in the LM ruling, whereby we ask the state body that is to execute the EAW whether or not its independence is respected, is, in my opinion, highly unreliable . . . and questionable.
>
> (EAW_E18_C)

> But if we were to be cut off from this international legal network completely, I would be distressed. . . . We have really been trusted. . . . This mutual trust was really built and shaped for a long time.
>
> (ENA_E19_C)

Although there were only 20 cases of refusal to execute the EAW in the examined files, in 89 cases (i.e. a third of the cases in which the perpetrator was apprehended), the Member States submitted questions to the Polish courts, asking for:

- clarification of the information on the act committed;
- clarification of issues related to the rights of defence, including, for example, whether the defendant can be heard by the court at the trial, whether a

professional defence counsel has been appointed, whether there will be prompt notification of dates of the trial and of the judgement;

- provision of details of the procedural aspects of the pre-trial proceedings;
- definition of the severity of the penalty to be imposed or
- clarification of issues related to the independence of the judiciary, for example, whether disciplinary proceedings are initiated against judges, the procedure for appointing court presidents and whether the executive branch has an influence on the activities of the courts by issuing written guidelines.

5. Costs of EAW

As mentioned earlier, the efficiency of EAW may also be analysed from economic perspective. In such a case, a comparison should be made between the costs of using this instrument and the benefits resulting from its execution and, consequently, from transporting the wanted person to Poland. The first cost connected with the EAW procedure, which is very difficult to estimate, is the time and remuneration of justice administration staff (judges, court secretaries and assistants) involved in drafting appropriate documentation. These costs are not itemised in any reports. One external court expense after the EAW has been issued is the translation of the warrant into English (and later also into other languages when corresponding with the state executing the warrant). This has been pointed out by court staff:

> However, the main costs are the translations. These are certified translations. It all depends on how many of them there are. Because we exchange these letters . . . so there are also translation costs, and it all compounds.
>
> (ENA_E28_C)

According to the procedure in force, an English translation of the EAW is handed over to the police who are obliged to organise and carry out a convoy from the country of arrest to the relevant penitentiary unit in Poland in the event of arrest of a wanted person. The basic and most serious cost for the Polish authorities in the EAW procedure is the transport of the detainee to the country (Gardocka, 2011, p. 16). This expense is in fact difficult to estimate, as the data provided by the Police Headquarters only include the costs directly related to the organisation of the convoy (flight or plane tickets) and do not include the labour costs of the officers who escort the person being transferred:

> It is difficult to calculate these costs when it comes to the police, because, of course, a police officer also has to do a lot of work . . . just to collect information which shows that a person is abroad, but, in my opinion, this is incalculable.
>
> (ENA_E1_P)

Ten years ago, the National Police Headquarters annually allocated more than €4.25 million per year for such convoys (Gardocka, 2011, p. 42). In 2014, the average cost of a regular flight convoy was over €2,750, while a collective convoy by a chartered aircraft was slightly over €250 per person (Nepelski & Struniawski, 2015, p. 102). It follows from the decision of the Court of Appeal in Gdańsk (case number II Akz 679/18) that the cost of a convoy from the Netherlands to Poland estimated by the National Police Headquarters was €1000. Police officials drew attention to the wide variety of costs depending on the situation:

> For one transfer this range can be very different. It varies from several thousand to over ten thousand zlotys. When it comes to extradition, it may even amount to tens of thousands.
>
> (ENA_E2_P)

We should mention that it is only in exceptional circumstances that convicted persons are ordered to pay the costs of a convoy, as our research (interviews with convicted persons as well as the examination of files) has shown that the courts very rarely recover such costs from detainees. Usually, the state treasury pays these costs.

> Of course, the police issue what's called a calculation of the charges for escorting to the contracting authority; however, in criminal cases, as with the European Arrest Warrant, this is included in the case file and is counted only as budgetary costs.
>
> (ENA_E4_P)

> The costs of escorting, well, let us say, they are not charged. In the very beginning, there was a practice of charging these people with these expenses, but they were unrecoverable. There is no chance of that happening.
>
> (ENA_E28_C)

On this subject, it is worth mentioning Article 5 TEU, which refers directly in Paragraph 4 to the principle of proportionality, meaning that actions within the EU (and thus the use of its mechanisms) must be applied in such a way as to contribute to achieving the objectives enshrined in the Treaties. The high importance of this principle among the principles governing the functioning of the EU is demonstrated by the fact that Protocol No. 2 on the application of the principles of subsidiarity and proportionality was annexed to the TEU and specifies their content. The principle of proportionality is sometimes interpreted to mean that Member States should use the tools provided by European law prudently and not to further their own interests but only those of the EU. In view of the high costs incurred by Member States in issuing and executing EAWs, it is worth considering the seriousness of the offence when deciding whether to use the EAW in a person search procedure. The paradox and abuse of this measure by Polish courts is shown by the following statement:

> A man stole € 175. The convoy costs several thousand zlotys, and the appointment of an expert also costs several thousand zlotys. The man is convoyed to Poland, pays some €100 bail and returns.
>
> (ENA_E1_P)

6. Collaboration

Measuring efficiency only makes sense if the team involved in a task is properly staffed. Every link in the chain of this collaboration must function correctly, first, so that the objective can be achieved and, second, so that no infringement occurs in the execution of the objective. This is also the case with the EAW. Proper national and international collaboration is essential for this mechanism to work efficiently. This collaboration takes place at different stages and involves different people and institutions. In principle, none of them is assigned solely to dealing with the EAW. It is one of many tasks that they carry out. For this reason, it is important that collaboration on the EAW does not obstruct the seamless implementation of other tasks. In the course of the interviews, we asked experts about which Polish and foreign entities they cooperate with when executing the EAW, how they evaluate that cooperation, whether there are any difficulties and how they could possibly be solved in order to improve the collaboration. The study has shown that the assessment of the cooperation is not uniform. Usually, collaboration with Polish officials is better rated, while problems, if they do occur, are related to a few selected countries. Experts who did not perceive major problems in collaboration stressed that it is often only the human factor that is at fault, and that sometimes a phone call and a conversation is enough.

> To be honest, I have never encountered any difficulties in exchanging this information with any country. . . . There has never been a situation where, for example, we had to lodge a complaint or ask for some kind of intervention. . . . So it seems to me that this is a well-functioning mechanism and procedure.
>
> (ENA_E15_BG)

Our data come from interviews with several dozen persons. They show what the respondents' experience is in terms of collaboration with individual states in the execution of the EAW. The data are obviously not exhaustive, but what is important is that they reveal similarities in the assessments of different countries by experts from various institutions. The experts reported good collaboration mainly with Germany and Lithuania. Germany, in particular, was given a high rating, and respondents evaluated working together with this country very favourably. However, there were far more statements in the survey suggesting that collaboration with other countries was poor, especially with Italy, Greece and the UK. There were many examples of inadequate cooperation on the part of these countries, and only a few are given later. The general problem is poor communication with these countries, as well as the length of time they take to carry out specific tasks: "But there are these countries . . . if you want something done wrong, contact Italy or Greece. They can even hang up on us when we call them" (ENA_E1_P).

The cooperation with Eurojust is rated very highly by the experts. As they said, "they are very fast, that is, we do not use it too often, but if there is already the third or fourth reminder to a foreign authority and there is no information, we use Eurojust" (ENA_E28_C).

Organising the surrender of a person under the EAW requires time-consuming steps. It is therefore important that Poland has timely information on such plans. Although they are usually communicated, there are also cases when Poland learns about them at the last possible moment: when the plane is landing at the airport. This is particularly true of the United Kingdom.

> As far as cooperation with the British is concerned, we also had [such a situation] recently, when British policemen brought us perhaps twenty or thirty . . . Polish citizens who had just been deported. Except that there were maybe only five or six wanted persons, but also without any prior information that such a convoy, such a deportation, would be carried out. We simply found out at the moment when the plane was taxing to the parking bay that the employees of the man hunting agent's company were not allowed on board, but the British were waiting here for our assistance, to collect all these gentlemen from them. . . . It happens sometimes with the British that they play this trick on us.
>
> (ENA_E20_BG)

The police play a major role in the implementation of EAW, as they are responsible for convoying wanted persons. In this regard, they cooperate with border guards, so that, for example, the border control of persons returning from outside the Schengen zone is not burdensome and often is not done in the traditional manner. This is what a police officer said about the collaboration:

> on many occasions the Border Guard assisted us in escorting that person through the terminal to the car. They made their crossings available to us many times, and if necessary, they provided assistance.
>
> (ENA_E4_P)

Experts from convoy departments said that they were in regular contact with prison officials, so there were no problems with admitting a person returning from abroad to prison at almost any time of the day or night.

> they are admitted basically at whatever time we arrive with the person. Of course, we try to do this as quickly as possible, immediately after the plane has landed so that the person can be in the penitentiary as quickly as possible.
>
> (ENA_E4_P)

This is especially important because, according to the file study, out of 336 cases examined, in more than 80% of cases the EAW was issued at the stage of executive proceedings, and thus wanted persons are transferred directly to prisons to serve their sentences. This has also been confirmed by the findings of other studies (Gardocka, 2011, p. 25; HFHR, 2018, p. 24). The collaboration of the convoy department with the prison service depends on the number of individuals being escorted. When convoying one person at a time, the police contact the relevant facility directly (in Poland, admissions of escorted persons generally take place in one Warsaw prison) and establish the details of the admission, including the time of the admission. The police also provide information on the exact number of persons, as well as their status: whether they are temporarily arrested or convicted. All this information is important for the placement of these people in prison.

Adverse situations arising from improper state-to-state cooperation have a bearing on, for example, the failure to count the period of imprisonment in a foreign prison as part of the sentence. The start of a sentence is considered to be the moment when a person is brought to prison and a so-called Reception Card is drawn up. The police officers who take the person over at the Polish border are responsible for filling in this card. Experts from the prison service said in interviews that they not only apply to the court to credit the time spent in a foreign prison but also monitor the case further. However, sometimes such decisions come late, because it is necessary to ask another country to specify the period the wanted person spent in a foreign prison.

Another problem is the failure to transfer the prison records of a person detained abroad. The lack of knowledge of what happened at the initial stage of incarceration is a problem for the prison service when it comes to working with the person. It is also often to the detriment of those being surrendered. One expert told the following story:

> I had the opportunity to speak quite recently with one inmate who was surprised because after being transported here she found out that she was being sent to a prison facility. She said that she had already served several years in the Netherlands and worked there, was eligible for prison leave, and suddenly found herself in a secure correctional institution. But we had an empty file, in which there was one page, the first page of some preliminary interview, and nothing more, and we couldn't say to her, 'well, you're right, because you really have some progress here, you have built some trust' – we had nothing.
> (ENA_E13_PS)

Rarely did the experts talk about mechanisms that could improve collaboration under the EAW. Instead, they emphasised that the human factor is at fault. The Schengen Information System (SIS), the largest database into which Schengen states enter information on wanted persons undeniably facilitates the execution of the EAW. According to some experts, one common database accessible to all institutions dealing with the EAW (e.g. the police, border guards, prison service and courts) would be helpful, but data protection concerns prevent such a step being taken. Liaison officers also assist, especially the police, in carrying out their tasks under the EAW.

Conclusions

In order to answer the question whether the EAW is an efficient instrument, it was first necessary to define this concept. The literature shows that to operationalise efficiency, scholars most often identify specific indicators to be measured. We used a similar approach in our analysis. We identified three measures of efficiency: the speed of judgements, the accuracy of judgements and the costs of the EAW. We also assumed that the guarantor of EAW efficiency is proper cooperation of persons involved in the implementation of this procedure, both at the national and international levels. This measurement allows us to conclude that, in general, the EAW procedure should be regarded as efficient, but we would like to emphasise that this assessment is made solely on the basis of an analysis of the measures given. It therefore refers strictly to the technical aspects. It does not take into account an assessment of the purpose for which the EAW instrument was created. As a side note, it is worth pointing out that it would be reasonable to consider whether it makes sense to bring a wanted person to Poland after many years of his/her absence, especially when he/she has already managed to settle down abroad and the act that he/she committed is a minor offence or the penalty is not very severe. Turning, however, to technical issues and the favourable assessment of the EAW's efficiency, it is worth recapitulating that this assessment is confirmed by the speedy execution time of the procedure from the moment the EAW is issued to the moment the wanted person is apprehended. In every fourth instance, the procedure is completed within a month, and in three-quarters of the cases it does not exceed six months. The accuracy of issued rulings is also positively evaluated. In most cases, the wanted person is detained and handed over. Refusal to execute the EAW is rare: this happens in less than one in ten cases. The analysis of reasons for refusals shows that the biggest problem is the enforcement of EAW in cases where there was a joint judgement or the judgement was issued *in absentia*. In recent years, the number of refusals and questions from foreign courts about the rule of law has also been growing, but these issues should not be linked to questions of the efficiency of the instrument itself but rather to problems of the Polish justice system. Some of the reasons for refusals, such as issuing EAWs against persons wanted for a short custodial sentence (e.g. up to six months or up to a year), or against persons wanted for a minor offence or for a non-criminal act in the country where the EAW is executed, can certainly be reduced by not issuing EAWs in such matters. This would have a beneficial effect not only of lowering the EAW refusal rate but also of improving the handling of the remaining cases. The number of EAW issued in Poland is very high. The costs involved are also significant. If we consider only the convoy, the costs range from several to a dozen thousand Polish zloty. One of the metrics that we used, namely the time between the commission of the act and the issuance of the EAW, proved inadequate for measuring the efficiency of the EAW, which should not be analysed in isolation. Studies show that individuals who committed offences many years earlier are brought back to serve their sentences: in three-quarters of cases this period is up to eight years, and in one in five cases it is from 10 to 16 years after the offence was committed. It must be remembered, however, that this period includes the pre-trial and trial proceedings conducted in Poland. Although the average duration of EAW proceedings in 2019 was less than nine months, depending on, in particular, the complexity of the case, criminal proceedings last longer: about 14% of them last more than 12 months, and about 1% even more than 8 years. It also appears that the factor which is supposed to guarantee the efficiency of the EAW is somewhat failing. Cooperation goes well only with some countries, while it is virtually non-existent with others, starting from a lack of contact to delays in providing important information such as the period of imprisonment in a foreign prison, which is essential for the correct assessment of the remaining sentence to be served. It seems that much can still be done to improve collaboration with several countries.

Notes

1 The Council Framework Decision of 13 June 2002 on the European arrest warrant and the surrender procedures between Member States (2002/584/JHA – hereinafter referred to as the Framework Decision).
2 This procedure was dictated by previous experience in conducting this type of research concerning, for example, refusal to send files or giving permission for a smaller number of files to be made available than requested, but it also seemed necessary insofar as the research was conducted during the COVID-19 pandemic, which, especially in its initial stage, affected the organisation of the work of Polish courts.
3 'Experiences of Poles deported from the UK in the context of the criminal justice system involvement' (Grant No. UMO-2018/30/M/HS5/00816).

References

Bober, M., Gąciarek, P., Jurkiewicz, J., Kościerzyński, J., Krasoń, M., & Zabłudowska, D. (2020). *Justice under pressure: Repressions as a means of attempting to take control over the judiciary and the prosecution in Poland: Years 2015–2019*. Iustitia.

Brodersen, K. H., Glerum, V. H., & Klip, A. (2020). *The European Arrest Warrant and in Absentia judgments*. Eleven International Publishing.

Council of Europe. (2018). *European judicial systems Efficiency and quality of justice* (No. 26; CEPEJ STUDIES). https://rm.coe.int/rapport-avec-couv-18-09-2018-en/16808def9c

Dandurand, Y. (2014). Criminal justice reform and the system's efficiency. *Criminal Law Forum*, *25*(3–4), 383–440. https://doi.org/10.1007/s10609-014-9235-y

Easton, J. (2018). Where to draw the line? Is efficiency encroaching on a fair justice system? *The Political Quarterly*, *89*(2), 246–253. https://doi.org/10.1111/1467-923X.12487

European Commission. (2021). *Statistics on the practical operation of the European arrest warrant – 2019*. https://commission.europa.eu/publications/replies-questionnaire-quantitative-information-practical-operation-european-arrest-warrant_en (accessed 28 March 2023).

Fair Trials. (2018). Beyond surrender. Putting human rights at the heart of the European Arrest Warrant. *Fair Trials*. www.fairtrials.org/sites/default/files/publication_pdf/FT_beyond-surrender_B5_web_spreads.pdf

Gardocka, T. (2011). *Europejski Nakaz Aresztowania. Analiza polskiej praktyki występowania do innych państw Unii Europejskiej z wnioskiem o wydania osoby przez trybu europejskiego nakazu aresztowania* [European Arrest Warrant. Analysis of Polish practice of requesting other EU states to surrender a person by means of European Arrest Warrant]. Institute for Justice. https://iws.gov.pl/wp-content/uploads/2018/08/AR_Gardocka-T_-ENA-2011.pdf.

HFHR. (2018). *Praktyka stosowania europejskiego nakazu aresztowania w Polsce jako państwie wydającym. Raport krajowy* [The practice of applying the European Arrest

Warrant in Poland as an issuing state: Report on Poland.] Helsinki Foundation for Human Rights. www.hfhr.pl/wp-content/uploads/2018/07/ENA_PL.pdf

Hofmański, P., Górski, A., Sakowicz, A., & Szumiło-Kulczycka, D. (2008). *Europejski nakaz aresztowania w teorii i praktyce państw członkowskich Unii Europejskiej* [The European Arrest Warrant in the theory and practice of European Union Member States]. Wolters Kluwer Polska.

Joński, K. (2016). *Efektywność sądownictwa powszechnego – Podstawowe problemy.* [Efficiency of the ordinary judiciary: Basic problems]. Institute for Justice.

Joński, K. (2017). *Instytucja asystenta a efektywność pracy sędziego – analiza pionów karnego i cywilnego pierwszej instancji sądów okręgowych* [The institution of the assistant and the efficiency of a judge's work: Analysis of criminal and civil divisions of first instance of district courts]. Instytut Wymiaru Sprawiedliwości.

Klaus, W., Włodarczyk-Madejska, J., & Wzorek, D. (2021). In the pursuit of justice: (Ab)use of the European Arrest Warrant in the polish criminal justice system. *Central and Eastern European Migration Review*, *10*(1), 95–117. https://doi.org/10.17467/ceemr.2021.02.

Klimczak, J. (2020). Szybkość postępowań sądowych w Polsce i w innych państwach Europy [Speed of court proceedings in Poland and other European countries]. In P. Ostaszewski (Ed.), *Efektywność sądownictwa powszechnego – oceny i analizy* [Efficiency of the judiciary: Evaluations and analyses] (pp. 273–292). Institute for Justice.

Klimek, L. (2015). *European Arrest Warrant.* Springer International Publishing. https://doi.org/10.1007/978-3-319-07338-5

Królak, S. M., Dzialuk, I., & Michalczuk, C. (2006). *Współpraca sądowa w Unii Europejskiej. Akty prawne, uzasadnienia, komentarze* [Judicial cooperation in the European Union: Legal acts, explanatory memoranda, comments]. Wydawnictwo Naukowe Scholar.

Mathis, K. (2009). *Efficiency Instead of Justice?* (D. Shannon, Trans., Vol. 84). Springer. https://doi.org/10.1007/978-1-4020-9798-0

Ministry of Justice. (2017). *Justice-Measures 2007-I H1 2017.* https://isws.ms.gov.pl/

Ministry of Justice. (2019). *MS-S5o Report in criminal and misdemeanour cases.* Ministerstwo Sprawiedliwości.

Ministry of Justice. (2020a). *EAW-European Arrest Warrant 2004–2020.* https://isws.ms.gov.pl/pl/baza-statystyczna/opracowania-wieloletnie/

Ministry of Justice. (2020b). *MS-S5o Report in criminal and misdemeanour cases.* Ministerstwo Sprawiedliwości.

Ministry of Justice. (2020c). *Average duration of court proceedings 2011–2020.* https://isws.ms.gov.pl/pl/baza-statystyczna/opracowania-wieloletnie/

Mitsilegas, V. (2020). After Brexit: Reframing EU-UK cooperation in criminal matters. In R. M. Pereira, A. Engel, & S. Miettinen (Eds.), *The governance of criminal justice in the European Union: Transnationalism, localism and public participation in an evolving constitutional order*. Edward Elgar Publishing.

Nepelski, M., & Struniawski, J. (2015). Kompetencje Policji w zakresie wykonania Europejskiego Nakazu Aresztowania [Police competences in the execution of the European Arrest Warrant]. *Warmińsko-Mazurski Kwartalnik Naukowy, Nauki Społeczne*, *2*, 97–108.

Ostaszewski, P., Klimczak, J., & Włodarczyk-Madejska, J. (2021). *Przestępczość i wymiar sprawiedliwości w pierwszym roku pandemii COVID-19* [Crime and justice in the first year of the COVID-19 pandemic]. Institute for Justice Publishing.

Roghină, G. E. R. (2012). "Fair trial in an optimum and foresseable time" Council of Europe's recommendation through European Commission for the efficiency of justice and express legal provision in the new Romanian Code of Civil Procedure. *Juridical Current*, *15*(2), 44–59.

Siemaszko, A., & Ostaszewski, P. (2013). *Efektywność kosztowa sądownictwa powszechnego* [Cost-efficiency of the general judiciary]. Institute for Justice. https://iws.gov.pl/wp-content/uploads/2018/08/Efektywno%C5%9B%C4%87-s%C4%85downictwa-powszechnego-oprac-12–1.pdf

Siemaszko, A., Ostaszewski, P., & Włodarczyk-Madejska, J. (2020). Tendencje wpływu spraw do polskich sądów powszechnych [Trends in the inflow of cases to Polish common courts]. In P. Ostaszewski (Ed.), *Efektywność sądownictwa powszechnego – oceny i analizy* [Efficiency of the common courts: Evaluations and analyses] (pp. 85–208). Institute for Justice.

Włodarczyk-Madejska, J., Ostaszewski, P., & Klimczak, J. (2020). Efektywność pracy sędziów sądów powszechnych. Wyniki analizy wywiadów pogłębionych [Work efficiency of common law court judges: Results of analysis of in-depth interviews]. In P. Ostaszewski (Ed.), *Efektywność sądownictwa powszechnego – oceny i analizy* [Efficiency of the common courts: Evaluations and analyses] (pp. 293–398). Institute for Justice.

Zielińska, E. (2017). *Mediacja w sprawach karnych o przemoc w rodzinie – skala i efektywność w praktyce polskiego wymiaru sprawiedliwości* [Mediation in criminal cases of family violence: Scale and efficiency in the practice of the Polish justice system]. Institute for Justice.

7 Abruptly interrupted lives

The effects of executing the European arrest warrant procedures on Polish emigrants

Witold Klaus, Justyna Włodarczyk-Madejska and Dominik Wzorek

Introduction

The outcome of the issuance and enforcement of the European Arrest Warrant (EAW) is the forcible removal of a person to the issuing country, which is most often the country of origin. According to the Polish Ministry of Justice, between 2006 and 2020, Poland issued more than 70,000 EAWs (MoJ, 2021), although European Commission data show a lower number of 45,000 (EC, 2021, pp. 39–40).[1] Obviously, this does not mean that so many individuals were forcibly returned to Poland, as it is not uncommon for more than one warrant to be issued against a single person. Moreover, not all wanted persons are tracked down by other Member States and handed over to the Polish authorities. On average, the effectiveness of such searches measured by the number of persons actually handed over is 26% in the EU, while for Poland between 2005 and 2013 this figure was slightly lower at 21% (Klaus et al., 2021, pp. 103–104). In recent years, however, this efficiency has been growing and in 2019 the EU average was 66% (EC, 2021, pp. 11–12). These data show the effectiveness of Polish EAWs to be less than 30% and that slightly more than 13,000 people have been transferred to Poland from other EU countries between 2005 and 2019 (EC, 2021, pp. 39–40). However, our findings (see Włodarczyk-Madejska & Wzorek in this volume) and Polish unpublished statistical data (Table 7.1) demonstrate that the effectiveness of the warrants issued from 2018 to 2019 was much higher and reached about 70%: such was the percentage of wanted persons successfully transferred to Poland.

As can be seen, data on the number of EAWs provided by different institutions and in different formats are not consistent with each other, and it is especially difficult to calculate how many people were forcibly removed from other EU countries and returned to Poland. The total number of people who were forcibly returned as a result of searches by the Polish criminal justice system is certainly much higher than the 13,000 reported by the EC, but it should not exceed 21,000 people as Polish data state. Thus, the number of forced returns compared to all re-emigrants is therefore not especially high, as it ranges between 1% and 2% of the total number of people returning to Poland. Nevertheless, it cannot be considered insignificant or marginal, especially because the forced returns bring a number of adverse, often long-term consequences not only for the returnees themselves but also for their

DOI: 10.4324/9781003254584-8

Table 7.1 The number of EAWs issued by Polish courts and enforced by Member States between 2004 and 2020

Year	*Number of EAWs issued by Polish courts*	*Number of EAWs exercised by EU Member States*
2004	1,619	19
2005	1,265	90
2006	1,226	257
2007	2,035	614
2008	2,926	989
2009	2,641	1,444
2010	2,124	2,076
2011	2,117	1,897
2012	2,030	1,823
2013	1,847	2,009
2014	1,961	1,730
2015	1,611	1,639
2016	1,426	1,541
2017	1,568	1,436
2018	1,497	1,146
2019	1,593	1,256
2020	1,268	966
Total	**30,754**	**20,932**

Source: Unpublished data from the Ministry of Justice

families. The second important reservation about these data is that we can only count the people who were forcibly returned to Poland. What we do not know is how many of their family members followed them back home.

During our research,[2] we talked to Polish nationals targeted by EAW measures to learn about their stories and find out why they left Poland, how their lives turned out abroad, and what consequences the forced return to the country had for them and their families. The objective of this chapter is to look at the consequences of this process for those sought by the justice system and forced to return to Poland. We will examine not only the returned persons themselves but also their families, whether they stayed in the country to which they emigrated or moved back to Poland. We concentrate not only on the experience of being removed due to EAW and the resulting imprisonment but also on the issues of reintegration into Polish society after the forced return, both for the arrestees themselves and their families. But we will begin with some general information on the causes of emigration and re-emigration (rather voluntary), as well as on the size of these two groups of Polish citizens on the move.

1. Emigration from and re-emigration to Poland

To illustrate the issue of forced returns to Poland, we should begin by discussing the emigration of Poles. According to various data, between 2 and 2.5 million people with Polish citizenship live abroad (GUS, 2020; Karolak, 2020, p. 103). Mass emigration, mainly to other European Union countries, began in 2000 and gained momentum after Poland's accession to the EU in 2004. In 2004, about 1 million Poles stayed outside Poland for at least two months, while in 2016 this number exceeded 2.5 million people. As many as 88% of them were residing in other EU countries. More and more people chose long-term stays of more than 12 months (Garapich et al., 2018, pp. 209–211). In the record-breaking 2006, about 50,000 people left Poland with the intention to emigrate permanently; in 2019, the figure dropped to about 11,000 people. The main destinations of migration have remained virtually the same for years: Germany, the UK, the Netherlands, Ireland, Italy and Norway have been dominant, but some changes can be observed between 2018 and 2020, such as a decline in the number of Poles permanently residing in the UK and an increase in the number of emigrants living in Germany and Ireland. Another change that can be observed in the last 20 years is the reduction of migration to the previously popular (mainly in the 1980s and early 1990s) United States and Canada. The main motive for leaving (for about three-quarters of the migrants) is finding work and improving the living conditions and standard of living. Another reason for leaving Poland is the wish to study abroad: in 2019, about 8,000 Poles studied in the UK, while around 5,000 Poles were enrolled at universities in Germany (GUS, 2020, 2021; Okólski & Salt, 2014).

Statistically speaking, the Polish emigrant between 2000 and 2019 was typically a person aged 20–49. Gender does not differentiate general migration trends as men and women migrate equally often, but it is important for migration destinations: women more often choose Italy and Germany, while for men it is the UK, the Netherlands and Ireland (GUS, 2020, pp. 87–89).

Research by Grabowska-Lusińska (2010) shows that around 30%–50% of emigrants declare the intention to return to Poland. This tendency is higher for those staying abroad for a short time (the longer the period of stay, the lower the willingness to return), as well as for younger (20–29 years) and better-educated people. The intention to return is less dependent on economic success than on the degree of integration within the host society and the relationship with the country of origin, that is, Poland. Still, in general, a great deal of variation can be seen as regards the motives for return, which escape simple explanations (Snel et al., 2015). These include decisions connected with one's professional situation (the opportunity to use the experience gained abroad, the belief that one can live a better life in Poland because the cost of living is lower here), as well as personal or family situation (the migrants feel that they are attached to Poland and feel most comfortable there, they miss home and their loved ones left behind, they want their children to have closer contacts with their grandparents, they want to raise their children in a Polish community, they need to take care of their elderly parents, and they are pressured by their family to return, which is experienced especially by women). When speaking about the reasons for return, we should also not forget the effects of Brexit and the precariousness of staying (or losing the right to stay) in the UK (Budyta-Budzyńska, 2017, pp. 24–29; Duda-Mikulin, 2018; Grabowska-Lusińska, 2010, p. 32; Matejko, 2010, p. 35; Radziwinowiczówna et al., 2020). When abroad, migrants who plan to return to Poland take special care to maintain contacts with family and friends in their home country. Thanks to such contacts, it is easier for migrants to socially readapt after returning to Poland. These social networks are especially important for those who have been abroad for many years (Matejko, 2010, p. 36).

As Karolak (2016, p. 25) estimates, between 2004 and 2014 alone almost 600,000 Poles opted to return from the UK only to Poland. Most migrants returned without any detailed plans, and one in three counted on the education and experience they gained abroad to help them find a job in Poland without any problems. Only one in 12 people had already secured a job before they returned (Grabowska-Lusińska, 2010). It is worth noting that "[p]reparedness pertains not only to the willingness of migrants to return home, but also to their readiness to return" (Cassarino, 2004, p. 271). Failures to adequately prepare, to gather the right information and different material resources (savings) and to (re)build social contacts result in disillusionment with return. That is why, unfortunately, many re-emigrants do not succeed at all in the local labour market. They do not feel welcome in Poland, and their experience from abroad is not appreciated. This applies especially to young people, women and residents of smaller towns (Karolak, 2020). Migrants who lived abroad with their families are better prepared to return. As a rule, in this group, it is the man who first returns to Poland and when his professional and housing situation becomes stable, he is joined by his partner and children (Matejko, 2010, p. 35). This pattern is basically the same as family emigration patterns that are linked to men's career development (Erlinghagen, 2021). Sometimes, however, the return to Poland cannot be planned or postponed. This is the case of people who return to Poland forcibly, including those who once committed crimes and are prosecuted by the criminal justice system, usually to serve their sentence in a Polish prison, or are deported from EU countries for other reasons (Brandariz, 2021; Mantu et al., 2021).

When discussing the process of re-emigration, we cannot, however, overlook the migrant's rootedness in the country to which they emigrated. It is of great importance for reintegration processes how a person organised their life abroad and whether and what kind of ties they maintained with Poland during their stay abroad, in other words, what their social anchors (Grzymala-Kazlowska, 2016) and social networks (Kuschminder, 2017) are like and where they are located. This is because we believe that the process of reintegration after a prolonged absence in the country of origin (which should then certainly not be called home, as this one was, in fact, built in a different place) differs little in principle, in terms of the social aspects, from the processes accompanying integration in the country of immigration.

> Reintegration is therefore not only an insertion back into the culture and life of the country of origin, but it is a process. Much like integration, return migrants must go through a process of reintegration, and how they reintegrate will be dependent upon their experiences and choices. . . . Networks have a critical role in this process as they provide access to resources and information regarding return and reintegration. The returnees' reintegration

> strategy is thus based on the four categories such as: cultural maintenance, social networks, self-identification, and access to rights, institutions, and labour markets.
>
> (Kuschminder, 2017, p. 43)

The reintegration process is even of a greater importance when a person was abroad for a long time since they come back to a society being sometimes at least a bit different than the one they had left. Additionally, during long-term emigration, the country of origin could also have been idealised (Bucholc, 2013).

We also realise that the very term 'reintegration' implies that a certain person was previously, before their departure, socially integrated in their home country (Khosravi, 2018, pp. 10–11). This may not always be the case, and is especially true for people who have had contact with the criminal justice system and have a criminal record(s). These migrants often cannot be considered integrated in Polish society: in many cases they were already on the fringes of society or excluded from it before their departure (Klaus, 2021). The term 'reintegration' is also often equated with the issue of assimilation: a full return to the culture of the country of origin without taking into account the experiences abroad and the change that occurred in the person as a result. In other words, the concept does not envisage any involvement of the society of the country of origin (Kuschminder, 2017, p. 16).

2. Methodology of the research

Our research included 31 interviews with Poles with different experiences of being forcedly returned, which we conducted between 2020 and 2021. By far, the largest group removed from a single country were 12 interviewees returned from the UK; there were also people transferred from such countries as the Netherlands, Austria, Ireland, Germany, Belgium and Spain. Our interviewees were aged between 25 and 75, with an average age of nearly 44. They included 27 men and 4 women. This gender disproportion is mainly due to the fact that, in general, crimes are the domain of men: males constitute approximately 95% of the detainees in Polish prisons (CZSW, 2021, p. 4). Men are also the majority of those sought by European Arrest Warrants in Poland and make up about 95% of the total (Klaus et al., 2021, p. 106). It is the stories of returnees that we want to tell in this chapter in order to show how the actions of the justice system have affected their lives and those of their families.

When conducting the study, we found our interviewees at different points in their lives: some had already served their sentences and had been released, but the vast majority were still in prison. This was due to our recruitment tactic. We recruited individuals for the study in three ways: (1) through Facebook, on selected discussion groups for Polish emigrants; (2) through representatives of non-profit organisations involved in providing support and assistance to persons who have served a sentence of imprisonment, with whom we had previously conducted expert interviews; (3) through the Central Board of the Polish Prison Administration, which we asked to provide us with information about prisoners who had ever been transferred to Poland under an EAW or under other international prisoner transfer procedures and who, at the time of the study, were serving a sentence in one of Poland's prisons. We describe the stories of these individuals in this chapter. Sadly, most of the respondents we were able to reach had no experience with reintegration in Poland because they were still incarcerated. In general, we found it a great research challenge to recruit people with such difficult experiences as forced removal from another EU Member State or the UK to Poland as a result of committing a crime (either in the country of origin or in a host country).

In the chapter, we also quote the experts that we interviewed. We spoke to 36 people, including police officers, judges, probation officers, prison and border guard officers, court administrators, and members of non-profit organisations that provide support and assistance to persons who have served a sentence of incarceration (see more in: Klaus in this volume).

3. The reasons behind emigration from Poland

For the majority of our study participants, and generally for most emigrants, the key reason for the decision to leave was the desire to make a complete overhaul of their lives. The departure was a turning point: it was supposed to be the start of a new, better life and a break with previous experiences. Thus, it can be said that this is a group of life-style migrants (Benson & O'Reilly, 2009). Decisions to leave are made in different circumstances. For some people, the tipping point was some significant life event (Gaspar, 2015). One example is Marta,[3] who, after losing a well-paid job she cared about, spontaneously made the decision to leave, and chose the country entirely by chance:

> Why did I end up in Spain? I lived in S., I had a good job there, a flat. And it so happened that I was fired [from my job]. . . . I bought champagne, got drunk with it, spread out a map of the world and said: Wherever I point my finger is where I'm going: whether to Japan, China or America, I would have gone there. And since my finger landed on Spain, I was in Spain within a week.
>
> (Marta)

Other people were forced to leave due to financial circumstances and wanting to improve their family's material status, like Tomasz, who planned to go to work and return to Poland after saving some money:

> A friend found me a job in Germany. I just wanted to get back on my feet. Here in Poland, when the baby was born, I invested some of my money in a house to be able to live normally. The money ran out and I took whatever job I could get. Any job. And that's why I went to Germany.
>
> (Tomasz)

Katarzyna also hoped for an improvement in her family's standard of living after leaving the country. She and her husband decided to move to the UK to earn money to repay the loans they had taken out in Poland and, in the long term, to provide a better life for their growing family, especially their children. Katarzyna also mentioned that an important reason for her to move was the support offered by British public institutions to families like theirs, which allows them to have a much better family life than in Poland.

> In Poland I had a fantastic job, quite a good life, but we simply lived on credit, as it often happens in Poland. . . . So my husband went to London for six months to earn money, and then he started to persuade me to join him. . . . He found out how the life of such growing families looks there. . . . The social services there are very good, I mean the subsidies, benefits and so on. We calculated everything . . . and I took this risk and followed my husband with a small child in my arms towards a new life.
>
> (Katarzyna)

In the cases discussed previously, the motive is generally a desire to improve one's overall standard of living, to provide good conditions for the whole family, for children, not only in economic but also in broader social terms. Importantly, people wishing to change their lives did not plan to return to Poland but rather to settle permanently in the country they had moved to.

However, family migrations were rare among our respondents. It was mostly people who had no strong family ties or major personal commitments in Poland that decided to emigrate. One example is Marek, who did not start his own family and only left his mother and other relatives in Poland. As he points out, he had little to lose by emigrating while he could gain a much better standard of living than in Poland. Marek stressed that the living conditions in the UK and the decent pay he received for his work had deterred him from criminal activities (he had already served two previous prison sentences in Poland).

> In Poland I didn't really have any prospects or anything. I had a friend there [in the UK] who had already been there for a few years. He had just come to Poland for vacation. So I talked to him and he suggested: 'if you want, come with me. I'll get you a job there to start with, then you'll get started, you'll pick up the language a bit.' . . . I liked it there and stayed. I got regular money every week. I could afford to support myself and to pay for a flat. I didn't have to look for other ways to get money. It was enough to go to work regularly.
>
> (Marek)

Polish research on multiple offenders shows that many of them perceive going abroad as an important element which can help them desisting from committing further crimes: by employing them (and jobs being difficult to find in Poland for people with a criminal record, as mentioned by Wojciech) and providing decent money, and most importantly, by separating them from their delinquent peers (Klaus, 2021, pp. 469, 492–494). For some people, this is also an opportunity to avoid the stigma of being a convict, a chance to be viewed differently, as a valuable person, not a criminal, as in Kamil's story.

> Finding a job will also be a problem [in Poland], because I called a few places and they asked about a clean criminal record. I don't want to hide it [my imprisonment], but if I mention it, I just get rejected. . . . [The certificate of no criminal record] is an obstacle to finding a job, to returning to a normal life.
>
> (Wojciech)

> You know, I'll tell you honestly, if I hadn't had that extradition, I would have stayed there [in the UK] for the rest of my life. I loved that country because those people didn't look at me like 'you're a criminal', but they looked at me like 'Kamil, there's a new life here, a new job' and said 'here you have new opportunities'. And you know, it was really just a kind of a motor for me, it gave me a push. There was never a time when I didn't want to go to work. I worked 104 days in a row most of the time, so you know, you could say I was a workaholic.
>
> (Kamil)

Leaving Poland was, therefore, both a chance for a better future and an escape from problems. This was also the case with Andrzej, who was aware that he was heavily addicted to drugs, and that his drug use was linked to being around other addicted people. He also reported that he had a strong sexual addiction to various women, which caused him a lot of conflicts and difficulties in social interactions. Hence, he decided to break with his friends, run away from his problems and leave Poland.

> In the meantime [between many stays in penal institutions], I also . . . relapsed into using [psychoactive] substances. Well, being in such a dishonest relationship, based on sex, you can't go far, because these were also addictive, and certainly dysfunctional [women]. So well, this had consequences such as the break-up of my relationship with my son, which I tried to rebuild after 3 years in prison, but I didn't succeed in that.
>
> (Andrzej)

Some people build and organise their lives in a new country, meet new partners and put down roots. This was the case of Sebastian, who met a girlfriend during his stay in the UK who came to him and forced him to move out of the flat he was renting with his friends:

> The woman told me that the condition for her to come to me was that I had to have a flat on my own and so on, that she would not live with five guys.
>
> (Sebastian)

Since the group we studied consisted of people who had come into conflict with the law, for some of them the main impulse to leave Poland was pending criminal proceedings or a conviction. A number of our interviewees admitted that they wanted to escape from the consequences of a conviction and the order to serve a prison sentence. Piotr regrets his escape because it was only after he was apprehended that he realised that serving the sentence immediately after the conviction would have caused less complications in his life than being detained many years later.

> I got a two-year sentence for burglary and theft. . . . And I left Poland. I didn't want to go to prison, I was so scared. And frankly speaking, in hindsight, I would have preferred to serve my sentence, to have peace now and just build my life.
>
> (Piotr)

For those fleeing trouble in Poland who are later arrested in other countries and then transferred to serve their sentences, being brought back to the country causes various difficulties to mount. One expert in the study pointed out that often these individuals, besides escaping punishment, also had other unfulfilled obligations: unpaid bills or debts with other people. Subjecting them to forced return brought back old problems that piled up in the short time after they were transported to Poland.

> These are people who left in order to avoid serving their sentences and came back to Poland, and suddenly it turned out that in the meantime the bailiff contacted them, or some office did, that the bills had not been paid. . . . and often, apart from the fact that they must serve their sentence, they have to deal with such everyday problems.
>
> (prison officer; ENA_E13_W)

As is evident, the migration trajectories of the removed persons we interviewed followed different paths. Most migrated on their own, without their families, while others, after some time abroad, chose to bring their family or join a person who had managed to make living arrangements for the whole family. The reasons for migrating also varied: from the necessity to earn more money to increasing the standard of life of the whole family in new surroundings. Understandably, in our group of respondents, there were people who consciously left Poland in order to avoid detention.

4. Between two societies: social anchoring in the host and the sending country

For most of our respondents, the purpose of emigration was to build a new life abroad, so in our interviews we searched for answers to the question of how they came to be in the new society and how they became rooted in it. Different researchers define acculturation in a new society in different ways. Some invoke the concept of integration and its different facets (Ager & Strang, 2008; Berry, 1992; Garcés-Mascareñas & Penninx, 2016). These approaches lay special emphasis on systemic and group issues and questions related to public policies and to migrants finding their place in this puzzle. Others propose different approaches, which are more centred on the individual. They explore the processes of uprooting, anchoring and embedding into the new, host society, which, however, are not linear and have different speeds in different areas. They may accelerate or regress, depending on individual life experiences (Grzymala-Kazlowska & Phillimore, 2018; Ryan, 2018; Trąbka & Pustułka, 2020). One concept that allows us to analyse and describe the process of developing footholds in a way that is more consistent with its fluid nature is the idea of 'social anchoring' which:

> refers to the process of finding significant reference: grounding points which allow migrants to restore their socio-psychological stability in new life settings. The anchors that people use allow them to locate their place in their world, give form to their own sense of being and provide them with a base for psychological and social functioning. In this way, anchoring represents a means of both adaptation and integration.
>
> (Grzymala-Kazlowska, 2016, p. 9)

Social anchors can be understood as very official or simply legal signs of someone's attachment to the new society (like citizenship). But they are also related to economic dimensions of life: financial resources, consumed goods and types of economic activity. On the other hand, though, anchors can be understood in a very individual, subjective way and can be related to one's self-concept, individual values, beliefs and memory (Grzymala-Kazlowska, 2016, p. 9). In other words, social anchors are those elements of visible and invisible identity that show belonging and adaptation to the new society. This theoretical approach allows us to take a closer look at elements of social life of our researched group that could be identified as social anchors. But what we are planning to do in this chapter is to broaden that perspective and focus not only on host countries where our respondents had been living before they were arrested (which is obvious when applying this term) but also to look for anchors (social networks) left back in the country of origin, that is, Poland, which could (or could not) be used after expulsion in the reintegration process.

The first evidence that our interviewees were finding their feet in the new society was legal employment. Most of them told us that in the new country it was easier to find a well-paid, long-term and stable job than in Poland:

> No, there is no problem with that [with work]. . . . I was a sailor, a ship mechanic by training, but there I got into the construction industry. By coincidence. The family says: 'listen, I have highlanders here, they deal with wood and parquet floors'. And I had no clue about that. 'That' s okay, they'll teach you'. And after 2 weeks I was actually doing woodworking with them,

> and it went on like that for 10 years. And I specialized in wood and parquet. I also worked on building whole houses for over two years.
>
> (Karol)

However, language skills were an important barrier to finding stable employment. Paweł said that it was difficult for him to find a good, prestigious job without a good command of English. People who left educational facilities early and are from lower class of the society rarely had had an opportunity to learn any foreign language; they also lack skills in learning on their own. And when one works long hours, in a low-paid, physical job, they do not necessarily have opportunities to enrol at any classes.

The language barrier is a major obstacle to joining a new society and becoming rooted in it, to meeting people and establishing new relationships at work and then in other spheres of life. It can therefore be a factor that makes immigrants decide to stick with their compatriots. This was the case for Paweł, who after his first experience working in a restaurant and the challenges of communicating in English, finally decided to change jobs and got hired at a company where he could work with other Poles and speak Polish:

> I worked two whole days washing dishes in an Italian restaurant, but when I saw what was going on, that my language was a big obstacle, because I could only say two or three words in English. . . . That's the main barrier, everyone who comes here and doesn't know English, is then directed to Poles, and so it works out somehow later.
>
> (Paweł)

Many of our interviewees migrated with Polish friends or to join Polish friends. They lived and spent their free time together. On the one hand, living in a Polish community abroad is an opportunity to maintain a network of contacts with people with similar experiences. Such a network can be very helpful when things go wrong. For this reason, it was not surprising that most of our interviewees told us that they lived in the Polish diaspora.

> You know, I went with a friend. Then I met some other guys, also from Poland. Also, let's say, guys with problems, but they were all right. They helped me find a job, they helped me find a flat.
>
> (Sebastian)

This approach cuts them off from their host society; they do not learn the language or meet friends outside the diaspora. Thus, they do not create anchors in the new society but living abroad they also do not have contacts with society in the country of origin. One may say that they are integrated into the diaspora which is a part of the society, so in other words they are integrated into the host society but differently than it is usually perceived (Carens, 2013, p. 167).

But we also found another tactic, where some respondents decided to widen their circle of friends and try to include people with different backgrounds. This was part of their migration strategy and may have stemmed from a general distrust of other Poles. For example, for Kamil, contacts with Poles were rather unwanted because he was afraid of being cheated and constantly criticised by his compatriots:

> I steered clear from Poles, because Poles only look for ways to scam others out of money. And the worst thing is when a Pole from abroad comes, who doesn't know his way around, they promise him mountains of gold, and then it's a disaster. So I tried, you know, to avoid these Poles.
>
> (Kamil)

Establishing contacts with members of the host society usually came with some struggles and required overcoming prejudices and stereotypes about Poles. This was the experience of Grzegorz, who complained that his neighbour, an older Turkish woman, was afraid that the group of Poles he was part of had moved into a neighbouring house. Such a situation could have been an obstacle to living in a new society, but for Grzegorz it created an opportunity to prove his belonging and attachment to the new society and its values.

> In the Netherlands our neighbour was a lady of Turkish origin, an older woman. At the beginning, when we moved in there, she said: 'Polish guys – that's no good'. But when she met us, she couldn't believe we were from Poland . . . because no one of us drank alcohol. You know, we only worked 10–12 hours a day and there were no parties, nothing. We would clean the house, the garden, everything.
>
> (Grzegorz)

Some of our interviewees underlined how much they liked the host country, how attached they were to the new society, that they shared its values. On the other hand, they became detached from Polish society. They appreciated not only the sights but also the people who lived there, their hospitality, openness and kindness. This feeling of being welcomed and accepted helps enormously in adapting to the new society and makes immigrants believe that their life is better than in Poland. For some of our interviewees (like Marcin), migration was not only a step towards a better life but also a step away from the criminal life in Poland and the social stigma attached to it.

> If a person leaves his motherland, where he grew up, is far from his family, and feels that he is welcomed there as if he were part of the region – because that is how they do things in the Balkans – then there is certainly some attachment. I can even say emotional attachment. This is because of the mentality of the people there. They are simply hospitable. I did not notice

> anything like jealousy or envy there. If you have something there, you are called a successful person. Here in Poland, unfortunately, I am called a thief, a criminal, and a scam.
>
> (Marcin)

> This kindness of people. We started to see the change in ourselves . . . when you go to Poland you can see huge differences. . . . in general, everything there (in the UK) is made for people . . . with more kindness. Their manners are better . . . there are so many people from different parts of the world and everyone is forced to be polite to each other . . . because everyone comes from a different culture.
>
> (Katarzyna)

Others also raised political issues by stressing their connection with the country to which they emigrated rather than with Poland and the current government.

> I am more attached to England and the people there than to Poland. Because when I arrive in Poland, it is just like during the communist times.
>
> (Szymon)

Other respondents, on the other hand, dreamed of returning to their home country, as they did not like the weather in the UK, the deteriorating economy, and they were thinking of having to take care of their elderly parents back home. So they were contemplating buying a house in Poland with the money they earned abroad and moving to their motherland when they retire.

Our respondents had different attitudes towards their ties to Poland and to the relatives or friends they left behind. In this respect, they can be divided into two groups. Some of them tried to maintain some kind of relations with Poland. These relationships were different and depended on who of their relatives stayed in the country and how long the emigration lasted. Others had no such relations at all or these were extremely shallow and sporadic. Some of our interlocutors tried, as best they could, to spend holidays with their families in Poland. As Sebastian indicates, he was in Poland several times a year and spent time with his family and friends.

> When I was in London, I went to Poland twice a year. . . . I was in Poland for every Christmas and Easter, and for longer holidays. I still have my mom, because my dad passed away, so I used to come here and so on, I have siblings, I have friends.
>
> (Sebastian)

For Jacek, coming to Poland for Christmas every year was not only a chance to rest but also to keep in touch with his children, who were in the care of his ex-partner. For a few days during the holiday season, he looked after them and spent time with them.

> Every December I used to go to Poland for Christmas. I used to take the children for three or four days. I'd rent a flat, my ex-girlfriend would let me have the kids for Christmas and after three or four days I'd drop them off and go back to England.
>
> (Jacek)

Some people were visited by family from Poland:

> My mother was there three times to visit me, she flew in. My brother came to visit me twice, he came with his family, his wife too, and with his children once.
>
> (Bartek)

> We haven't been in Poland for a long time since we left. . . . from 2007 to 2015 we hadn't been in Poland at all. We're also in a pretty comfortable situation here, because someone visits us all the time, it's just more convenient for us. Our parents visit us several times a year, as well as friends and acquaintances from Poland. The last time we went to Poland was for my 40th birthday, so it was about two years ago.
>
> (Joanna)

Many study participants kept in touch with family and friends on a regular basis via phones and various instant messengers (Skype or Messenger) or Facebook. The frequency of this contact varied, depending on the needs of the interviewees and their families. Some of them talked every day. Others admitted that these relationships had weakened over time and became less frequent.

But for some people the reason for fleeing the country and staying abroad was being searched by the police. In rare cases, these people did not maintain any contact with their families, not even by phone. Others, like Marcin, were very much affected by the separation from their loved ones and were relieved to finally see their families when they were apprehended by the police.

> I had never been to Poland at all! . . . because I couldn't, I was afraid they would detain me at the border.
>
> (Marek)

> I was afraid that I would be arrested and taken to prison, so I did not go back to Poland, I lived there [abroad].
>
> (Bogdan)

> So all in all . . . something kept drawing me in . . . I kept thinking about coming back. Even when they arrested me, I was glad, so to speak, I wasn't depressed or upset. It was like I was waiting for it. That's how I would call it.
>
> (Marcin)

Łukasz, on the other hand, decided to bring his family to live in the UK in order to keep in touch with them.

> When bringing my family here, I knew that sooner or later the police would catch me anyway. If I hadn't brought my family here, I would probably still be in hiding today. Because I had my ways . . . after so many years of hiding . . . and so on. . . . But I chose contact with my family rather than . . . well without contact . . . I didn't want my children . . . wouldn't recognize me.
>
> (Łukasz)

There was also a group, however, that simply stopped all contacts with the country. Old acquaintances had faded because of time and distance (e.g. contacts with high school friends) or because of the stay in prison (as in Paweł's case). Paweł's comparison between living abroad and incarceration as similar processes of dissolving relationships is also interesting. In the case of other respondents, the closest family members have passed away and contact with distant relatives is rare (e.g. a phone call once a year). Sometimes relationships with family were never particularly close, so there were no ties to loosen (as in Maciej's case).

> There was a lot of us at home . . . we have contact with each other, but you know, we don't have that kind of contact. We lived together, so it was a bit different. Everyone went their separate ways and, you know, there is contact by phone, but it's no great contact. My brother doesn't visit me, because he doesn't have the need to. What for? It's enough that I call him and talk to him, and I think that's enough for now.
>
> (Maciej)

> You know, whether you are abroad or in prison, at the beginning, those first contacts are nice, but after some time they fade away. So the same as in Poland, I got out of prison after a few years, so I left and I wanted to visit my friends and at some point I was standing on the street and I said: Fuck, I don't know anyone here, do I? Where are all these people? I went to one address, to another, one person is in jail, one is dead, one is somewhere abroad. And basically for this period of 6 months after I came out I didn't meet up with anyone.
>
> (Paweł)

The quotes show a very different picture of the process of becoming established in a new country. For some people this happened faster, especially for those who lived abroad with their families. Others lived in the Polish diaspora because they felt better there and because they could not speak the language of the country to which they emigrated and could not integrate into the new society. The frequency with which they contacted their families also varied. For some of them, it was close and frequent. For others, these ties loosened with the time spent abroad and disappeared altogether in some cases. Family ties were also hampered greatly because of the EAW.

5. The consequences of the EAW procedure on persons being transferred and their family members

Incarceration is difficult both for the detainee and their family, exposed to disorganisation due to emerging tensions caused by the inability to perform basic family duties. These tensions can be alleviated, provided that each party has the proper skills, abilities and will. Otherwise, the relationship may break down. The problems faced by the families of detainees (especially female partners) are mainly of an economic nature, but they are compounded by issues such as child-rearing, loneliness and stigmatisation from the community, causing shame and guilt over the partner's conviction (Crewe, 2009; Warr, 2016). These difficulties are even greater when someone is no longer connected with the country depriving them of their freedom; a person whose transfer to Poland interrupts their often well-ordered life as an emigrant. Forced return to Poland entails a number of adverse consequences, just to mention the loss of work or of contact with family and friends (especially those living in diaspora). And returning those people directly to a Polish prison and all processes connected with removal remind to a large extent the experience of foreign prisoners known from other research. While any imprisonment carries with it a number of pains and frustrations, some of these hardships, especially those associated with being away from families and loved ones, they are even greater when one is detained in a crimmigration prison (Ugelvik & Damsa, 2018). The family may have been partly in Poland, but they could have also been in the country to which the detainee emigrated. This made it difficult for them to visit in person and left only the possibility of telephone contact (albeit limited, as calls abroad are quite expensive) or online, remote contact. The latter was relatively rare in Polish prisons before the pandemic and only became more widespread during the pandemic, though also not without some problems (Dawidziuk & Kotowska, 2021).

Hence, many people awaiting a forced return to their country of origin fight to prevent it and stay in the country of emigration. They show evidence of their long stay, family and social ties. They had no plans to return to Poland, and the struggle to stay was important not only for them personally but also for their families (Martynowicz, 2018, pp. 281–282; see also Martynowicz in this volume). This process makes them feel victimised, frustrated and terrified about having to return to a place they feel no connection to as they had left it long before and had left little or nothing behind (Ugelvik & Damsa, 2018, p. 1034).

Removal to Poland changes the convict's family situation. At least three scenarios are possible: (1) the returned person loses contact with the family, (2) the returnee does not lose contact with the family but the family stays abroad, and (3) the family follows the returnee to Poland, and changes their lives completely. Often, as prison officials said, especially before the Covid-19 pandemic, the third scenario took place: "when a man was deported,[4] the family also followed him" (prison officer, ENA_E14_W). Our respondents stressed how difficult this moment was in their families' lives:

> [My partner] came back, she is currently in Poland. . . . She didn't want to be there [abroad] on her own because she was there alone without a family. . . .

> She took it very badly. She cried for some time. . . . She was sad and upset. . . . It all happened suddenly, from one day to the next it all fell apart.
>
> (Marek)

> She also had time to sort everything out and she packed, I mean my partner, together with the sixteen-month old baby. She packed her bags and flew to Cracow to my parents' place. They offered her one room there, where she started to live. . . . The purpose of this was so that we could be together and she could visit me here in prison, because there are visits every week. And so it went on for. . . . I had a 4-year sentence, but it went on for 2.5 years . . . because I was released on early parole for good behaviour.
>
> (Karol)

Our research shows that generally the returnee's parents live in Poland, while their own families – partners and children – usually stay abroad, as do their friends. Sometimes families do not survive this ordeal:

> after he was deported for those six months [to prison], his family fell apart because his wife with their three children left him. He lost the opportunity to work there and he lost his flat. These are the consequences of the delayed execution of the sentence
>
> (probation officer, ENA_E26)

However, it should also be noted that very few of our interviewees had families who lived abroad with them.

Some forced returnees have no contact with their families who stayed in Poland. Sometimes this is because that family (especially parents) are no longer alive. Our interviewees talked about their families in Poland in different contexts. For some, it was a chance to return to something and someone after being released from prison. But others felt ashamed of having to admit failure to the family. As Marta said: "I was ashamed to tell my family that I was in prison". The literature demonstrates that guilt or shame is experienced by many prisoners (Farrall et al., 2010; Maruna, 2001). For our respondents, this shame involved a combination of two uniquely shameful elements: being in prison and being forcibly returned – no matter of the legal scheme of this return be it deportation, extradition or execution of EAW (Radziwinowiczówna, 2022; Turnbull, 2018). Experts who work with these individuals witnessed this problem:

> They have no [family in Poland] – and if they do, the ties are broken, they don't want to renew the ties, because sometimes grandmothers live there, sometimes grandfathers or uncles, but they don't want to reconnect with them. Especially when someone came from the West with empty pockets and no success – as a total failure. People don't want to brag about their failures.
>
> (NGO social worker, ENA_E9_F)

In the interviews, however, experts stressed that this shame is usually felt only at the beginning, and that later the contacts are renewed. Being able to conceal one's stay in prison from the family depends on two things: the financial situation of the prisoner (e.g. whether they have money to do shopping while serving the sentence) and the length of the sentence as it is much easier to hide this fact when the sentence is short, as one of the prison officers explained:

> I talked to deportees who were very ashamed to contact their Polish families, ashamed that they had returned to Poland like that. So they did not contact them during their sentences. . . . [Such] people . . . need help here [in prison], so . . . the shame continues, but the prisoner needs money for cigarettes. . . . this is where the shame gets pushed to the side at some point. . . . the length of the sentence is very important. If someone has 3–4 months to serve, they can pretend in front of their family that it never happened. But if the sentence is two, three, four, five years, it is difficult to pretend for five years that they are not in prison. So as a rule, then, this contact is instantaneous. But as I have said, that situations in which the prisoner does not inform the family in Poland that they are in a Polish prison can be counted on the fingers of one hand, and always when the sentence is very short.
>
> (prison officer, ENA_E14_W)

Incarceration not infrequently leads to weakened or even broken relationships with partners. Especially if these relationships are shallow, although this is influenced by many different factors, such as the length of the sentence or individual attitude (Klaus, 2021, pp. 452–456), but also by the conditions of serving the sentence, as Tomasz pointed out:

> It is because of these Polish prisons that contact with the family is totally broken. Because those people [family members] don't know what is going on. . . . here in Poland . . . there is no way of telling them what is going on, what you need, because [during a phone conversation] someone is standing over you or shouting, so either I cannot hear, or they cannot hear me. And it's better not to talk! And relationships get ruined because of that. And now you have to work very hard to rebuild them, at least the ones that you can.
>
> (Tomasz)

One of the reasons why family bonds are broken is that they are not maintained. When the family remains abroad, therefore, keeping in touch mainly boils down to conversations via Skype or telephone. Face-to-face visits of prisoners with families abroad are very rare. Prisoners said that the most difficult thing for them was to stay in touch, especially with their children abroad. On the other hand, the prison officers we talked to stressed that the intensity of contact depends on the relationship with the family and not on the distance between them, and it does not matter whether the family lives in the country or abroad. Contact with the Polish family is also necessary in order to facilitate the prisoner's reintegration into the Polish society after leaving prison. If they stay in touch with their Polish families, they may have a place to go back to when they finish doing their sentence.

Being released with no family support in Poland and no place to stay is an obstacle, for example, in obtaining a conditional early release. In order to be granted parole, it is necessary to provide a permanent address of residence in Poland. Sometimes people returning to the country do not have such an address; thus, they do not meet the formal requirements to exercise this right. It also happens that after serving the sentence, a re-emigrant with no ties in Poland ends up in a shelter for the homeless or in other institutions like in the case of Dariusz, who said: "I am leaving prison in Poland and I don't have anywhere to live. And this is where my problem begins". The experts also admitted this fact:

> Of course, they won't be released on parole, because if someone is released on parole they . . . have to have an address, because a community interview has to be done. I don't think a social worker would go to London to do a community interview, so it's [refusal of early release] right away. . . . And see how inconsistent it is, too, because . . . it's not about the process of social rehabilitation, whether this person has been re-socialized well or not, it's simply about technical obstacles – meaning they don't have anywhere else to go, so they won't go out. Well, they have to provide some kind of address. . . . We have a major dilemma, what to do in such a situation? Because abroad – if they have someone to come back to, if they have a job there, they can start afresh faster, it will be easier for them than here in Poland, where there is nothing, nothing to keep them, where it is difficult to find a job.
>
> (NGO social worker, ENA_E11_F)

One of the prisoners' fears is whether they will find a job once they are released, which is difficult for those with a criminal record. On top of the lack of a place to stay, financial difficulties, fear of returning to the criminal world, and social reluctance to help, unemployment is one of the reasons that most often leads to committing another crime. These are also the obstacles to reintegration (Klaus, 2021). Surveys among entrepreneurs show their reluctance to hire those with a criminal record: only 1/5 of companies hired ex-prisoners, with some employers unaware of the employee's past at the time of hiring. Fifteen per cent of company owners declared that they would never employ a person with a criminal record regardless of their qualifications. Only one in four respondents felt that the mere fact that someone had been incarcerated would not be a barrier to employment (RCPS, 2012, pp. 41–42). On the other hand, employers who have hired convicted offenders have mostly favourable opinions of them (two-thirds of respondents), and 90% rate their work well (Banerski, 2011, pp. 33–34, 37).

The stigma of having been an offender makes it difficult not only to find work after leaving prison but also to become re-established and re-integrated into society. For fear of how society will react, many people do not want to return to the neighbourhoods they used to live in, especially those ex-convicts who come from small towns and villages where people know each other. So they move to another location and become more anonymous to society (Klaus, 2021). Many, especially young people, decide to go abroad again: if not to the country where they used to live (because, for example, they have an entry ban), then to another one. There may be different motives for this decision. Many people have left everything in the country to which they emigrated:

> most of them [re-emigrant prisoners] declare that the moment they step outside the [prison] gate they will go straight to the airport and fly back, because in their minds they still live there. They came from abroad, they're used to it, that's where their life was, that's where their families often stayed, that's where they went to the store, that's where they went to the hairdresser's and that's where they live in their minds.
>
> (prison officer, ENA_E14_W)

Some, like Karol, realised that life abroad is more comfortable and easier and that this is where he can pursue his passions. Others had lived abroad for many years; they know the realities in that country, unlike in Poland, and have someone to come back to (like Piotr).

> I could afford to go on vacation twice a year. . . . To pursue my hobby; I ride motorcycles. To buy myself such a motorcycle which I always dreamt about – such mundane things, which here [in Poland] are unattainable for a physical worker like me. So it kind of makes me want to go back there.
>
> (Karol)

> I felt at home there [in the Netherlands]. . . . I know what everything is like there and it's really easier and I didn't have such problems as in Poland. . . . I feel more connected to the Netherlands. I spent a lot of time there, 12 years, it's such a long time and I can't imagine living in Poland after I leave prison. There is simply someone there waiting for me, I have some plans connected with that. I know I have friends there who will help me to get back on my feet after I get out. . . . I know it is easier with work and I know the language.
>
> (Piotr)

Sometimes, they escape from bad environment, from their friends from the past, who have caused them a lot of trouble, including trouble with the law. For them, cutting themselves off from this company, from Poland, is like cutting themselves off from their old lives:

> I do not want [to go] there [to my family home], because I know that I can start drinking again there. Because I would see my family right away, my friends, and I don't want that, because I know how it would end.
>
> (Michał)

According to the experts, the people who stay in Poland are usually older or those who have well-functioning families here:

> Those who stay in Poland have families, most often they have children, families here. People who also have support from family, from relatives who . . . offer them a place to come back to after they leave prison, they have a flat, their parents are still alive, or their wife or partner is still alive, they have some connections so that they can get a job somewhere quickly.
>
> (probation officer, ENA_E23)

However, it may be difficult for parolees to leave the country because they are subject to various obligations, including probation. They may petition the court for permission to serve the probation term remotely, abroad, or for the probation to be revoked. However, the experts pointed out that the probation is practically never lifted, and it is only exceptionally that the court agrees for a parolee to go abroad and contact the probationer remotely by phone, e-mail or instant messenger. Usually the first few months of probation are spent in Poland anyway, in order for the probationer to be supervised regardless of the fact that this supervision is really artificial and not very helpful in terms of social reintegration (Klaus, 2021).

In this chapter, we have not been able to describe the process of reintegration into Polish society of the forced returnees, because we collected too few such accounts during our research. Therefore, this chapter focuses on the first and very narrow stage of this process, namely incarceration in a Polish prison and attempts of the returnees to adjust to life there (also in terms of their relationships with their families) and the visions of their lives once they will be finally released. The remaining elements of the process could only be planned and predicted by our respondents. And as we can see, most of them were instead thinking about re-emigration, that is, returning to the country from which they had been removed.

Conclusions

Research by Marta Erdal and Ceri Oeppen (2017) shows that two factors are important in the process of returning to one's country of origin and finding one's feet in a new reality: agency and preparedness. The first factor concerns what prospects a person has in their home country and what barriers limit their opportunities for development or decision-making, including (which is extremely important) the possibilities of further international migration. The second factor involves not only the technical and organisational preparation for return but also the mind-set, which is strongly tied to agency (Cassarino, 2004; Erdal & Oeppen, 2017).

Neither of these factors is present in the case of our respondents. They were not the ones who decided if and when they wanted to return to Poland. Most of them were more than surprised by this fact, and their lives were unexpectedly and abruptly interrupted. Even those who were in hiding did not know when they would be caught and did not prepare for this contingency. It is also worth noting that the vast majority of our respondents did not anticipate at all that a removal to Poland would take place (because they were not aware that they might be sought by the Polish criminal justice system) and that it would be carried out in such a way. Therefore, they were by no means prepared for it. The procedure also robbed them of any element of agency: they were arrested, forcibly transferred, and then imprisoned in Poland. The experience of deprivation of liberty itself greatly reduces agency. This occurs both at a psychological level, with cognitive adaptation described as a 'condemnation script' (Maruna, 2001), and at a practical level, with a real decrease in life opportunities, including job opportunities (Farrall et al., 2010). The overall process, therefore, has had inordinately negative effects not only on the respondents and their wellbeing but also on their family members.

Some forcible removals (but not in the case of the EAW) also mean that returnees are unable to get back to the country that they had emigrated to, as they receive an entry ban. Thus, it affects their capacity to start a new life after leaving prison, although some of our respondents were determined to leave Poland. However, the application of these bans varies in practice. In the UK, it translates into a real inability to return. In other countries, especially those being part of the Schengen area, these individuals may go back, but they will not be able to live fully 'normal' lives. They will always be hiding from law enforcement or immigration authorities because their stay will be irregular. They will have to keep a low profile and work in the black market. If they are apprehended, they will be subject to yet another forced return, albeit of a different kind, as most likely they will not be deprived of liberty, except in cases of administrative detention on the grounds of their illegal stay in a Member State (see CJEU ruling in case C-719/19). There are, nevertheless, exceptions to this rule, like in Norway, which administers a custodial sentence for breaking the return ban (Mulgrew, 2018, p. 86). Some people will choose to take this risk, especially since they will be able to return again soon after their departure. Others will prefer to avoid such a life, especially if they have families. For them, emigration to another EU country is a safe option, as the entry ban covers only the country in which they lived. This is a particular form of return mobilities (King, 2017), available only to EU citizens. This is what many people are counting on, as they do not see a real possibility of building a life in Poland from scratch, especially with the stigma that comes with being an ex-convict.

Notes

1 The significant divergence between data presented by Polish Ministry of Justice and by the EC report (which bases on data received from Member States, in this case provided by Polish authorities) is impossible to explain. The differences in presenting data or in counting those events (number of arrest warrants versus number of people being subjected to this procedure) might contribute to this divergence, but we did not manage to confirm this hypothesis as a detailed methodology of data gathering was not provided.

2 The project, called 'Experiences of Poles deported from the UK in the context of criminal justice system involvement', was generously funded by the National Science Centre, Poland (Grant No. UMO-2018/30/M/HS5/00816).

3 The names of the interviewees have been changed.

4 Most of our respondents – both experts and returnees – in their interviews used the word ‘deportation’ (in rare cases also extradition) to describe the experience of a forcefully returned person or the procedure itself, despite the legal definition of this transfer – which could be deportation, extradition, transfer under EAW procedure or transfer of prisoner (under conditions described in Council Framework Decision 2008/909/JHA of 27 November 2008 on the application of the principle of mutual recognition to judgements in criminal matters imposing custodial sentences or measures involving deprivation of liberty for the purpose of their enforcement in the European Union).

References

Ager, A., & Strang, A. (2008). Understanding integration: A conceptual framework. *Journal of Refugee Studies*, *21*(2), 166–191. https://doi.org/10.1093/jrs/fen016

Banerski, G. (2011). *Zmiana na lepsze. Raport z realizacji projektu „Proces aktywizacji zawodowej i społecznej byłych więźniów*” [Change for the better: Report on the implementation of the project *Process of professional and social activation of former prisoners*]. SMG/KRC Poland-Media.

Benson, M., & O’Reilly, K. (2009). Migration and the search for a better way of life: A critical exploration of lifestyle migration. *The Sociological Review*, *57*(4), 608–625. https://doi.org/10.1111/j.1467-954X.2009.01864.x

Berry, J. W. (1992). Acculturation and adaptation in a new society. *International Migration*, *30*(s1), 69–85. https://doi.org/10.1111/j.1468-2435.1992.tb00776.x

Brandariz, J. A. (2021). The removal of EU nationals: An unaccounted dimension of the European deportation apparatus. *Central and Eastern European Migration Review*, *10*(1), 13–33. https://doi.org/10.17467/ceemr.2021.06

Bucholc, M. (2013). Outside the moral circle polish political refugees in Norway: Between the established and the outsiders. *Human Figurations*, *2*(3). http://hdl.handle.net/2027/spo.11217607.0002.303

Budyta-Budzyńska, M. (2017). Emigracja powrotna – Zyski i straty, kapitały i przekazy migracyjne. Na przykładzie reemigracji z Islandii do Starych Juch [Return emigration: gains and losses, migration capitals and transfers. The case of re-emigration from Iceland to Stare Juchy]. *CMR Working Papers*, *101*(159). https://depot.ceon.pl/handle/123456789/15191

Carens, J. (2013). *The Ethics of Immigration*. Oxford University Press.

Cassarino, J. P. (2004). Theorising return migration: The conceptual approach to return migrants revisited. *International Journal on Multicultural Societies*, *6*(2), 253–279.

CJEU (Great Chamber) 22 June 2021, Case C-719/19 FS v Staatssecretaris van Justitie en Veiligheid, ECLI.EU.C.2021.506.

Crewe, B. (2009). *The Prisoner Society: Power, Adaptation and Social Life in an English Prison*. Oxford University Press.

CZSW. (2021). *Roczna Informacja Statystyczna*. Centralny Zarząd Służby Więziennej [Annual Statistical Information. Central Board of Prison Service].

Dawidziuk, E., & Kotowska, K. (2021). Nowe technologie w komunikacji skazanych i tym czasowo aresztowanych ze światem zewnętrznym [New technologies in communication of convicts and pretrial detainees with the outside world]. *Archiwum Kryminologii*, *43*(2), 151–194. https://doi.org/10.7420/AK2021.31

Duda-Mikulin, E. A. (2018). Should I stay or should I go now? Exploring Polish women’s returns “home”. *International Migration*, *56*(4), 140–153. https://doi.org/10.1111/imig.12420

EC. (2021). *Statistics on the practical operation of the European arrest warrant – 2019.* European Commission. https://ec.europa.eu/info/sites/default/files/law/search_law/documents/eaw_statistics_2019_swd_2021_227_final_08_2021_en.pdf

Erdal, M. B., & Oeppen, C. (2017). Forced to return? Agency and the role of post-return mobility for wellbeing among returnees to Afghanistan, Pakistan and Poland. In Z. Vathi & R. King (Eds.), *Return Migration and Psychosocial Wellbeing: Discourses, Policy-Making and Outcomes for Migrants and their Families* (pp. 39–55). Routledge.

Erlinghagen, M. (2021). Migration motives, timing, and outcomes of internationally mobile couples. In M. Erlinghagen, A. Ette, N. F. Schneider, & N. Witte (Eds.), *The Global Lives of German Migrants: Consequences of International Migration Across the Life Course* (pp. 157–171). Springer International Publishing.

Farrall, S., Bottoms, A., & Shapland, J. (2010). Social structures and desistance from crime. *European Journal of Criminology*, *7*(6), 546–570. https://doi.org/10.1177/1477370810376574

Garapich, M. P., Grabowska, I., & Jaźwińska, E. (2018). Migracje poakcesyjne z Polski [Post-accession migrations from Poland]. In L. Magdalena & M. Okólski (Eds.), *25 wykładów o migracjach* [25 lectures on migration] (pp. 208–220). Wydawnictwo Naukowe 'Scholar'. https://ksiegarnia.pwn.pl/25-wykladow-o-migracjach,764493242,p.html

Garcés-Mascareñas, B., & Penninx, R. (Eds.). (2016). *Integration Processes and Policies in Europe*. Springer International Publishing. https://doi.org/10.1007/978-3-319-21674-4

Gaspar, S. (2015). In search the rural idyll: Lifestyle migrants across the European Union. In K. Torkington, I. David, & J. Sardinha (Eds.), *Practising the Good Life: Lifestyle Migration in Practices*. Cambridge Scholars Publishing.

Grabowska-Lusińska, I. (2010). Poakcesyjni migranci powrotni w badaniach poza statystyką publiczną [Post-accession return migrants in research beyond public statistics]. In I. Grabowska-Lusińska (Ed.), *Poakcesyjne powroty Polaków* (pp. 27–33). Centre of Migration Research.

Grzymala-Kazlowska, A. (2016). Social anchoring: Immigrant identity, security and integration reconnected? *Sociology*, *50*(6), 1123–1139. https://doi.org/10.1177/0038038515594091

Grzymala-Kazlowska, A., & Phillimore, J. (2018). Introduction: Rethinking integration. New perspectives on adaptation and settlement in the era of super-diversity. *Journal of Ethnic and Migration Studies*, *44*(2), 179–196. https://doi.org/10.1080/1369183X.2017.1341706

GUS. (2020). *Sytuacja demograficzna Polski do 2019 r. Migracje zagraniczne ludności w latach 2000–2019*. Główny Urząd Statystyczny.

GUS. (2021). *Demographic situation of Poland until 2019. Foreign migrations of the population between 2000 and 2019*. Central Statistical Office.

Karolak, M. (2016). From potential to actual social remittances? Exploring how polish return migrants cope with difficult employment conditions. *Central and Eastern European Migration Review*, *5*(2), 21–39. https://doi.org/10.17467/ceemr.2016.02

Karolak, M. (2020). Returning for (dis)integration in the labour market? The careers of labour migrants returning to Poland from the United Kingdom. In S. Hinger & R. Schweitzer (Eds.), *Politics of (Dis)Integration* (pp. 101–120). Springer International Publishing.

Khosravi, S. (2018). Introduction. In S. Khosravi (Ed.), *After Deportation: Ethnographic Perspectives* (pp. 1–14). Palgrave Macmillan.

King, R. (2017). Conclusions. Exploring the multiple complexities of the return migration – psychosocial wellbeing nexus. In Z. Vathi & R. King (Eds.), *Return Migration and Psychosocial Wellbeing: Discourses, Policy-Making and Outcomes for Migrants and their Families* (pp. 257–273). Routledge.

Klaus, W. (2021). Sidła i udręki, czyli co stoi na przeszkodzie procesu odchodzenia od przestępczości? [Snares and pains, or what stands in the way of departing from crime?] In W. Klaus, I. Rzeplińska, P. Wiktorska, & D. Woźniakowska-Fajst (Eds.), *Karierowicze kryminalni? Aktywność przestępcza w dalszych losach nieletnich*. Wydawnictwo INP PAN. https://zenodo.org/record/5590327

Klaus, W., Włodarczyk-Madejska, J., & Wzorek, D. (2021). In the pursuit of justice: (Ab)use of the European Arrest Warrant in the Polish criminal justice system. *Central and Eastern European Migration Review*, *10*(1), 95–117. https://doi.org/10.17467/ceemr.2021.02

Kuschminder, K. (2017). *Reintegration Strategies: Conceptualizing How Return Migrants Reintegrate* (1st ed., 2017 edition). Palgrave Macmillan.

Mantu, S., Minderhoud, P., & Grütters, C. (2021). Legal approaches to 'unwanted' EU citizens in the Netherlands. *Central and Eastern European Migration Review*, *10*(1), 35–53. https://doi.org/10.17467/ceemr.2021.07

Martynowicz, A. (2018). Power, pain, adaptations and resistance in a 'foreign' prison: The case of Polish prisoners incarcerated in Northern Ireland. *Justice, Power and Resistance*, *2*(2), 267–286.

Maruna, S. (2001). *Making Good. How Ex-Convicts Reform and Rebuild Their Lives*. American Psychological Association.

Matejko, E. (2010). Reintegracja poakcesyjnych migrantów powrotnych na polskim rynku pracy- wyniki analizy jakościowej [Reintegration of post-accession return migrants into the Polish labour market: Results of the qualitative analysis]. In I. Grabowska-Lusińska (Ed.), *Poakcesyjne powroty Polaków* [Post-accession returns of Poles] (pp. 34–47). Centre of Migration Research.

MoJ. (2021). *ENA – Europejski Nakaz Aresztowania w latach 2004–2020* [European Arrest Warrant 2004–2020]. Ministry of Justice. https://isws.ms.gov.pl/pl/baza-statystyczna/opracowania-wieloletnie/

Mulgrew, R. (2018). The role of oversight in foreign-national only prisons: Counteracting the disapplication of rehabilitation. *Crime, Law and Social Change*, *70*(1), 77–92. https://doi.org/10.1007/s10611-017-9720-4

Okólski, M., & Salt, J. (2014). Polish emigration to the UK after 2004, why did so many come? *Central and Eastern European Migration Review*, *3*(2), 11–37.

Radziwinowiczówna, A. (2022). Violence that builds sovereignty: The transnational violence continuum in deportation from the United States. *Journal of Ethnic and Migration Studies*, *48*(5), 1095–1112. https://doi.org/10.1080/1369183X.2020.1850244

Radziwinowiczówna, A., Kloc-Nowak, W., & Rosińska, A. (2020). Envisaging post-Brexit immobility: Polish migrants' care intentions concerning their elderly parents. *Journal of Family Research*, *32*(3), 473–494. https://doi.org/10.20377/jfr-352

RCPS. (2012). *Sytuacja osób opuszczających zakłady karne na terenie województwa łódzkiego. Raport z badania* [Situation of people leaving penitentiary institutions in the Łódzkie voivodeship: Report from the survey]. Regional Centre of Social Policy in Łódź.

Ryan, L. (2018). Differentiated embedding: Polish migrants in London negotiating belonging over time. *Journal of Ethnic and Migration Studies*, *44*(2), 233–251. https://doi.org/10.1080/1369183X.2017.1341710

Snel, E., Faber, M., & Engbersen, G. (2015). To stay or return? Explaining return intentions of Central and Eastern European Labour migrants. *Central and Eastern European Migration Review*, *4*(2), 5–24.

Trąbka, A., & Pustułka, P. (2020). Bees & butterflies: Polish migrants' social anchoring, mobility and risks post-Brexit. *Journal of Ethnic and Migration Studies*, *46*(13), 2664–2681. https://doi.org/10.1080/1369183X.2020.1711721

Turnbull, S. (2018). Starting again: Life after deportation from the UK. In S. Khosravi (Ed.), *After Deportation: Ethnographic Perspectives* (pp. 37–61). Palgrave Macmillan.
Ugelvik, T., & Damsa, D. (2018). The pains of crimmigration imprisonment: Perspectives from a Norwegian all-foreign prison. *The British Journal of Criminology*, *58*(5), 1025–1043. https://doi.org/10.1093/bjc/azx067
Warr, J. (2016). The prisoner: Inside and out. In Y. Jewkes, B. Crewe, & J. Bennett (Eds.), *Handbook on Prisons* (pp. 586–604). Routledge.

8 Conditional residence – prisons and beyond

How 'criminality' shapes uncertain futures in the times of crimmigration

Agnieszka Martynowicz

Introduction

The focus of this chapter are the practical, life-altering consequences of the administration of transnational justice, namely of the use of the European Arrest Warrant (EAW). The *Council Framework Decision of 13 June 2002 on the European arrest warrant and the surrender procedures between Member States* (EAW FD)[1] was agreed by EU members with the purpose of speeding up extradition proceedings between those states. The EAW system is based on the principle of mutual recognition and trust in the judicial decisions in the different Member states and was – at least in theory – designed to prevent political interference in the extradition process (Home Affairs Committee, 2013). In the UK, the implementing legislation – the *Extradition Act 2003* – came into force in 2004. The UK was party to the EAW until the end of the so-called transition period post-EU exit that came to an end on 31 December 2020. On 1 May 2021, the EAW system was replaced in the UK by a new arrangement of 'Surrender', contained in Title VII of the *Trade and Cooperation Agreement 2021* (TACA).[2] In essence, the new TACA mechanism mirrors the prior arrangements under the EAW, allowing for simplified extraditions between the UK and EU Member States to continue.

As stated elsewhere in this collection, there has been considerable focus in legal literature on the implementation of the EAW over the years since its introduction. Yet, despite the obvious cross-border element of its practical use and consequences for thousands of people (and their families), a consideration of its consequences for forced mobility is largely absent within border criminologies. This is a significant gap in our understanding of bordering processes, given that the scale of the movement of people on foot of the EAW is quite considerable. Between 2009 and 2021, for example, the UK sent 12,315 people to EU states on foot of the EAW and TACA (National Crime Agency, 2021).[3] Poles, on whom this chapter focuses in much of its content, constituted by far the largest group at 5,995, with Lithuanians and Romanians a very close second and third at 1,117 and 1,112, respectively (National Crime Agency, 2021). To contribute to addressing the research gap, and following in the footsteps of other chapters, this chapter considers the practical impact of EAW proceedings in two contexts.

DOI: 10.4324/9781003254584-9

First, based on the findings of my doctoral research in male prisons in Northern Ireland undertaken in 2014 and 2015, and supported by a review of EAW judgements from Northern Irish courts, the chapter lays bare the personal costs for both arrestees and the families of the Requested Person (RP) being subjected to EAW proceedings. For those imprisoned in the course of such a process, those costs include, but are not limited to, barriers in access to prison-based services; difficulties in obtaining and understanding legal advice; mounting challenges to extradition and negotiating the impact on family lives (see also Klaus, Włodarczyk-Madejska and Wzorek in this volume). The chapter focuses on the family aspect, and on some details of how challenges were mounted by those prisoners to the EAW process.

Second, the chapter discusses the implications of the EAW process (and, potentially also of the new TACA surrender process) on continued residence of EU nationals in the UK following its departure from the EU. As readers will be all too aware, on 23 June 2016 the UK Government held a referendum on the country's continued membership of the European Union. With the franchise restricted (with some exceptions) to British citizens, those who were entitled to take part in the referendum decided that the UK should leave the Union. This decision was taken by a majority of 52% to 48%, and 'Brexit' became reality on 31 January 2020.[4] As a result of the vote, the lives of millions of EU citizens resident in the UK were thrown into turmoil, their fate and the legal status becoming part of negotiations of the future relationship between the UK and other Member States of the EU (for very detailed analysis, see Barnard & Leinarte, 2019). After the referendum, many EU citizens resident in the UK felt a deep sense of rejection by their adopted home and many, including the author of this chapter, felt like objects, rather than subjects, in the referendum debate, outsiders rather than holders of rights (see e.g. Burrell & Schweyher, 2019).

The EU citizens outside of prison walls or not entangled in the workings of the criminal justice system at least had options open to them; these included, but were not limited to, confirming residence rights or applying for British citizenship to try to guarantee their right to stay. EU nationals inside the prisons across the UK were and are highly unlikely to be able to avail of the latter option, as criminal conviction is now a barrier to citizenship (Bosworth, 2011). When 'Brexit' was becoming reality, and EU nationals were asked to *apply* for a new immigration status, conditionality of residence on 'good behaviour' also became clear, with the introduction of "suitability requirements" and 'criminality checks' in the new EU Settlement Scheme (EUSS) (Home Office, 2022)[5] that replaced residency guarantees of the EU Citizenship Directive.[6] Hence, the second focus of the chapter, using data from research interviews undertaken with legal and immigration support practitioners in 2021, is on the consequences of EAW proceedings (historical or otherwise) for attaining continuous residence in the UK after Brexit. Expanding into a theoretical discussion, the chapter considers our understanding of the EAW as a measure of 'forced mobility' and the notion of a 'criminal justice system' that crosses international borders with ever-increasing intensity. Finally, the chapter comments on the conditionality of residence of EU citizens in the UK before and after Brexit.

1. Bordering 'the unwanted'

According to De Giorgi (2010, p. 150), the modern 'punitive turn' against migrants and migration dates back to the 1970s when the most industrialised European countries "imposed a virtual stop on labor *[spelling original]* migration as a consequence of rising unemployment rates, economic stagnation, and the unfolding of a broad crisis of the industrial economy". Kalir (2019, p. 22) traces the "violent, criminalising and overall dehumanising assault by the Western states" on migrants and refugees, in particular those from the Global South, to the early 1990s and the end of the Cold War. Whichever historical point of departure we take, in the latter part of the twentieth century, migrants have increasingly been portrayed as "inherently dangerous" to Western societies, "posing an existential threat to the body politic, to our way of life, as well as more tangible threats to our standard of living, our public services, our safety and security" (Webber, 2012, p. 5).

The 'threat' embodied by the figure of 'a migrant' fed into public imaginations, by both media and politicians (see e.g. Eberl et al., 2018; Grande, Schwarzbözl & Fatke, 2019; De Noronha, 2018; Radziwinowiczówna & Galasińska, 2021), gives governments of all ideological shades the platform to engage in a "war on migration" (Webber, 2012, p. 5). Such 'war' is fought through the introduction of restrictive immigration legislation and complex regulations, stemming from deeply embedded State racism, xeno-racism and xenophobia (Webber, 2012; Bhui, 2013, 2016; Kalir, 2019), now mainstreamed into liberal democratic political systems (Hutter & Kriesi, 2022). "[P]revention of entry, containment and deportation" (Kalir, 2019, p. 22) all serve as the tools of mobilisation against the 'migrant threat'. However, such mobilisation is not used against all migrants in equal measure. As Webber (2012, p. 5) argues, those highly mobile migrants whose "youth, salary, qualifications and talent" are sought by governments to prop up the states' economic system are often welcomed – and even invited by the government and corporations – into labour markets and wider societies (see also Bhui, 2016). The poor and the persecuted, on the other hand, are met with "real-life militarised external border controls [and] fully fledged and virtually unregulated internal border police force" (Webber, 2012, p. 5).

When it comes to migrants who – at any point – have been in contact with the criminal justice system, hostility against them is often "rooted in a widespread view that non-citizens convicted of crimes are particularly undeserving of sympathy because they have betrayed the hospitality of the society that let them enter and live in the state" (Gibney, 2013, p. 218). As such, they are the one constant 'enemy at the gates' of bordered states. As Aliverti (2016, p. 138) contends, nationality is "the last category that allows legally sanctioned differential treatment", in particular – although not exclusively – in criminal justice context. Migrants accused of or convicted of criminal offences are placed at the hard frontier of the state, with prisons, other places of detention and criminal courts now an intrinsic part of the migration control systems in many liberal democratic states (Bosworth, 2011; Kaufman, 2015; Turnbull & Hasselberg, 2017; Martynowicz, 2016b; Kalir, 2019).

This bordering of the unwanted is "a ritualized method of reasserting state authority, reinforcing a collective resentment against the groups assumed to disrupt the national order" (Phillips, 2012, p. 16). As Fekete and Webber (2010, p. 2) argued over a decade ago, deportation is now constructed as a "reasonable and proportionate way to guarantee public security against a foreign enemy" and has largely been normalised as such in Western democracies (see also Bosworth, 2011). "Separation, segregation and expulsion" argue Fekete and Webber (2010, pp. 2–3) "are new penal principles passed off by politicians as a proportionate response to the menace of foreign criminals". As Wacquant (1999, p. 216) adds, in European states, the prison systems are asked "not only to curb crime, but also . . . to hold at bay populations judged to be disreputable, derelict and unwanted" and *foreigners* are the primary group of interest for the prisons' new role. Although at first sight *extradition* (and in the case of the current chapter, its incarnation in the form of the European Arrest Warrant) appears to be a criminal justice tool one step removed from the *crimmigration* system of the control of mobility of the 'unwanted', as this chapter will later argue, the scale of the movement of people in the context of EAW now justifies its consideration in this context.

2. Methodology

The empirical material on which this chapter is based combines evidence from two separate pieces of research. First, it uses interview and observation data from my doctoral research with male Polish prisoners in Northern Ireland, undertaken in 2014 and 2015. During the research, 18 prisoners[7] who were incarcerated in HMP Maghaberry[8] and HMP Magilligan[9] contributed either individually or in small groups through in-depth, semi-structured, qualitative interviews. Eleven were interviewed in high-security conditions, five in medium-security conditions, and two in both (at different stages of their respective sentences). Six of those interviewees were held on foot of a European Arrest Warrant in the high-security prison, awaiting the outcome of their extradition proceedings. While this chapter is not really concerned with the details of the *procedure* of extradition under EAW, it is important to state that the process of decision-making by the courts in those cases was simplified to enable a speedy transfer of the person subject to the warrant. Once the UK authorities issued a certificate recognising a request from another EU Member State, the person sought was then arrested and brought before a judge. First, full judicial hearing had to be set within 21 days in cases where the person did not agree to extradition straight away (House of Commons Library, 2017). Once the judge was satisfied that conduct by the person alleged in an EAW is an 'extradition offence', that there were no legal barriers to extradition, and that extradition will not (disproportionately) breach the person's human rights, he or she then had to order the extradition. The decision to extradite could be appealed within seven days. Normally, extraditions should have taken place within ten days of any judicial decision becoming final (House of Commons Library, 2017). I mention this procedure for context, as five of the EAW interviewees were in custody for a short time; only one spent over 22 months in Maghaberry Prison while contesting the warrant and it is in those short windows of time that the interviews took place. I also met informally with another prisoner who was in the process of challenging his EAW through the courts; some anonymised notes of this encounter formed the background (rather than data) for my analysis.

In addition to interviews with prisoners, a small number of staff whose roles included specific duties relating to 'foreign national' prisoners were also interviewed, as were a number of representatives of prison monitoring and oversight bodies. The study included observations of aspects of prison regime, and in particular the quarterly Foreign National Forum in each of the prisons (designed as a 'consultative' meeting with this group of prisoners) and monthly Equality and Diversity Meetings (which, while including prisoner representatives, were more formal meetings for core staff responsible for equality issues). Research material also included informal discussions with both prisoners and staff.

For the purposes of this chapter, the interview data from the PhD project was supplemented with a review of EAW and Surrender cases reported by Judiciary NI between January 2004 and December 2022.[10] The searches of terms 'European Arrest Warrant', 'Extradition Act 2003', 'District Court',[11] 'Sad Okregowy',[12] 'Poland' and 'Republic of Poland' returned 12 cases, which were then subjected to thematic analysis. Citation details of those cases are available in the Reference list at the end of the chapter.

Second set of data used in this chapter comes from interviews conducted in the first half of 2021 under the auspices of the research project[13] on extraditions and deportations of Polish nationals undertaken by Klaus, Włodarczyk-Madejska and Wzorek (see Chapters 4, 6 and 7 in this volume). Co-ordinated by Witold Klaus and myself, interviews with five solicitors, one Polish-English interpreter, three advisors/support workers and one representative of detention monitoring organisation were conducted by an independent researcher between February and November 2021.[14] Finding practitioners who were *specifically* involved in support for EU nationals threatened with deportation and extradition proved to be a significant challenge, especially given that those subject to EAW proceedings often do not come to the attention of support organisations. However, and helpfully, the interviews provided significant material on the implementation and impact of the EU Settlement Scheme (EUSS). Given the timing of the research, amid very intensive period of applications to the Scheme before its deadline of 31 June 2021, this was perhaps not surprising. It is this material that allowed me for some *initial* analysis of the potential impact of the Scheme on the future of individuals and their families with a past involvement in EAW proceedings, and it is here where the data from my PhD research in 2014 and 2015 and the new information 'collided' in relevance on the, earlier unpredicted, continuum of bordering experience.

3. 'I've put all my eggs in one basket'

Since the mid-2000s, there has been an increased interest in the situation of 'foreign national' prisoners and their experience of both prison and deportation systems.

Burgeoning literature included official monitoring reports (HMIP, 2006, 2007), academic accounts of their experiences and treatment in several jurisdictions (see e.g. Bosworth, 2011; Brosens, 2019; Kaufman, 2015; Martynowicz, 2013, 2018; Ugelvik & Damsa, 2018) and theoretical analysis of the role of imprisonment in bordering practices (see e.g. Aliverti, 2016; Bosworth et al., 2016; Fekete & Webber, 2010). This increased interest expanded our knowledge and understanding of *foreignness* in the prison context; however, as I argued elsewhere (Martynowicz, 2013) despite this intensified focus, 'foreign national prisoners' were often treated in the extant literature as a rather homogenous group. More nuanced discussions of differential experiences by either gender, 'race' or nationality remain rare (some examples include Martynowicz, 2016a; Matos, 2016; Park & Jeffries, 2018). It is a rather important omission, given the constitution of the 'foreign national prisoner' populations. In the UK, for example, this 'group' accounted for 12% of the total prison population (at 9,682 detainees) in the first quarter of 2022,[15] with the largest national groups among those being Albanian (14% of the 'foreign national' prison population), Polish (9%), Romanian (8%), Irish (7%), Lithuanian (4%) and Jamaican (4%). While there are some experiences that those detainees will have in common (e.g. difficulties in access to prison services, HMIP, 2006, 2007), others – such as experience of racism, xenophobia and xeno-racism – will vary (see also Introduction to this volume).

What is even rarer – and, arguably until the publication of the current volume nearly non-existent – is the differentiation of experiences by *reasons* for which 'foreign nationals' might have been imprisoned in the first place. Specifically, there is dearth of literature that focuses on people who experience prison detention as the result of extradition proceedings such as those under the European Arrest Warrant. In the UK context, this is perhaps not surprising as while some information exists on the scale of extraditions (in particular under the previously used EAW, National Crime Agency, 2021), when it comes to prison statistics, 'foreign national prisoners' are not differentiated by reasons for detention or, in fact, by remand/sentenced status (MOJ, 2022). This, combined with the fact that many people detained on foot of extradition processes are not in prisons for long (if at all), adds to their invisibility in the analysis of either transnational mobility or experiences of imprisonment or experience of bordering processes in this context.

In my own doctoral research (albeit now somewhat dated), 30% of interviewees were awaiting court decisions about their EAW. Unlike those serving a sentence, they tended to be less interested in the prison regime (perhaps beyond ensuring that they had some contact with other Polish prisoners and access to some Polish food in the prison shop). Often, their actual prison existence was quite mundane. Marcin[16] busied himself with painting models in his cell, while Jarek tried to kill time-solving crossword puzzles. Occasionally, he went to English classes, "mostly to drink coffee and have a chat with the other Polish guys". Marek was a keen reader and because he had very good English, he was able to use the prison library regularly. Mostly, they were keen to 'stay out of trouble' for as long as their EAW cases were being considered, displaying compliance with the prison regime (see also Martynowicz, 2018).

Understandably, their central concern was the EAW court process. They were focused on speaking to lawyers; submitting evidence of long-term residency, family life and evidence of community links to Northern Ireland; providing medical evidence, and so on, in attempts to challenge EAWs. Marcin was in regular contact with his solicitor and was adamant that he will fight the extradition to the very end: "I have not lived in Poland for 9 years now, and I am not planning on going back!" he exclaimed during the interview. Cezary complained about access to legal representation, in particular about the fact that his solicitor often turned up for consultations without an interpreter. Cezary previously served part of a prison sentence for an offence committed in his time in Northern Ireland and was arrested on the basis of EAW when he was 'signing in' at a police station as part of his bail conditions for that sentence. His family lived in Northern Ireland, and he was adamant that he wanted to continue to live there too.

Piotr was keen to correct information sent to the courts but was getting frustrated with his solicitor's 'indifference'. Not knowing much English, Piotr was having difficulties communicating with his lawyer, which only added to his uncertainty of where the EAW process was at. He also found it difficult to trust his legal representation without being able to fully understand what was going on: "If I had any English, I would defend myself better", he remarked. During an interview Piotr stated that a decision to extradite him had actually been taken nearly a month previously. It was his understanding that the courts in Northern Ireland were "waiting on some papers" to arrive from Poland, but he did not know what they were and therefore was unaware if the extradition was going ahead or not. At the same time, staff in the prison thought that his extradition was 'imminent' (E&D Co-ordinator, Maghaberry). If it was, he appeared not to have been informed about his possible imminent departure.

Marcin, Piotr and Cezary resisted both *the process* and the potential *outcome* of extradition proceedings. Their family and working lives were intertwined with their new 'home' and they spoke of lives that were well established and, in large measure, better than the ones left behind in Poland. Their objections to removal were often framed in economic terms; they wanted to provide better, more secure financial futures for their partners and children. Some, like Piotr, explained that he and his family put "all the eggs in one basket" when deciding to come to Northern Ireland, leaving no practical or emotional connection to Poland and their previous lives. Marcin spoke at some length about how his child had better education in Northern Ireland that could meet their complex learning needs. Resisting extradition was therefore important not just for him but for the wellbeing of his family. This accords very much with the initial reasons for migration of many Eastern European migrants into the UK post-2004 enlargement of the EU (for a review of literature on reasons for migration into the UK, see Burrell, 2010; for Northern Ireland context, see Bell et al., 2009) who placed finding work and improving their families' prospects very much at the top of their migration agenda. In this context, it is understandable that the desire to continue their lives in a country which often provided those improved opportunities featured so prominently in their reasons to challenge extradition. This determination to resist transfer under EAW stood in stark contrast to the cases of interviewees who had no deep family connection in Northern Ireland. Marek, who left Poland in the middle of his appeal court case concerning drug possession offence, expressed his willingness to go back to Poland as soon as he could and complained that on previous date for his EAW hearing, he spent eight hours in a court holding cell but was not updated on what happened in the case. Jarek's case in Poland was at the investigative stage, and he was sought to provide evidence; he appeared resigned to the fact that he will be extradited soon after we met for the interview.

While awaiting extradition decisions, EAW arrestees clearly experienced the pain of the threat of expulsion. Their anxiety relating to expulsion was exacerbated by the fact that their removal (even short term) would also affect their children and families: they would not only face separation from their loved ones, but their family's financial stability was also often threatened. That family situation/the right to family life is significant in a large number of extradition cases was borne out of the analysis of Northern Irish EAW cases for this chapter: in 9 out of 12 of them, Article 8 (EHCR) rights were raised as a reason to stay extradition. However, challenges to the EAW on Article 8 grounds can be gruelling, and there often is no realistic prospect of them being successful without significant evidence of disproportionality of removal in all case circumstances. As one advisor interviewed in the second research reflected in 2021:

> if anyone thinks that they won't be extradited because they have a wife here, or a child or a grandchild, unfortunately they are seriously mistaken.
>
> (Interview P02)

The impact on families can, as he further remarked, be 'traumatising'. The interviewee could not recall many families who followed the arrestees to the requesting country to stay there for the duration of the person's sentence. As he put it, families often 'have nothing to go back to' and therefore, in his experience, make the decision to stay behind in the UK. This can, in some cases, be "heart-breaking":

> [if] you have a wife who has cancer, and she may no longer be here when you come back. And that's still no reason enough [*to overturn an EAW*].
>
> (Interview P02)

This often-traumatising effect is borne out by some of the testimonies of family members in EAW court cases analysed for this chapter.[17] In *The Republic of Poland v. Tumkiewicz* (2015),[18] the High Court judges were presented with Mr Tumkiewicz'es wife's statement that she and their son (who was born and raised in Northern Ireland) would not be able to visit him in prison, was he to be extradited to Poland. Evidence from a medical expert, Dr Harbinson, confirmed that the spouse suffered from depression as a direct result of his imprisonment in the course of the extradition proceedings, the threat of extradition and the negative impact it would have on their son's relationship with his father. As the judgement noted in Paragraph 7:

> Dr Harbinson concluded that extradition would undoubtedly exacerbate the depression and that treatment would be unlikely to be effective.

Although some of this evidence was challenged by another medical expert examining the mother's mental state, they still recognised that Mr Tumkiewicz'es arrest had some detrimental impact on their son's activities. Crucially, yet another expert who spoke to Mr Tumkiewicz'es five-year-old son concluded (as reported at Paragraph 10 of the judgement) that:

> The child . . . needed his father in his daily life . . . it was not in the best interests of the child or his mother for his father to be extradited and it would place increased stress on a vulnerable family unit.

However, in this case – and in accord with the advisor's assessment expressed in the 2021 interview – this impact was not enough to stay the extradition. The authorities were therefore permitted to transfer Mr Tumkiewicz to Poland to serve the remainder of his sentence.

The impact on families can sometimes be seen as manifestly unfair when delays occur in bringing people to 'justice' across national borders, especially when the reasons for delay can be blamed on mistakes by the authorities in either the Requesting or Sending state (see also Klaus in Chapter 4 and Włodarczyk-Madejska and Wzorek in Chapter 6 of this volume). Such were the circumstances in the case of *Poland v. Sebastian Gorski* (2015),[19] where there was a four-year delay in the execution of the EAW. This was despite the fact that Mr Gorski was in contact with the authorities in Poland to get his National ID *after* his suspended sentences were activated there and before he left the country. It was also even though he was in contact with the police and courts in Northern Ireland *after* the EAW was issued, and therefore his whereabouts known to the authorities. Between mid-2008 (when he arrived in Northern Ireland) and his eventual arrest under the EAW in February 2014, Mr Gorski and his wife had two children, neither of whom knew any other 'home' than Northern Ireland. Expert evidence in the case confirmed distressing psychological impact on both Mr Gorski's wife and on him (he attempted to take his own life in prison as a result of the EAW proceedings), as well as on their young children. The court accepted that, was Mr Gorski to be removed to Poland to serve a prison sentence there, his relationship with the children would suffer significantly (they would not be able to visit for financial reasons), and his wife's mental health was likely to deteriorate. However, even in those circumstances, it was the *culpable delay* in executing the warrant rather than the family situation that caused the judge in the case to refuse extradition. As the learned Judge Smyth stated at Paragraph 50 of the judgement:

> I accept that had it not been for the culpable delay in this case, *the family circumstances of the RP would be insufficient to justify a refusal* to return him to Poland when weighed against the important public interest that the U.K. should honour its Treaty obligations.
>
> (emphasis added)

In the nine Northern Irish cases available for analysis for this chapter that raised Article 8 grounds in challenge to extradition, only two did not proceed to the person's transfer. In both, including the case of Gorski discussed earlier, it was the *culpable delay* in arrest that was decisive, and *not* the impact (at times very serious) on family lives.

4. Conditionality of residence

Residence outside of the country of citizenship is often conditional, and this is no different in the context of EU membership. As the previous section shows, this conditionality is evident (and subject to very serious constraints of 'justice') in the EAW process. Moreover, legal instruments such as the EU Citizenship Directive, include multiple exemptions to the right to reside based on behaviour, criminal record, financial situation and more. The *myth* of the freedom of movement is quickly undermined when one regards all the grounds on which a person's 'freedom' of movement within the EU could be curtailed, including their presence being 'conducive to public good' or them not being a 'threat to public safety' (see e.g. Brandariz, 2021); grounds that are as broad as they are often discriminatory in their application (Klaus & Martynowicz, 2021).

In the UK context, it is important to consider the consequences of Brexit on the situation of EU nationals and the significant changes to how they can now claim and exercise the right to stay. Here, conditionality of residence is evident in the implementation of the EUSS, designed as part of the UK's *Withdrawal Agreement*[20] from the Union with the aim of providing new immigration status to EU and EEA citizens. With some minor exceptions (most notably for Irish citizens), millions of EU and EEA citizens residing in the UK by 31 December 2020, and no longer able to avail of the protections of EU Directives on free movement, were required to apply to the Scheme to secure their continued right to work and live here.[21] The UK government refused the calls for the Scheme to be declaratory in nature, instead making an application to it compulsory. The differentiation in status (Settled or Pre-settled) is based on the length of uninterrupted residence in the UK (generally over or under five years). On the face of it, such a distinction appears simple and relatively easy to evidence. However, as multiple reports outline, the application and evidentiary processes were/are anything but simple and a variety of vulnerabilities (including age, gender, nationality and ethnicity) were identified as barriers to effective engagement with the Scheme (see e.g. Independent Chief

Inspector of Borders and Immigration, 2019; Sumption & Fernández-Reino, 2020; Jablonowski & Pinkowska, 2021). Due to its compulsory nature, the EUSS can also be seen as one of the largest exercises in the creation of electronic residence database in UK's history. When it comes to EU and EEA citizens in the UK, this is a fundamental shift in policy and practice as, until UK's departure from the EU, it had neither a system of compulsory registration (Elfving & Marcinkowska, 2021) nor a requirement for residence documentation beyond an EU passport. Those EU nationals who failed to apply to the Scheme by 30 June 2021[22] will have "automatically and irreversibly" lost their "entitlement to stay in the UK, and accrued periods of residence and/or work will be negated, disproportionately impacting upon the disadvantaged and vulnerable" (O'Brien, 2021, p. 432).

It is now well documented that EU and EEA citizens have been experiencing "geopolitical and emotional insecurity" (Burrell & Schweyher, 2019, p. 193; see also Elfving & Marcinkowska, 2021) as a result of Brexit (Hall et al., 2022). As Hall et al. (2022) point out, the UK's decision to leave the EU and the resulting uncertainty over future status of EU citizens in the country (some with a very long history of residence) has threatened the relative guarantee of their access to resources such as the right to reside, healthcare, accommodation and education, and previously effectively unlimited access to the labour market. The fact that it took well over three years between the Brexit Referendum (June 2016) and the completion of the *Withdrawal Agreement* (November 2019) for details of the future system of protection of citizens' rights to emerge from UK-EU negotiations, did nothing to assuage the concerns. While many questions were raised about the gendered and age-related impact of the new Scheme (see e.g. O'Brien, 2021), as Burrell and Schweyher (2019, p. 194) noted, the whole Scheme is "wrapped up in moral overtones of deservingness based around standards of 'suitability' and warnings against criminality". For those who do not fit neatly into the moral 'clean slate', the right of continued residence can become solely dependent on the relationship between them and criminal justice. It is this aspect of the new Scheme that I turn to next.

5. Brexit and the 'criminality check' – consequences for 'new' residence status

Perhaps predictably, a history of contact with the criminal justice system proved one of the main barriers to achieving the new residency status. From its inception, the EU Settlement Scheme included the condition of *suitability* for continued residence. The Home Office amended guidance (2022, p. 154) states that:

> The assessment of suitability must be conducted on a case by case basis and be based on the applicant's personal conduct or circumstances in the UK and overseas, including whether they have any relevant prior criminal convictions, and whether they have been open and honest in their application.

At the same time, the guidance requires a self-disclosure (in the process of the application for status) of certain criminal convictions. Despite concerns dating back to 2019 about the clarity of the requirement, and whether or not it includes *all* convictions (UNLOCK, 2019), the guidance is still quite complex, stating that adult applicants:

> are required to provide information about previous criminal convictions in the UK and overseas, and are only required to declare *past criminal convictions* which *appear in their criminal record in accordance with the law of the State of conviction at the time of the application*. There is no requirement to declare *spent offences*, cautions or alternatives to prosecution, for example fixed penalty notices for speeding.
>
> (Home Office, 2022, pp. 154–155, emphasis added)

While on the face of it, there was no need to disclose spent convictions, the differences between legal systems of *what* is considered spent and *when* could inevitably lead to much confusion. Given the reach of the Scheme into 'overseas criminality' (through the requirement of disclosure of offences committed outside of the UK), it is also clear that residence decisions will have intersected with transnational justice, including with former and 'legacy' EAW processes.

Already at the dawn of the EUSS, Martynowicz and Radziwinowiczówna (2019) identified the issue of the 'criminality checks' as a point of vulnerability for those needing to avail of the Scheme's application process, raising the concern that EU nationals with 'criminal past' will become "instantly, and more easily, deportable". Two years later, Radziwinowiczówna and Lewis (2021, p. 11) stressed, "Criminal record is an important factor contributing to abstaining from applying under the EUSS". This is not surprising, as disclosure of criminal convictions in the process of EUSS application can lead to being considered for deportation. The Home Office *can* refer the applicant for assessment for removal, even where they did not come to their attention previously. As a solicitor working in a migrant support organisation (and interviewed for our research in 2021) confirmed:

> we are seeing people who are afraid to apply for [settled] status because they don't want to disclose their criminal record and they don't want to be considered for deportation if they were not previously.
>
> (Interview P06)

And as another interviewee remarked, the chances of getting the new residence status in the case of contact with the criminal justice system were, in his view, low. As this advisor remarked:

> there is the general [Home Office] policy of referring every case, even when there is a minor criminality, to the Immigration Enforcement and the HO [Home Office] is clearly keen not to grant Settled Status to people when they have [criminal record] and they are not required to do so.
>
> (Interview P04)

This means that 'honest' disclosure of convictions can have double-edged consequences, no status and removal, while, in a rather Kafkaesque twist, non-disclosure (even accidental) can lead to same (Home Office, 2022, Rule EU16a).[23] This raises questions about how prior contact with the criminal justice system would inevitably lead to (some) people becoming undocumented in the UK. Conscious of the fact that some of their clients will choose to 'go underground' rather than expose themselves to the possibility of transfer through application for a new immigration status, one advisor reflected:

> They openly say: I would rather function in the "underground" . . . than go to prison. We will have to face an avalanche of human misery caused by Brexit and the fact that those people would not be able to stay here [*had they applied for the new residence status*]. They will be pushed to the margins of society.
> (Interview P02)

Additionally, a lack of understanding of what a period of imprisonment in *any* country means for the EUSS application complicated matters for many. As one advice practitioner interviewed in 2021 explained:

> Our clients . . . do not realise that every stint in prison, any arrest, breaks the continuity of residence in the UK. . . . We have clients who think they can apply for permanent residence because they've lived here for 10, 15 years and only left to serve the sentence elsewhere. . . . That's not the case.
> (Interview P02)

As a consequence, even if the application for the new immigration status was/is not automatically rejected on the basis of criminal record, many of those whose residence *was* broken due to time of imprisonment, including in the country of origin following a transfer on the back of EAW, are/were unable to avail of the more secure Settled Status (based on five years unbroken residence in the UK). If granted the less-secure Pre-Settled Status instead, they will only be able to apply for more permanent residence in five years' time. Moreover, their application for Settled Status when they become eligible in the future is likely to be subjected to the same scrutiny (with respect of checks against criminal records), meaning that the *conditionality and uncertainty* of their residence will potentially continue for a number of years, including depending on when their convictions become 'spent'.[24] This will potentially keep them in a situation of having to go through the same criminal records check in five years, possibly facing removal in the future. There is also no guarantee that the rules of granting of the Settled Status will not change in the future as no immigration rule is set in stone.

Those in prisons – including those detained on foot of the EAW – were faced with practical difficulties during the application window, not only in gaining access to the necessary documentation that would prove their identity or the length of their prior residence but also to the very basics such as a paper copy of the application. When paper (rather than digital-only) application was actually provided, which was not until around two weeks before the Scheme's deadline of 30 June 2021 (Interview P03), all applications had to be made with the use of a phone app or a laptop, neither of which are available in prisons. Calls to the Home Office's Resolution Centre (the first point of contact to request a paper application) were rarely possible as the cost of phone calls from prisons is prohibitive for many. Limits on out-of-cell time were also a factor, and such time was severely restricted during the Covid-19 pandemic, introducing an additional barrier. With the deadline for applications set for June 2021, one legal manager of a support organisation stated that attempting to secure access to the application process for EU nationals in prisons was like working in "a wilderness" (Interview P03). As they reported, imprisoned applicants sometimes were also being pre-judged by Home Office staff:

> I once called the Resolution Centre myself, for someone who wanted a paper application form, and they essentially told me that it wasn't worth applying because my client was in prison, so they were likely to be refused. And we made it very clear that it wasn't up to them to decide.
>
> (Interview P03)

As can be seen from the summary of issues in the previous discussion, the 'suitability' requirements and 'criminality checks' under the EUSS have the potential to wreak havoc over the lives of EU nationals who have been in contact with the criminal justice system. For some, the application process will have meant deportation, for others, weeks and potentially months of uncertainty awaiting decision on their residence while the Home Office considers their future. For others, and we might never find out for how many, the EUSS' 'criminality check' will mean an undocumented, insecure, and precarious existence for many years to come.

Conclusions: the invisible prisoner of transnational justice

The European Arrest Warrant was conceived as a measure simplifying the extradition between Member States of the European Union on the basis of 'mutual trust' between the various European criminal justice systems. In theory, its core assumption – bringing fugitives to justice – can hardly be criticised. In practice, however, over the years it has been subjected to numerous critiques, from allegations of misuse of the system (Fair Trials International, 2021) to questions over its effectiveness and efficiency (see Włodarczyk-Madejska and Wzorek in this volume) and the meaning of 'justice' in EAW context (see Klaus in Chapter 4). What has been considerably less visible in academic and activist critique of the EAW is the far-reaching impact of its use on the lives of EU migrants and their families. While deportability of EU nationals has been in focus for some time, the EAW itself has – until the publication of this collection – been largely absent from discussions of bordering practices. This despite the fact that this expansion of the reach of national criminal justice systems across borders contributes to thousands of people being moved between countries each year. The UK alone transferred on average just over a 1,000 people a year to other EU Member States between 2009 and 2021 (National Crime Agency, 2021).

EAW detainees and their families are not just largely invisible in academic literature, but also in prison systems and in systems of legal and practical support for migrants. In the UK, the figure of the 'foreign criminal' (De Noronha, 2018) is a complex one, but the nomenclature used in reporting of 'foreign national offending' here means that they are treated like a homogenous, undifferentiated group. This makes it much harder, if not impossible, to find out how many detainees facing extradition there even are in the system at any given time, adding to their invisibility. The fact that EAW detainees are subjected to a criminal justice, rather than immigration enforcement process, means that they rarely come to the attention of support agencies that may otherwise have an interest in/assist those subjected to processes such as deportation. This is not, by any means, a criticism of any of the organisations involved in assistance; rather, the invisibility is related to the nature of the EAW process itself as a *justice* matter. This alone can engender feelings quite separate from support for other vulnerable migrants, as 'fugitives from justice' are unlikely to garner much sympathy for their plight.

Yet, just as with deportation, extradition can present enormous challenges to the arrestees and their families. As the (very brief) review of extradition cases in Northern Ireland, undertaken for this chapter, shows, these can be life-altering (see also Klaus, Włodarczyk-Madejska and Wzorek in this volume about the impact observed by people who were forcefully returned to Poland due to issuance of an EAW). From impact on children's well-being, to the consequences for mental and physical health of the detainees, spouses and children, extradition proceedings break the continuances of well-established lives, financial stability, educational support and community links and, in the case of Brexit and the EUSS, can also put even more conditions on legal residence well into the future.

As this chapter tried to argue, there is a specific group of EU nationals in the UK now that are at risk of becoming new subjects of the 'Departheid', questioning Kalir's (2019, p. 30) assertion that "they are not considered threatening, even when administratively lacking the right documentation" – and they are those who, at some point in their lives, have been in contact with the criminal justice system. Given the obstacles identified in this chapter to acquiring legal status as a result of 'criminality', there are potentially thousands[25] of EU migrants in the UK who have, almost overnight, become undocumented as a result of Brexit, the EUSS and new residency requirements. Illegalisation through inaccessibility of a residence status has serious consequences that, as clearly shown in the UK by the 'Windrush Generation Scandal' (House of Commons, 2020), extend way beyond the threat of expulsion. In the UK context, the implementation of the 'hostile environment' policy means that access to the basic support available (at least in theory) to 'lawful residents' – welfare, education, healthcare, and accommodation – are restricted as soon as the person is unable to provide evidence of such residence. As such, the 'avalanche of human misery' is almost certainly already here, with some EU nationals forced behind the invisible bars of the prison of undocumented status, leading existence on the margins in the shadows of society.

Notes

1 2002/584/JHA (at: https://eur-lex.europa.eu/legal-content/EN/TXT/?uri=CELEX%3A0 2002F0584-2009032).
2 *Trade and Cooperation Agreement between the United Kingdom of Great Britain and Northern Ireland, of the one part, and the European Union and the European Atomic Energy Community, of the other part*, Treaty Series No. 8 (2021)(at: www.gov.uk/government/publications/ukeu-and-eaec-trade-and-cooperation-agreement-ts-no82021).
3 As this data covers the calendar years, 2021 figure includes the first transfers under the new TACA surrender procedure.
4 With the so-called transition period until 31 December of the same year.
5 The publication date reflects the most recent version of the EUSS Guidance (at: https://assets.publishing.service.gov.uk/government/uploads/system/uploads/attachment_data/file/1115086/EU_Settlement_Scheme_EU__other_EEA__Swiss_citizens_and_family_members.pdf).
6 *Directive 2004/38/EC of the European Parliament and of the Council of 29 April 2004 on the right of citizens of the Union and their family members to move and reside freely within the territory of the Member States amending Regulation (EEC) No 1612/68 and repealing Directives 64/221/EEC, 68/360/EEC, 72/194/EEC, 73/148/EEC, 75/34/EEC, 75/35/EEC, 90/364/EEC, 90/365/EEC and 93/96/EEC* (at: https://eur-lex.europa.eu/legal-content/EN/TXT/?uri=CELEX%3A02004L0038-201106).
7 This number of interviewees needs to be seen in the context of the relatively small overall population of Polish prisoners incarcerated in Northern Ireland at the time. For example, on 31 March 2014 (during the first phase of my project), there were 23 Polish prisoners across the four prisons that hold adults in the jurisdiction (research notes).
8 A high-security prison accommodating remand and sentenced prisoners.
9 A medium-security prison accommodating sentenced prisoners only. HMP Magilligan also contains an open prison unit.
10 Judiciary NI is an online service for Northern Ireland's Courts, where judgements, decisions and directions are published as public record. The timeline of cases (January 2004 to December 2020) was chosen to reflect the time for which the EU Directive on European Arrest Warrant applied to Northern Ireland before UK's exit from the EU (until December 2020) and also to catch any cases either a) delayed by the Covid-19 pandemic or b) considered under the new Surrender procedure implemented in UK/EU justice cooperation post-Brexit. I have chosen cases in Northern Ireland to coincide with the locum of the original doctoral research and limited the search to cases involving Polish nationals for coinciding with the focus on said project.
11 This was the court of first instance in all EAW requests in Northern Ireland between 2004 and 2020, and remains so under the Surrender procedure.
12 Again, this is the court of first instance issuing all EAW requests in Poland.
13 This research was part of the project 'Experiences of Poles Deported from the UK in the Context of the Criminal Justice System Involvement', funded by the National Science Centre, Poland, under Grant No. UMO-2018/30/M/HS5/00816.
14 Witold and I are very grateful to Patrycja Pinkowska for her assistance with this project, and in particular in accessing the relevant interviewees.
15 The most recent official statistics available, published in July 2022 by the UK Ministry of Justice here: www.gov.uk/government/statistics/offender-management-statistics-quarterly-january-to-march-2022/offender-management-statistics-quarterly-january-to-march-2022#population. The overall statistics include 725 'non-criminal' detainees (i.e. those held under immigration and not criminal justice powers of detention).
16 All arrestees quoted in this chapter have been given pseudonyms.
17 I do not propose here a full analysis of the *legal* arguments against and for extradition. I use the material from the cases to illustrate impact on families, quite outside of the

legal and legalistic arguments of issues such as proportionality and public interest which form a large part of judicial decisions on extradition.

18 *The Republic of Poland v. Pawel Tumkiewicz*, [2015] NIQB107.

19 *Court in Sad Okregowy, Poland v. Sebastian Gorski* [2015] NICty 1.

20 *AGREEMENT on the withdrawal of the United Kingdom of Great Britain and Northern Ireland from the European Union and the European Atomic Energy Community* (2019/C 384 I/01) (at: https://eur-lex.europa.eu/legal-content/EN/TXT/PDF/?uri=CELEX:12019W/TXT(02)&from=EN)

21 The basic rules of the EU Settlement Scheme are available at: www.gov.uk/settled-status-eu-citizens-families

22 There was some, limited, scope for late applications but this is an exception.

23 "where, in relation to the application and *whether or not to the applicant's knowledge*, false or misleading information, representations or documents have been submitted (including false or misleading information submitted to any person to obtain a document used in support of the application), which is or are material to the decision whether or not to grant the applicant indefinite leave to enter or remain or limited leave to enter or remain . . ., you may refuse the application, provided that it is proportionate to do so" (Home Office, 2022, p. 21).

24 At the time when this book is going to print (end of December 2022), the necessity of the second application is in doubt, following the successful High Court challenge in the case of *Independent Monitoring Authority v. Secretary of State for the Home Department* [2022] EWHC 3274 (Admin). The Court stated that EU citizens who have been granted pre-Settled Status should not become unlawfully resident if they fail to apply for the more secure Settled Status once their five year-residency requirement is met, as their rights will already have been protected under the *Withdrawal Agreement* after the first application. As of 28 December 2022, the Home Office is planning to appeal.

25 There is no proper way of assessing how many people may be affected. The Office of National Statistics estimated the number of EU nationals residing in the UK in mid-2020 at 3.5 million (https://blog.ons.gov.uk/2021/07/02/are-there-really-6m-eu-citizens-living-in-the-uk/). Yet, by end of June, the Home Office received 6 million applications to the EUSS, 5.4 million of which were 'concluded' (ibid; 'conclusion' could be either successful or unsuccessful application). By March 2021, around 6% of those were 're-applications' (multiple applications can be needed to reasons such as a requirement for supplementary documentation, appeals, etc). Radziwinowiczówna and Lewis (2021, p. 10) cited Government estimates of eligible EU nationals who were yet to apply to the EUSS as of June 2021 to be anything between 130,000 and 820,000. How many of those will elect not to apply for reasons stated in this chapter is impossible to know.

References

Aliverti, A. (2016). Doing away with decency?: Foreigners, punishment and the liberal state. In A. Eriksson (Ed.), *Punishing the other: The social production of immorality revisited* (pp. 124–144). Oxon: Routledge.

Barnard, C., & Leinarte, E. (2019). Brexit and citizens' rights. *European Journal of Legal Studies, SI*, 117–152. https://doi.org/10.2924/EJLS.2019.005

Bell, J., Caughey, A., Hansson, U., Martynowicz, A., & Scully, M. (2009). *'. . . easy life, great people, bad weather'. A report on the experiences of migrant workers in Northern Ireland.* Belfast: Department for Employment and Learning.

Bhui, H. S. (2013). Introduction: Humanizing migration control and detention. In K. F. Aas & M. Bosworth (Eds.), *The borders of punishment. Migration, citizenship, and social exclusion* (pp. 1–17). Oxford: Oxford University Press.

Bhui, H. S. (2016). The place of 'race' in understanding immigration control and the detention of foreign nationals. *Criminology & Criminal Justice*, *16*(3), 267–285. https://doi.org/10.1177/1748895816646613

Bosworth, M. (2011). Deportation, detention and foreign national prisoners in England and Wales. *Citizenship Studies*, *15*(5), 583–595. https://doi.org/10.1080/13621025.2011.583789

Bosworth, M., Hasselberg, I., & Turnbull, S. (2016). Imprisonment in a global world: Rethinking penal power. In Y. Jewkes, B. Crewe, & J. Bennett (Eds.), *Handbook on prisons* (2nd ed., pp. 698–711). Oxon: Routledge.

Brandariz, J. A. (2021). The removal of EU nationals: An unaccounted dimension of the European deportation apparatus. *Central and Eastern European Migration Review*, *10*(1), 13–33. http://doi.org/10.17467/ceemr.2021.06

Brosens, D. (2019). Prisoners' participation and involvement in prison life: Examining the possibilities and boundaries. *European Journal of Criminology*, *16*(4), 466–485. https://doi.org/10.1177/1477370818773616

Burrell, K. (2010). Staying, returning, working and living: Key themes in current academic research undertaken in the UK on migration movements from Eastern Europe. *Social Identities*, *16*(3), 297–308. http://doi.org/10.1080/13504630.2010.482401

Burrell, K., & Schweyher, M. (2019). Conditional citizens and hostile environments: Polish migrants in pre-Brexit Britain. *Geoforum*, *106*, 192–201. https://doi.org/10.1016/j.geoforum.2019.08.014

De Giorgi, A. (2010). Immigration control, post-Fordism, and less eligibility: A materialist critique of the criminalization of immigration across Europe. *Punishment & Society*, *12*(2), 147–167. https://doi.org/10.1177/1462474509357378

De Noronha, L. (2018). The figure of the 'foreign criminal': Race, gender and the FNP. In M. Bhatia (Ed.), *Media, crime and racism* (pp. 337–358). London: Palgrave Macmillan.

Eberl, J. M., Meltzer, C. E., Heidenreich, T., Herrero, B., Theorin, N., Lind, T., Berganza, R., Boomgaarden, H. J., Schemer, C., & Strömbäck, J. (2018). The European media discourse on immigration and its effects: A literature review. *Annals of the International Communication Association*, *42*(3), 207–223. http://doi.org/10.1080/23808985.2018.1497452

Elfving, S., & Marcinkowska, A. (2021). Imagining the impossible? Fears of deportation and the barriers to obtaining EU settled status in the UK. *Central and Eastern European Migration Review*, *10*(1), 55–73. https://doi.org/10.17467/ceemr.2021.04

Fair Trials International. (2021). *Reinforcing procedural safeguards and fundamental rights in European Arrest Warrant ('EAW') proceedings*. https://www.fairtrials.org/articles/publications/reinforcing-procedural-safeguards-and-fundamental-rights-in-european-arrest-warrant-proceedings/

Fekete, L., & Webber, F. (2010). Foreign nationals, enemy penology and the criminal justice system. *Race and Class*, *51*(4), 1–25. https://irr.org.uk/app/uploads/2016/12/ERB_69.pdf

Gibney, M. J. (2013). Deportation, crime and the changing character of membership in the United Kingdom. In K. F. Aas & M. Bosworth (Eds.), *Borders of punishment: Migration, citizenship, and social exclusion* (pp. 218–236). Oxford: Oxford University Press.

Grande, E., Schwarzbözl, T., & Fatke, M. (2019). Politicizing immigration in Western Europe. *Journal of European Public Policy*, *26*(10), 1444–1463. https://doi.org/10.1080/13501763.2018.1531909

Hall, K., Phillimore, J., Grzymala-Kazlowska, A., Vershinina, N., Ögtem-Young, Ö., & Harris, C. (2022). Migration uncertainty in the context of Brexit: Resource conservation tactics. *Journal of Ethnic and Migration Studies*, *48*(1), 173–191. https://doi.org/*10.1080/1369183X.2020.1839398*

HM Inspectorate of Prisons (HMIP). (2006). *Foreign national prisoners: A thematic review*. London: HMCIP.

HM Inspectorate of Prisons (HMIP). (2007). *Foreign national prisoners: A follow-up report*. London: HMIP.

Home Affairs Committee. (2013). *Pre-Lisbon Treaty EU police and criminal justice measures: The UK's opt-in decision*. London: The Stationery Office.

Home Office. (2022). *EU Settlement scheme: Suitability requirements* (Version 8.0). https://assets.publishing.service.gov.uk/government/uploads/system/uploads/attachment_data/file/1089107/EU_Settlement_Scheme_suitability_requirements.pdf

House of Commons. (2020). *Windrush lessons learned review. Independent Review by Wendy Williams*. https://assets.publishing.service.gov.uk/government/uploads/system/uploads/attachment_data/file/874022/6.5577_HO_Windrush_Lessons_Learned_Review_WEB_v2.pdf

House of Commons Library. (2017, April 18). *The European Arrest Warrant, briefing paper no.07016*. https://researchbriefings.files.parliament.uk/documents/SN07016/SN07016.pdf

Hutter, S., & Kriesi, H. (2022). Politicising immigration in times of crisis. *Journal of Ethnic and Migration Studies*, *48*(2), 341–365. http://doi.org/10.1080/1369183X.2020.1853902

Independent Chief Inspector of Borders and Immigration. (2019). *An inspection of the EU Settlement Scheme November 2018 – January 2019*. https://assets.publishing.service.gov.uk/government/uploads/system/uploads/attachment_data/file/799439/An_inspection_of_the_EU_Settlement_Scheme_May_WEB.PDF

Jablonowski, K., & Pinkowska, P. (2021). *Vulnerability in the EU Settlement Scheme: Looking back, going forward. A review of evidence from Law Centres' casework*. Law Centres Network. https://the3million.org.uk/sites/default/files/files/Vulnerability%20in%20the%20EU%20Settlement%20Scheme%20%28LCN%20report%2C%2021%20Jul%202021%29.pdf

Kalir, B. (2019). The Draconian Governance of illegalized migrants in Western States. *Conflict and Society*, *5*, 19–40. https://doi.org/10.3167/arcs.2019.050102

Kaufman, E. (2015). *Punish & expel. Border control, nationalism, and the new purpose of the prison*. Oxford: Oxford University Press.

Klaus, W., & Martynowicz, A. (2021). Introduction: Unwanted citizens of EU Member states and their forced returns within the European Union. *Central and Eastern European Migration Review*, *10*(1), 5–12. http://doi.org/10.17467/ceemr.2021.05

Martynowicz A. (2018). Power, pain, adaptations and resistance in a 'foreign' prison: The case of Polish prisoners incarcerated in Northern Ireland. *Justice, Power and Resistance*, *2*(2), 267–286.

Martynowicz, A. (2013). Warehouses for the deportable foreign national prisoners in the UK. *Archiwum Kryminologii*, *XXXV*, 305–331. https://doi.org/10.7420/AK2013K

Martynowicz, A. (2016a). Not so multicultural prison: Polish prisoners in a transitional prison system. *Criminology & Criminal Justice*, *16*(3), 337–349. https://doi.org/10.1177/1748895815599579

Martynowicz, A. (2016b). Uncertainty, complexity, anxiety – Deportation and the prison in the case of Polish Prisoners in Northern Ireland. *Archiwum Kryminologii*, *XXXVIII*, 425–439. http://doi.org/10.7420/AK2016O

Martynowicz, A., & Radziwinowiczówna, A. (2019). *Brexit, EU Settlement scheme and the forced (im)mobility of EU Citizens in the UK*. www.law.ox.ac.uk/research-subject-groups/centre-criminology/centreborder-criminologies/blog/2019/04/brexit-eu

Matos, R. (2016). Trajectories and identities of foreign national women: Rethinking prison through the lens of gender and citizenship. *Criminology & Criminal Justice*, *16*(3), 350–365. https://doi.org/10.1177/1748895815603776

Ministry of Justice. (2022). *Offender management statistics quarterly: April to June 2022*. www.gov.uk/government/statistics/offender-management-statistics-quarterly-april-to-june-2022/offender-management-statistics-quarterly-april-to-june-2022#:~:text=Foreign%20National%20Offenders%20(FNOs),of%20the%20total%20prison%20population

National Crime Agency. (2021). Table: Wanted from the UK – EAW-TACA statistics – financial year 2021–22. www.nationalcrimeagency.gov.uk/what-we-do/how-we-work/providing-specialist-capabilities-for-law-enforcement/fugitives-and-international-crime

O'Brien, C. (2021). Between the devil and the deep blue sea: Vulnerable EU citizens cast adrift in the UK post-Brexit. *Common Market Law Review*, *58*(1), 431–470. https://doi.org/10.54648/cola2021025

Park, M. J. Y., & Jeffries, S. (2018). Prisoners of identity: The experiences of ethnic minority Vietnamese women categorised as foreign in Cambodian prisons. *Women's Studies International Forum*, *69*, 56–66. https://doi.org/10.1016/j.wsif.2018.05.001

Phillips, C. (2012). *The multicultural prison: Ethnicity, masculinity, and social relations among prisoners*. Oxford: Oxford University Press.

Radziwinowiczówna, A., & Galasińska, A. (2021). The vile Eastern European': Ideology of deportability in the Brexit media discourse. *Central and Eastern European Migration Review*, *10*(1), 75–93. http://doi: 10.17467/ceemr.2021.01

Radziwinowiczówna, A., & Lewis, O. (2021). *The post-Brexit legal framework for international migration in the UK: Differentiated deportability of poor Europeans?* CMR Working Papers No. 126/184. www.econstor.eu/bitstream/10419/259398/1/1771954728.pdf

Sumption, M., & Fernández-Reino, M. (2020). *Unsettled status 2020: Which EU Citizens are at risk of failing to secure their rights after Brexit?* Oxford: The Migration Observatory. https://migrationobservatory.ox.ac.uk/wp-content/uploads/2020/09/Report-Unsettled-Status-2020.pdf

Turnbull, S., & Hasselberg, I. (2017). From prison to detention: The carceral trajectories of foreign-national prisoners in the United Kingdom. *Punishment & Society*, *19*(2), 135–154. https://doi.org/10.1177/1462474516660695

Ugelvik, T., & Damsa, D. (2018). The pains of crimmigration imprisonment: Perspectives from a Norwegian all-foreign prison. *The British Journal of Criminology*, *58*(5), 1025–1043. https://doi.org/10.1093/bjc/azx067

UNLOCK. (2019). *EU Nationals, settled status and criminal records. Policy briefing – September 2019*. www.unlock.org.uk/wp-content/uploads/EU-nationals-settled-status-and-criminal-records-Sept-2019.pdf

Wacquant, L. (1999). 'Suitable enemies': Foreigners and immigrants in the prisons of Europe. *Punishment & Society*, *1*(2), 215–222. https://doi.org/10.1177/14624749922227784

Webber, F. (2012). *Borderline justice: The fight for refugee and migrant rights*. London: Pluto.

9 Schengen as a European criminal justice instrument – the power of evaluation

Martin Nøkleberg and Helene O.I. Gundhus

Introduction

The Schengen agreement, signed in 1985, is considered pivotal to the European integration project, as it is designed to support the free movement of persons and cross-border mobility by the removal of internal border checks (Cooper, 2015). By making movement across internal borders in Europe easier, the agreement is assumed to promote the use of the four freedoms (free movement of persons, capital, goods, and services) and thus provide citizens and businesses with new opportunities to pursue with positive economic externalities (Davis and Gift, 2014). However, the removal of intra-Schengen border checks and controls came at a cost, and to compensate for the perceived security deficit their abolition might cause, compensatory measures covering various areas were established. In particular, comprehensive rules and standards for control practice on external Schengen borders were laid down to strengthen the outer perimeter of the Schengen area, along with an increase in police and judicial cooperation between Schengen countries, common visa and asylum policies, and the adoption of databases such as the Schengen Information System (SIS) and the European Dactylographic System (Eurodac) (Aas, 2011; Van der Woude, 2020; Fjørtoft, 2022). The Schengen framework is thus designed to establish harmonisation and standardisation across signatory countries (Paul, 2017), particularly as the Schengen *acquis* leaves no room for national exemptions, compelling Schengen states to adhere to common rules and standards.

Although the ambition to achieve harmonisation across countries is often framed as an attempt to ease the movement of persons and provide new opportunities, previous observers have pointed out that the border-free Schengen Area in fact operates as a significant instrument for European social exclusion by aiming to set up impenetrable external borders (Mathiesen, 1997). Moreover, in recent years, the tension between national security concerns and freedom of movement has become ever more acute, particularly as a result of ideas about the links between terrorism, security, migration and borders (Neal, 2009) and the 'migration–security nexus' (Pinyol-Jiménez, 2012), which has led to increasing securitisation of the border area because mobility is viewed as a security concern. Although, as Van der Woude (2020, p. 125) clearly shows, signatory Schengen countries have removed

DOI: 10.4324/9781003254584-10

systematic intra-border control, "this does not imply the end of the monitoring of cross-border mobility", since "border control in the Schengen Area has been continued and even strengthened in the form of patrols and police and immigration controls in the hinterland". Several observers have described the extensive control regime at the external border as being part of building 'Fortress Europe' (Huysmans, 2006; Steinhilper and Gruijters, 2018; Engelbert, Awad and Van Sterkenburg, 2019). Another crucial aspect of developments in the Schengen Area is the way that various recent events or crises have caused some Member States to reintroduce temporary internal border controls to counter the perceived risks associated with terrorism, unwanted immigration and the spread of the coronavirus (Gülzau, 2021). Such reinstatement of intra-Schengen controls has led scholars to ask whether the Schengen area is in 'crisis' (Fijnaut, 2015; Börzel and Risse, 2018; Casella Colombeau, 2020; Somer, 2020), as they may impede the ambition of free movement and cross-border mobility. Both its external and internal measures mean that Schengen acts as a criminal justice and security governance instrument influencing the European system and practice of border controls.

A well-functioning Schengen area depends, in large part, on the correct implementation of the Schengen *acquis*, because failure to implement the common rules fully can endanger the area and threaten trust between the Member States. To support the compensatory measures, strengthen mutual trust and improve the harmonisation between the Member States, evaluation and monitoring mechanisms are considered crucial aspects of Schengen cooperation, with peer evaluation seen as a defining feature: Schengen Member States evaluate each other, and this process and its results (e.g. recommendations and follow-up reports) may influence their border control practices. By its recommendations on how to remedy deficiencies, Schengen evaluation constitutes a significant governance instrument that works to enhance harmonisation across Schengen borders. One study, for instance, has shown how Schengen evaluation increased professionalism in the Norwegian police (Ulrich, Nøkleberg and Gundhus, 2020).

Previous research on evaluation processes suggests that evaluations do not take place in a vacuum (Raimondo, 2018). Although often portrayed as neutral or even technocratic exercises, they are "pervaded with power relationships and embedded in tensions between stakeholders as well as between values, institutions and belief systems" (Nordesjö and Fred, 2021, p. 3). Moreover, increasing politicisation has also been observed in the use of evaluations, particularly within the European Union (EU) (Hoerner, 2019; Stephenson, Schoenefeld and Leeuw, 2019), and it has been argued that politics and normativity are inherent to any policy evaluation (Bovens, Hart and Kuipers, 2008). In this chapter, we aim to unpack the development of Schengen by seeing evaluation and monitoring mechanisms as a form of power. We will look at evaluation as a governance instrument shaping the construction of Schengen as a criminal justice and security area. Taking the case of the Schengen evaluation of Norway as its point of departure, this chapter will explore how Norwegian police officers perceive and navigate the mechanism which enables a form of community of practice, and how they view the move towards tighter control by the European Commission in the evaluation process.

We will then look at how Frontex is becoming more important as a supranational agency within Schengen. The inclusion of vulnerability assessments in the evaluation mechanisms has implications for understanding Schengen, both as a political area and as an idea.

The chapter is divided into five sections. First, we briefly describe the main features of Schengen as a border control regime and outline the analytical tool used to explore Schengen evaluation as a form of power. The next section lays out the research design of the study. Following the conceptual and methodological considerations, we present an empirical analysis of the characteristics of the Schengen evaluation mechanism and of how it has developed. Examining how Norwegian police officers viewed their experience of Schengen evaluation, we analyse how, as a form of power, it affects practice. The final section discusses the main aspects of shifts in governmental instruments and the role and limitations of Schengen evaluation in shaping border control regimes in Europe.

1. Schengen as a border control regime, and the powers of evaluation

Although, through the abolition of internal controls, Schengen constitutes a 'borderless area' within Europe, this area still seems to be deeply concerned with border controls and bordering practices (Karamanidou and Kasparek, 2022; Van der Woude, 2020; Gülzau, 2021; Salomon and Rijpma, 2021). Much scholarly attention has been paid to the external borders of the Schengen area, with studies scrutinising control practices and border agencies present at the external borders, the processes of securitisation and militarisation, and the co-existence of security and human rights and humanitarian ideals (Bigo, 2009; Neal, 2009; Takle, 2012; Franko and Gundhus, 2015; Pallister-Wilkins, 2015; Casella Colombeau, 2017; McMahon and Sigona, 2018; Votoupalová, 2020).

The Schengen Borders Code (SBC) allows signatory states, under certain conditions, to reinstate internal border controls temporarily, and scholarly interest has increasingly been directed towards border checks at the internal borders of the Schengen area (Casella Colombeau, 2020). Previous studies have pointed out that various reasons have been invoked to justify such temporary reinstatement of controls. Since the early 2000s, most of them have been related to the hosting of important political meetings and events and generally lasted only a few days (Van der Woude and Berlo, 2015). The reinstatement of intra-Schengen controls in response to the major migratory flows into the EU in 2015 has been characterised as an EU-initiated collective securitisation of the Schengen space (Ceccorulli, 2019). During the same period, security concerns about global terrorism have also driven the reimposition of temporary border controls (Van der Woude and Berlo, 2015; Gülzau, 2021), and the Covid-19 pandemic has also recently served as justification for Member States to impose internal border controls (Wolff, Ripoll Servent and Piquet, 2020). Numerous Schengen members have expanded their use of temporary controls, retaining them for months or years. Consequently, it has been argued that the "prolongation of temporary internal border controls can be understood as the normalization of an exceptional measure legitimated through a shift from a frame of threat to a frame of risk" (Karamanidou and Kasparek, 2022, p. 2). In addition to reinstating temporary intra-Schengen controls, observers point out that Member States are also policing borders inside the Schengen area, as the SBC allows immigration and/or police checks to be carried out by national law enforcement officers (Van der Woude and Van der Leun, 2017; Van der Woude, 2020).

Another key aspect of the Schengen area is its evaluation and monitoring mechanism for monitoring and verifying that the Schengen *acquis* are being implemented in Member States. This mechanism is regarded as necessary to ensure high and uniform standards in the application of the acquis and to maintain a high level of trust between the Member States. The recommendations on addressing deficiencies identified in the evaluation reports, action plans and follow-up reports show the potential of Schengen evaluation to influence the practices of the police or border guards. As noted in the introduction, research has highlighted how evaluation processes are embedded in and shaped by norms, values, and belief systems, and organisations, institutions and stakeholders (Bjørnholt and Larsen, 2014; Raimondo, 2018; Nordesjö and Fred, 2021). It has also been noted that there may be power struggles and conflicts of interest between various stakeholders in evaluative practices (Morris and Clark, 2013; Eckhard and Jankauskas, 2020). Evaluations may also be used in a variety of ways, ranging from using their findings, knowledge and results to develop policy changes to using them to change the evaluation process itself (Alkin and Taut, 2003; Bjørnholt and Larsen, 2014). It is for this reason that evaluations may involve power relationships.

According to Nordesjö and Fred (2021), it is possible to discern how different forms of power are involved in evaluation practices, and they present three ways of thinking about evaluation and power. The first focuses on the instrumental power of evaluation. This represents the most intuitive form of power relation: evaluations, understood as value-neutral and objective scientific procedures, and their results, are intended to influence actions and decisions. However, this instrumental model has been criticised because its underlying rationale is difficult to validate (Nordesjö and Fred, 2021). The second view focuses on the power of the context of evaluations and draws attention to power dynamics created by it, and to the power to define preconditions for the evaluation processes in particular. For example, decisions about problem formulation or stakeholder involvement may affect the process or outcome of an evaluation (Nordesjö and Fred, 2021). Such influence has been described as an act of framing (Høydal, 2021). The third view focuses on performative power, with evaluations being seen as social practices that are "defined, shaped, and carried out in a social context by actors with interests and values", but that may also "shape perceptions, norms, and cognitions among actors, as well as various domains and aspects of organisations and society" (Nordesjö and Fred, 2021, p. 9). Thus, the performative aspects of the evaluation suggest evaluative practices have "the power to shape the purpose of the organisation and its activities in order to adhere to, and *perform*, the logic of the evaluation system" (Nordesjö and Fred, 2021, p. 10). These perspectives are relevant to our aim in this chapter, which is to understand the Schengen evaluation and monitoring mechanism as a form of power.

2. Research design

The empirical materials for this chapter are drawn from a larger project examining Schengen evaluation as an educational experience for the public service responsible for the main areas evaluated: the management of Schengen external borders, police cooperation, and the Schengen Information System and return (the forced return of persons illegally staying in a Schengen country) (see Ulrich, Nøkleberg and Gundhus, 2020 for a full description). This chapter uses data derived from two types of sources: (1) documentation of Schengen evaluation and (2) qualitative in-depth interviews with Norwegian police actors involved in Schengen evaluation.

The documentation consists of EU documents relating to Schengen evaluation in general, and documents concerning the four evaluations of Norway, which took place in 2000–2001, 2005, 2011–2012 and 2017. All the relevant documents were made available for the study. The recommendations resulting from evaluation reports and Council Conclusions/Council Implementing Decisions have been closely examined. Norwegian implementation reports submitted to the Schengen Evaluation Working Party or the Commission, which addressed the recommendations, have also been studied, together with documents showing how the recommendations were acted on. The main purpose of the document analysis was to explore the nature of the evaluations – especially as regards learning and enhanced professionalism. The analysis of documents was guided by one key question: To what extent did the follow-up measures actually result in the desired improvements which were declared to the Council? Can these changes be traced and documented?

To capture the experience of the participants, this chapter draws on 20 in-depth interviews with key actors in various positions in the National Police, conducted between 2017 and 2019. Those considered key actors were officials at the national level: people in the National Police Directorate (NPD), the National Criminal Investigation Service (NCIS), the Norwegian Police University College (NPUC) and the National Police Immigration Service (NPIS) – who were responsible for essential areas of Norway's participation in Schengen. Officials at various levels in the institutions discussed were interviewed. In addition, key actors were identified in some police districts – those responsible for the most important external border crossing points (BCPs) or Schengen internal borders.

The interviews covered topics such as the interviewees' experience of Schengen cooperation in general and of Schengen evaluation in particular, and their assessment of Schengen evaluation as a learning experience for the police. To facilitate analysis of the qualitative data used, the principles of thematic analysis were used (Braun and Clarke, 2006) and analytical categories and themes were identified inductively from the data. In this chapter, the analysis aims to identify overarching themes to do with police officers' experience of Schengen evaluation and its impact on police practice. The mixed-method approach taken for this research enabled there to be a comprehensive assessment of experiences and perceptions of Schengen evaluation in Norway.

3. The Schengen agreement and Schengen area

The Schengen Agreement, designed to abolish internal border control between five EU Member States, was drawn up in 1985. The five states were France, Germany, Luxembourg, Belgium and the Netherlands. The aim was to facilitate movement across internal borders, and thus support and enhance European integration and the use of the four freedoms (of persons, goods, services and capital). The agreement was an acknowledgement of the fact that border control between the five countries had become so superficial that its contribution to security and combating crime was considered minimal. It should also be noted that there had been a steep rise in the volume of cross-border traffic in Europe, and greatly increased labour mobility (Davis and Gift, 2014), which were important contributing factors to the agreement.

After the ratification of the agreement, it took five years to adopt the Convention Implementing the Schengen Agreement (CISA) in 1990, which was an intergovernmental convention regulating all the compensatory measures as well as the lifting of internal border control. The Schengen Convention came into force in 1995, and by then, Portugal and Spain had also joined. Thus, it seems that the idea of the Schengen Area quickly caught on, and when negotiations started for the new EU treaty to replace the Maastricht Treaty of 1992, it had become clear that the majority of EU Member States wished to belong to the passport-free travel zone of 'Schengen'. Following the Treaty of Amsterdam, which entered into force in 1999, the entire Schengen *acquis* became EU law. Since 1985, the Schengen area has been expanded several times and now encompasses 26 countries, of which 22 are EU Member States and four are Schengen Associated Countries. In many ways, Schengen is regarded as the quintessence of European collaboration (Davis and Gift, 2014).

4. The origin of Schengen evaluation and its evolution: from peer evaluation to super-national involvement

As noted, the Schengen Implementing Convention of 1990 set out comprehensive rules to regulate the abolition of border control within the Schengen area. In particular, these were rules for external border control on the perimeter of the area. The Schengen Information System (SIS) was part of the Convention, as was police cooperation between Schengen countries and a common visa policy. It should be noted, however, that the Implementing Convention did not establish a comprehensive monitoring and evaluation mechanism to ensure compliance with the Convention's rules and other rules based on or connected with them. Instead, as stated in Article 131 of the Convention, the Executive Committee was given overall responsibility for ensuring that the Convention was implemented correctly and was thus instrumental in laying the foundation of the evaluation mechanism later adopted.

In 1998, while Schengen cooperation was still inter-governmental and outside the EU, the Executive Committee adopted a set of rules establishing an evaluation mechanism, both for countries already belonging to Schengen and for candidate countries.[1] This led to the establishment of a 'Standing Committee on the evaluation and implementation of Schengen' – later to be known as SCH-EVAL within the EU. Its mandate was twofold: (1) to establish whether all preconditions for bringing the Convention into force in a candidate Schengen country had been fulfilled and (2) to ensure that the Schengen *acquis* was being properly applied by countries that had already implemented the Convention, by identifying shortcomings and proposing solutions. The Standing Committee was composed of high-ranking representatives from each signatory state and had considerable power to influence decisions and practice. This can be seen in the description of its tasks, which says the Standing Committee "shall draw up a report laying down a list of the criteria to be satisfied by the candidate States" and, in the case of States already applying the Convention, "shall provide the scope for detecting any problems encountered at external borders and for identifying situations which do not comply with the standard set in accordance with the spirit and objectives of the Convention".[2]

When Schengen cooperation was incorporated into the European Union in 1999, following the Treaty of Amsterdam, the Standing Committee became a Council Working Party: the Schengen Evaluation Working Party or SCH-EVAL. All the rules and procedures previously governing Schengen evaluation remained in force. The main task of SCH-EVAL was to prepare programmes for evaluations and then organise visits to Schengen countries being evaluated. Such visits were conducted by teams of experts from Schengen countries, accompanied by a representative of the General Secretariat of the Council and a Commission observer. During the evaluation visits, a 'Leading Expert' was appointed from the team. Compliance with the Schengen *acquis* was a central concern in evaluation visits, but the teams also attempted to identify best or good practice, which could help develop common standards in the various fields covered by Schengen cooperation. Procedure for the visits was based on the principle of full transparency. This meant that the country being evaluated could not deny access to any site or space, any documents or any personnel the evaluators wanted to talk to when they were checking routines or testing skills and knowledge. No superior officer could intervene to answer a question directed to a subordinate, nor could answers given be corrected subsequently. The answer given by the person directly addressed by the evaluators was to go into the report unchanged. An important implication of the principle of full transparency is that it compels everyone to prepare themselves properly for visits – which can be both a motivation for learning and a source of power. With its ambitions to improve practice and develop common standards, the Schengen evaluation mechanism is an instrumental use of evaluation: the evaluative practices are designed to improve the evaluand (Nordesjö and Fred, 2021). Such an understanding of evaluation is often inspired by models of rational or learning organisations, although these have been criticised for ignoring the presence of institutional norms, routines and belief systems (Raimondo, 2018).

From the outset, the evaluation and monitoring procedure was based on peer evaluation, a principle which follows naturally from the core idea of Schengen – the necessity for mutual trust between Member States, as each country is responsible for safeguarding its external borders on behalf of all the other Schengen countries.

Police and border experts from all the Schengen countries evaluated each other under the leadership of the working group (SCH-EVAL), which consisted of representatives from all participating states and was chaired by the EU Presidency country and supported by a secretariat. Following an evaluation, the evaluation team drafted a report, a finalised version of which was distributed to all Schengen states, ahead of discussion of it in SCH-EVAL. After this discussion, draft Council conclusions containing the main recommendations were developed. The role of the Council was to give final approval to the recommendations resulting from the evaluation, but obviously the process of peer evaluation could influence the Council Conclusions, as each report was discussed in SCH-EVAL. This can be understood as a soft form of political power, foregrounding the common project and the protection of the autonomy of national states (Fjørtoft, 2022). As we will show in greater detail later, this form of peer evaluation became a more technocratic form of power, after the changes in the evaluation mechanism adopted in 2013 and implemented and made operational in 2015.

The first country to be evaluated under this procedure was Greece, in 1999. The five Nordic countries (Norway, Sweden, Denmark, Iceland and Finland) were next in 2000–2001. They joined Schengen as a group, even though Iceland and Norway were not EU Member States but admitted under special conditions, as Schengen Associated Countries (SACs). In 2007, nine more EU Member States joined Schengen, after being evaluated in 2006–2007. Switzerland joined in 2008 and Liechtenstein in 2011, both as SACs.

The Schengen evaluation procedure continued to develop, especially after 2007, when the evaluations of the nine latest countries to join Schengen were fresh in people's minds. Lessons were clearly learnt during this period, which resulted in a thorough review of working methods, to make the evaluation system more efficient, fair and transparent, while ensuring equal treatment for all countries – both old and new Schengen members.[3] Evaluation teams became more professional, and training programmes were developed. Evaluation reports focused more on areas which needed improvement. There was also more scrutiny of follow-up processes. The contextual conditions of Schengen evaluation were changing, which had the potential to affect both the process itself and its results.

The 2009 Lisbon Treaty brought about a major change in the mechanism by giving the European Commission the right to formally propose new legislation in the areas of Justice and Home Affairs. The Commission immediately launched a proposal to reform Schengen evaluation, with the aim of strengthening follow-up on Council recommendations. It was proposed that the Commission should take the lead in evaluation processes. It should be noted that Member States were eager to preserve their influence in these, to balance that of the Commission, and there was a strong desire to retain as much of the principle of peer evaluation as possible. One interviewee said:

> The Schengen states' delegates to SCH-EVAL argued strongly in favour of preserving as much of Member States' authority as possible at crucial points in the evaluation process. And they succeeded: The Council would still be

the body competent to decide on recommendations, with SCH-EVAL as its advisory body.

(No 20)

Striking a balance of power between the Commission, the Union's executive branch, and the Member States represented in the Council and its subordinate bodies has always been a feature of the EU.

After lengthy discussion, the Regulation to reform Schengen evaluation was finally adopted by the Council in October 2013 and made operational in 2015 as the new Schengen Evaluation and Monitoring Mechanism (SEMM).[4] The most significant change was that the Commission took the main responsibility for planning, programming and selecting evaluation teams. Previously, these tasks had been performed by SCH-EVAL, chaired by the Presidency country and supported by the Council Secretariat. The new mechanism sets out clearer rules for reports, recommendations and follow-up to identified deficiencies. Close monitoring of the implementation of recommendations is another key feature. Each Schengen country is now evaluated every five years. In addition, unannounced and thematic evaluations are conducted to monitor compliance with the Schengen *acquis* in critical areas.

Although changes resulted from the reform of the Schengen evaluation regime in 2013, whereby the Commission took the leading role, core features of peer evaluation were still preserved and considered crucial to the mechanism. Evaluators continue to be nominated by the Schengen states, and each on-site team has two leading experts, one from the Commission and one from a Schengen state. Parity in evaluation visits and reporting is thus ensured, and the principle of peer evaluation is maintained at these stages of the evaluation process. The Council also retains its power to decide on the recommendations, assisted by the working group (SCH-EVAL), as before. The Council's role is to strengthen mutual trust, ensure better coordination at the European level and reinforce peer pressure and solidarity.[5] The Commission's role is however strengthened by its having responsibility for planning, programming and selecting evaluation teams, which can influence the character of the evaluation process. The Commission now has a stronger mandate to make plans and carry them out than it had in the former system, which was based entirely on peer evaluation. It has been suggested that the new evaluation mechanism seeks to be a more neutral approach (Kaasik and Tong, 2019) than the previous intergovernmental and peer-evaluation model.

Two new areas for evaluation were added by the Regulation – return and readmission and the abolition of controls on internal borders. Integrated Border Management (IBM), as a governance model, itself became subject to evaluation – along with the three border evaluations. This area of evaluation (borders and IBM) is now called management of external borders. In all evaluations, the functioning of the authorities that apply the Schengen *acquis* will now be subjected to scrutiny.

Schengen evaluation has become an ever more complex exercise involving mutual inspection and assessment; it involves many common regulations and standards, is supervised at the supra-national level of the EU (by the Commission and Council jointly), and is supported by non-penal sanctions and interventions. There is a strong element of competition between Schengen countries. After peer evaluation, they all want 'good grades' and strive to get them. There is thus peer pressure as well as peer evaluation. Schengen evaluation is also a continuous process. There is hardly any interval between the follow-up procedures and the start of preparations for the next evaluation.

Schengen evaluation is thus changing its form of power, from being just a system to check compliance with the Schengen *acquis* and observe best practices among peers, to being a way of assessing the Member States' application of broadly based principles pertaining to border control and border security strategy. It is now a more stringent test of the competence of personnel undergoing Schengen evaluation, and those administering it are more highly trained.

5. Community of practice – perceptions of Schengen evaluation

We will now show how different types of evaluation mechanism were perceived and enacted, taking empirical examples from the case of Schengen evaluation of Norway, which has been evaluated four times. After evaluation prior to joining Schengen, evaluations took place there in 2005, 2011–2012 and 2017. As the previous description shows, the numerous actors involved in Schengen evaluation do not operate in isolation. In fact, evaluation can be understood as a 'community of practice', which Wenger (1998) defines as groups of people who share a concern or a passion for a topic and where these individuals deepen their knowledge through regular interaction with each other.

As a Schengen Associated Country (SAC), from the start of its participation in Schengen Norway had the right to nominate police and border guards for evaluation visit duty. Prior to formally becoming a SAC, as part of implementation preparations (in 2000), Norwegian police officers took part in evaluation visits in order to gain an insight into Schengen requirements. The National Police Directorate of Norway soon saw the benefits of such participation: increased learning and better skills could be gained from studying other countries and Norway could be better prepared for evaluation and for training colleagues at the national level. In addition, it was important for Norway to demonstrate that, operationally, an associated Schengen country was on an equal footing with the EU Member States. Since the early 2000s, Norway has regularly participated in Schengen evaluation visits. A pool of Schengen evaluators was established, comprising experts in all areas of evaluation, including visa and data protection. Over the years, Schengen evaluation training courses have been extensively utilised to build up and renew the pool of experts. The National Police Directorate, NCIS, the National Police ICT Services, the National Police Immigration Service and several police districts with important external borders have members that belong to this pool.

The pool continues to be widely used under the evaluation mechanism adopted in 2013. In 2010, 13 evaluators took part, and this increased to 18 in 2015–2016. By the summer of 2018, the pool consisted of 32 experts, including representatives of the Data Protection Authority, the Ministry of Foreign Affairs and the Directorate of Immigration. An evaluator generally participates in two or more evaluations. Numerous interviewees stressed the importance of having such a pool of evaluators, as is illustrated by this description:

> You get a clear understanding of what is required and expected – what standard to aim at. And you make many personal contacts. We learn about good solutions from each other. We also see that we are not alone in having deficiencies.
>
> (No 3)

As a result, several Norwegian evaluators have built up considerable personal experience, with the potential for learning effects which can be utilised in their own practice. Establishing a network across Schengen countries is also considered of great importance, and networking between experts has been identified as a positive effect (Kaasik and Tong, 2019).

Many key actors interviewed for this study spoke of the new professionalism and thoroughness now displayed by Schengen evaluators. Evaluation teams are thus judged to have become more professional, with evaluators' qualifications now being scrutinised by the Commission prior to selection, and continuity being maintained within the teams as far as possible. One interviewee perceived these improvements:

> The quality of Schengen evaluation has improved since 2005. Back then there were no requirements concerning evaluators' qualifications. Since 2011, a lot has been learnt in Brussels, from good and bad experiences of evaluation visits. Now there are very competent evaluators.
>
> (No 12)

In Norway, each of the last three evaluations has clearly been more thorough than the one preceding it, and those being evaluated are subjected to closer scrutiny, especially since the adoption in 2013 of the procedure that came into operational effect in 2015. Professionalism has been enhanced: regular participation in the evaluation processes has led to the development of an 'evaluation culture', based on common training, personal relationships and mutual trust. Many evaluation teams became close-knit units, carrying out evaluation visits over several years to various countries. The development of an evaluation culture indicates the performative power of evaluation procedures. Schengen evaluation has become a continuous process which is to some extent circular (it consists of an initial questionnaire – evaluation visits – evaluation reports – recommendations to remedy deficiencies – action plans – assessment – reporting on progress – and then preparation for the next round). This fact can lead the police to shape their aims and activities to adhere to, and even carry out the logic of the evaluation system (Nordesjö and Fred, 2021).

However, evaluation cycles with no intervals between them may lead to what scholars have characterised as the 'performance paradox', in which "organisations and individuals learn how their performance is measured (and how it is not)" and as a result "they can put all effort into what is measured, and performance will go up" (Nordesjö and Fred, 2021, p. 6). In the case of Schengen evaluation, a Member State may find out what performance and measurement indicators are used and adapt their practice to do well in the evaluation. In Norway, preparations for the evaluation processes can be traced back to the first evaluation in 2000–2001. As we have seen, preparation increased and became more thorough following each successive evaluation. For example, in the 2005 evaluation, it consisted of selecting sites for evaluation visits, drawing up the schedule and organising the logistics, with some local preparations and rehearsals. By 2011–2012, preparations had become more detailed: they included pre-inspections by project personnel once the sites to be evaluated had been determined, to check on-site preparations and test knowledge and skills. Preparation for the 2017 evaluation was yet more comprehensive: the Nordic sites that were going to be visited worked together and carried out pre-evaluations, with Swedish and Danish evaluators working in Norway, and vice versa. The pre-evaluations were conducted as if a real Schengen evaluation visit was being carried out and were considered very worthwhile by numerous interviewees. One of them said:

> The pre-evaluation visits were modelled on real visits. Concrete feedback was given – things which needed to be corrected before the real evaluation.
> (No 9)

What this indicates is that considerable effort is made by the Norwegian police to meet evaluation criteria and perform well. It also points to effects which can be understood as processes of self-regulation or self-government. In evaluation research, it has been argued that such a Foucauldian-inspired understanding of power (i.e. governmentality arrangements producing self-governing subjects (Lemke, 2002)) means that the evaluand starts "operating in a certain way because they are aware *that* (and often even *how*) their practices will be measured and assessed" (Nordesjö and Fred, 2021, p. 6). One interviewee put it like this: "Evaluation is a kind of exam: it's assessment, measurement. . . . One psychs oneself up beforehand, preparing, planning and looking for weaknesses to 'close the gaps' and remedy weak spots" (No 5). Thus, inherent to the Schengen evaluation mechanism is the pressure to become self-regulating subjects adhering to the rules of the game.

6. Frontex vulnerability assessments – more powerful evaluations

Since 2015, there has been a widespread perception that the Schengen area is under constant threat, which has led to the ending of free movement across internal borders:

> Several terrorist attacks, the arrival of elevated numbers of irregular migrants at the EU's external borders as a consequence of the 2015 refugee crisis and more recently the outbreak of the COVID-19 pandemic have led to the reintroduction of internal border controls some of which are still in place today.
> (COM(2020) 779: 17)[6]

During this period, unannounced evaluations with more detailed rules became more important, marking a turn away from the peer evaluation learning approach. The growth of the Schengen area, the increased number of Schengen states, migratory pressure and the increasing importance of risk analysis are put forward as justifications for unannounced evaluations. In COM(2020) 779, the reason given is the change in the environment since the creation of the Schengen *acquis*. Powers to protect the border have been enhanced and have become more repressive (Hartwig, 2020). Since 2015, the Commission has recommended that Frontex might be granted a right to intervene, an idea that was not adopted. However, the revised article 8(1) in the Regulation (EU) 2016/1624[7] sets out a greatly expanded array of operational tasks for the Agency, and in 2019 these powers to protect the border were considerably increased (Hartwig, 2020). The most significant development is the creation of the European Border and Coast Guard uniformed Standing Corps of 10,000 operational staff,[8] which makes it possible for the agency to intervene more independently. Eurosur was also formally incorporated into the regulation of Frontex (Regulation (EU) 2019/1896)). Frontex no longer merely coordinates and supports Member States but has become an operational agency combating crime and changed its name to the European Border and Coast Guard Agency. Frontex has also become an observer of evaluation visits.

In 2016, SCH-EVAL was complemented by vulnerability assessment, conducted by Frontex. A vulnerability assessment network (VAN) comprising all Schengen states[9] provides assessments and recommendations of measures to be taken, thus increasing the extension of the Schengen control system. It is important to note that these assessments are concerned with the vulnerability of the border, not the vulnerability of human beings crossing it (Franko and Gundhus, 2015). Recommendations from these two sources can be mutually reinforcing. Schengen states must coordinate their replies to the Schengen questionnaire with an assessment of their national vulnerability provided to Frontex.[10] Frontex has thus now taken a much more important part in evaluations of the border (COM (2020) 779 final).

The new evaluation procedures, particularly the vulnerability assessments, appear a technical, neutral way of framing evaluations. According to Rijpma (2016), VAN is presented as purely technical – relying exclusively on objective data to identify operational weaknesses – in contrast to the more politicised previous Schengen Evaluation Mechanism, which relied more on peer-evaluation (see also Deleixhe and Duez, 2019). As argued by Fjørtoft (2022, p. 564): "Vulnerability assessment seems like a device to increase the legitimacy of the intervention mechanism and not simply a fact-finding device". Any failure to comply with the Agency's recommendation may, according to the logic, lead to a European intervention, making vulnerability assessments more effective tools to monitor states' border practices. The technical neutrality of the evaluation can also make it a more powerful political tool, which is justified by scientific objectivity and quantified indicators (Fjørtoft, 2022). In many ways, this highlights the performative power of evaluation as social practice. Technical neutrality gives the assessment a scientific aura, which shapes the aims of the organisation and the way it adheres to and performs the logic of evaluation systems (Nordesjö and Fred, 2021, p. 9).

Risk analysis as part of border control was initiated by EU Member States in 2002, and further confirmed in the Schengen Borders Code (Horii, 2016). It was operationalised as Common Integrated Risk Analysis Methodology (CIRAM), by Finland with nine other Member States (Belgium, Denmark, France, Germany, the Netherlands, Norway, Spain, Sweden and the UK), and the ad-hoc Risk Analysis Centre was set up in Helsinki. When Frontex was established in 2004, the Risk Analysis centre became part of Frontex, whose mandate was to develop and apply CIRAM. Frontex was given the important role of providing risk analyses on external borders, and these analyses also helped to determine where and when Schengen evaluations should be carried out. As Andersson (2014) argues, Frontex thought work is political in that it influences EU policymakers' perceptions (and policies), resource allocation and Member States' access to funding; it also defines the rationale and justifications for its own operations (see also Horii, 2016). Risk assessment aims to collect data by interviewing migrants and from other sources – not only aggregated data but also more and more personal data, which then feeds back into risk assessment because of the data collected and various types of subsequent evaluation (Gundhus, 2018). Risk analysis, therefore, reveals understandings of what security is, how it is threatened, and what solutions are necessary and appropriate (Horii, 2016). Risk analysis of the external border has been an important instrument for proposing activities and operations. From the beginning, the Risk Analysis Centre also has collaborated with EU's other intelligence agencies such as Europol.

Vulnerability assessments, by contrast, are designed as highly quantitative procedures relying on technical expertise to make them more powerful as objective scientific assessments. The CIRAM methodology, where risk is seen as a function of threat, vulnerability and impact, is mostly concerned with risk analysis of the external border and relies on a combination of qualitative methodology and more quantitative risk indicators (Paul, 2017; Gundhus, 2018; Fjørtoft, 2022). Fjørtoft (2022) argues that these risk analyses are more political than scientific expertise, since it states that "the main sources for measuring the magnitude and likelihood of the threats are intelligence, historical analysis, and expert judgement" (Frontex, 2012, p. 23). In principle, CIRAM's estimates can be reasonably accurate, however, it can be argued that "[i]n practice, a high level of assurance in measuring vulnerability is not warranted" (Frontex, 2012, p. 28). This being so, Fjørtoft (2022, p. 563) argues that "while the model is not devoid of statistical indicators, it is sceptical about relying too much on them". This approach has been changed by the implementation of the Vulnerability Assessment, which is a central component of the right to intervene:

> If a member state does not comply with the Vulnerability Assessment recommendations, or faces "disproportionate migratory pressures at the external borders," Frontex would be mandated to deploy European Border and Coast Guard Teams to the member state in question – even against the member state's will.
>
> (European Commission, 2015b, Article 18) (Fjørtoft, 2022, p. 564)

The appeal to technical expertise has therefore helped legitimise increasing the power not only of the Frontex agency but also of Schengen as a criminal justice instrument.

7. Intra-Schengen border management of EU nationals – the Norwegian case

As noted earlier, one of the main objectives of the Schengen *acquis* was to remove systematic border control between the participating states. However, as Van der Woude (2020) observes, under the Schengen Agreement, this does not mean the end of the monitoring of cross-border mobility or expulsions of EEA (European Economic Area) nationals. On the contrary, it involves a significant increase in international police cooperation, including special operations and cross-border cooperation between police forces, together with the deportation of irregular migrants. Police capabilities have also been widened by the exchange of data (such as fingerprints, DNA, vehicles) between police authorities (Van der Woude, 2020).

The tension between the ideal of free movement intra-Schengen and sovereignty practices peaked during the so-called migration crisis in 2015. As we have seen, this led to the re-introduction of border checks at the physical borders between Schengen states, and to the proliferation of the use of article 23 of the Schengen Borders Code, which "allows immigration and/or police checks to be carried out by national law enforcement agencies in border areas" (Van der Woude, 2020, p. 111).

In Norwegian Immigration law, it is made clear that EEA citizens in Norway have greater protection from being deported to another Schengen country than those with non-Schengen citizenship – the third-country nationals. Although EEA citizens have the right to freedom of movement, there are also grounds on which expulsion can take place of which the most common is that a person has committed a crime, such as a crime of violence or a drug or sexual offence.[11] It must also be decided if public order or safety is threatened, and "this condition will normally be met as long as a criminal offence has been committed".[12] Assessments of the future risk of the person committing further criminal offences will also be considered; if the EEA national has a family in Norway, this is weighed against the consequences for the family in a proportionality assessment.

National Police Immigration Service statistics show that one-third of forced returns are convicted offenders.[13] The most common nationalities among returned convicted offenders have been East Europeans. In 2022, according to UDI statistics,[14] the most common convicted returnees were Romanian (19%), Polish (14%) and Lithuanian (11%). These figures have been much the same for some years: in 2016 the most common such returnees were from Romania (16%), Poland (14%) and Lithuania (11%).

As the number of migrants grew during 2015–2016, a major concern was the failure to introduce a comprehensive registration procedure, which impacted the identification and protection of vulnerable asylum seekers (Boysen and Viblemo, 2018; Gundhus, 2021). As Gundhus (2021) argues, the introduction of simplified procedures, together with the general sense of crisis, led to tighter territorial control in Norway (Immigration Law §21). Ordinary police and regulatory actors were tasked with it, and this led to various combinations of border control and traditional law-enforcement rationalities, methods and objectives (Gundhus, 2020). Immigration law and criminal law were combined to determine who should be put under scrutiny. Minor offences and fines were used by the police districts as triggers for deportation processes, particularly as regards EU nationals. Police patrols were ordered to prioritise monitoring and ensuring migrants' compliance with the conditions of their residence permits, and greater efforts were made to check their identity and legal situation by concentrating on passports and false documents and making arrests for petty crimes such as shoplifting (Gundhus, 2017; Franko, 2020).

Pre-arrival policing therefore went hand in hand with checking people already in Norway (Gundhus, 2021). This particularly affected people from EEA countries who were guilty of minor offences and antisocial behaviour such as begging (see also Franko, 2020). The police rely on 'creative thinking' as well as coercive measures available to deal with such people (Aas, 2014; Gundhus and Franko, 2016). These include arrest and remand in custody, searches of personal belongings or dwellings, and surveillance and tracking of people's networks.

This results in the detection of minor offences and fines for disorderly conduct. In Norway, as in France, Sweden and the UK (Franko, 2020), this means that Eastern Europeans (usually after they have been in prison) are prime candidates for expulsion, whether they are from EU countries or not (see more in Franko, 2020, pp. 118–162). The focus of the Norwegian Operation Migrant[15] on asylum seekers therefore was to support existing orders that patrols should combine immigration law with criminal law to achieve high deportation targets. Efforts to control those coming from third countries outside Schengen have, in practice, turned into intra-Schengen control efforts targeting Eastern Europeans. This can be explained by the general political situation, which features strict immigration policies and strenuous efforts to deport foreign nationals and convicted EEA citizens.

The use of penal power that leads to the social production of the crimmigrant other justifies these practices in a welfare state (Franko, 2020). Using immigration law to target potential criminals goes beyond the intention of the law. Various processes inside and outside the country make migration a penal subject. The penal welfarism described by Barker (2018) is also affected by dynamic interactions with external processes separate from the internal logic of the welfare state. This move towards criminalising migrants chimes with the upgrading of the European border guard service to make Frontex even more of a law enforcement tool for detecting and fighting cross-border crime (Franko, 2020; Van der Woude, 2020).

Conclusions: from peer pressure to technocracy?

In this chapter, we have approached evaluations as social practices that are defined, shaped and conducted in a social context by actors that have varying interests and values, and where these practices shape actors' values, perceptions and norms (Nordesjö and Fred, 2021). Since epistemic and political approaches to evaluations overlap, we have analysed to what degree each type of approach is found in the evaluations, and the interactions and tensions between them.

We have shown that the development of evaluation culture increases the performative power of evaluation procedures. The fact that Schengen evaluation has become a continuous process shows that it can shape the aim of the police and their activities to adhere to, and even perform, the logic of the evaluation system (Nordesjö and Fred, 2021). However, unbroken evaluation cycles may lead to what has been characterised as the 'performance paradox', where organisations and individuals under evaluation find out how their performance is measured and put all their effort into meeting those requirements, to do well in the evaluation (Nordesjö and Fred, 2021). As has been pointed out, preparation for Schengen evaluation is a common practice.

Nordesjö and Fred (2021) show how different forms of power are part of evaluation practices, and they offer three perspectives to capture different ways of thinking about evaluation and power. The first looks at the instrumental power of evaluation. The second captures the contextual power of evaluations and draws attention to power dynamics related to the conditions surrounding evaluation, particularly the power to set preconditions for the process. The third is the performative power whereby evaluations are considered social practices that are 'defined, shaped, and carried out in a social context by actors with interests and values', but that at the same time may also "shape perceptions, norms, and cognitions among actors, as well as various domains and aspects of organisations and society" (Nordesjö and Fred, 2021, p. 9). In this chapter, the second and third perspectives of evaluation as power have been foregrounded. The analysis shows the importance of contextual aspects, as these have exerted pressure to change the old peer review system to standardised Schengen evaluations. One explanation for this is that the soft power system failed to achieve its aim once external pressure on the borders increased and affected the practice of free internal movement. However, we have also shown the importance of understanding the performative power of evaluations, whereby evaluation shapes organisational logics and justifies more technocratic expertise, at the expense of political power.

The three approaches to evaluation as power also conceptualise and theorise expertise differently. Fjørtoft's (2022) analysis of approaches to expertise in Schengen has been important here. He argues that expertise can be used either for its problem-solving function, in line with the instrumental power of evaluation, or politically; he points out that language, self-presentation, and signalling may be a source of authority and legitimacy. These are two contrasting approaches – political and epistemic – to the appeal of expertise. In the past, the EU and its agencies have been able to present themselves as technical and apolitical in order to claim legitimacy. Traditionally, Schengen evaluations relied less on technical expertise and foregrounded trust and peer to peer evaluations. Although this type of expertise, based more on experience than on scientific knowledge, can be used strategically to increase legitimacy through SCH-EVAL as a common project, it might be argued that the technical and scientific approach of the vulnerability assessment – paradoxically – is more in line with symbolic uses of expertise, which in a powerful way facilitates the right to intervene.

Notes

1 Decision of the Executive Committee of 16 September 1998 setting up a Standing Committee on the evaluation and implementation of Schengen – SCH/Com-ex (98) 26 rev def (at: EUR-Lex - 41998D0026 - EN - EUR-Lex (europa.eu))
2 Decision of the Executive Committee of 16 September 1998 setting up a Standing Committee on the evaluation and implementation of Schengen – SCH/Com-ex (98) 26 rev def (at: EUR-Lex - 41998D0026 - EN - EUR-Lex (europa.eu))
3 Council Conclusions on the legacy of Schengen evaluation within the Council and its future role and responsibilities under the new mechanism, Doc. No. 14374/1/14 REV1 LIMITED (at: 146074.pdf (europa.eu))
4 Council Regulation (EU) No 1053/2013 of 7 October 2013. The European Parliament (EP) was consulted, but the Regulation fell outside the remit of co-decision Council – EP (at: EUR-Lex - 32013R1053 - EN - EUR-Lex (europa.eu))
5 Council Regulation (EU) No 1053/2013 of 7 October 2013, recital 11 (at: EUR-Lex - 32013R1053 - EN - EUR-Lex (europa.eu))
6 Report from the Commission to the Council and the European Parliament on the Functioning of the Schengen Evaluation and Monitoring Mechanism pursuant to Article 22 of Council Regulation (EU) No 1053/2013 First Multiannual Evaluation Programme (2015–2019). COM/2020/779 final (at: EUR-Lex - 52020DC0779 - EN - EUR-Lex (europa.eu))
7 Regulation (EU) 2016/1624 of the European Parliament and of the Council of 14 September 2016 on the European Border and Coast Guard and amending Regulation (EU) 2016/399 of the European Parliament and of the Council and repealing Regulation (EC) No 863/2007 of the European Parliament and of the Council, Council Regulation (EC) No 2007/2004 and Council Decision 2005/267/EC (at: EUR-Lex - 32016R1624 - EN - EUR-Lex (europa.eu))
8 The standing corps should be composed of four categories of operational staff, namely statutory staff, staff seconded to the Agency by the Member States for a long term, staff provided by Member States for short-term deployments and staff forming part of the reserve for rapid reaction for rapid border interventions. Operational staff should consist of border guards, return escorts, return specialists and other relevant staff. The standing corps should be deployed in the framework of teams. The actual number of operational staff deployed from the standing corps should depend on operational needs. (Regulation (EU) 2019/1896 (58).
9 Regulation (EU) 2016/1624 of the European Parliament and of the Council of 14 September 2016 on the European Border and Coast Guard (at: EUR-Lex - 32016R1624 - EN - EUR-Lex (europa.eu)). A new Regulation on the European Border and Coast Guard was adopted in October 2019 (Regulation (EU) 2019/1896) and replaced the Regulation (EU) 2016/1624.
10 Interviews No 1 and 9.
11 www.une.no/en/case-types-and-countries/eea-cases/
12 www.une.no/en/case-types-and-countries/eea-cases/
13 www.politiet.no/om-politiet/dokumenter-strategier-og-horinger/dokumenter/?aktivFane=tema&enhet=1234&tema=35&side=2
14 www.une.no/en/case-types-and-countries/eea-cases/
15 Following the so-called migration crisis in Europe in 2015, the Norwegian police implemented Operation Migrant, which was the first national intelligence-led policing project, with the aim to predict crime challenges concerning increased migration to improve future resource allocation (Gundhus and Jansen, 2020).

References

Aas, K.F. (2011) '"Crimmigrant" bodies and bona fide travelers: Surveillance, citizenship and global governance', *Theoretical Criminology*, 15(3), pp. 331–346. Available at: https://doi.org/doi:10.1177/1362480610396643.

Aas, K.F. (2014) 'Bordered penality: Precarious membership and abnormal justice', *Punishment & Society*, 16(5), pp. 520–541. Available at: https://doi.org/10.1177/1462474514548807.

Alkin, M., & Taut, S. (2003) 'Unbundling evaluation use', *Studies in Educational Evaluation*, 29(1), pp. 1–12.

Andersson, R. (2014) *Illegality, Inc.: Clandestine Migration and the Business of Bordering Europe*. Oakland, CA: University of California Press.

Barker, V. (2018) *Nordic Nationalism and Penal Order: Walling the Welfare State*. London: Routledge.

Bigo, D. (2009) 'Immigration controls and free movement in Europe', *International Review of the Red Cross*, 91(875), pp. 579–591. Available at: https://doi.org/10.1017/S1816383109990385.

Bjørnholt, B. and Larsen, F. (2014) 'The politics of performance measurement: "Evaluation use as mediator for politics"', *Evaluation*, 20(4), pp. 400–411. Available at: https://doi.org/10.1177/1356389014551485.

Börzel, T.A. and Risse, T. (2018) 'From the euro to the Schengen crises: European integration theories, politicization, and identity politics', *Journal of European Public Policy*, 25(1), pp. 83–108. Available at: https://doi.org/10.1080/13501763.2017.1310281.

Bovens, M., Hart, P. and Kuipers, S. (2008) 'The Politics of Policy Evaluation', in R.E. Goodin, M. Moran, and M. Rein (eds) *The Oxford Handbook of Public Policy*. Oxford: Oxford University Press. Available at: https://doi.org/10.1093/oxfordhb/9780199548453.003.0015.

Boysen, K.R. and Viblemo, T.E. (2018) *The Changing Influx of Asylum Seekers in 2014–2016, Norway's Response*. Kristiansand: Oxford Research.

Braun, V. and Clarke, V. (2006) 'Using thematic analysis in psychology', *Qualitative Research in Psychology*, 3(2), pp. 77–101. Available at: https://doi.org/10.1191/1478088706qp063oa.

Casella Colombeau, S. (2017) 'Policing the internal Schengen borders – managing the double bind between free movement and migration control', *Policing and Society*, 27(5), pp. 480–493. Available at: https://doi.org/10.1080/10439463.2015.1072531.

Casella Colombeau, S. (2020) 'Crisis of Schengen? The effect of two "migrant crises" (2011 and 2015) on the free movement of people at an internal Schengen border', *Journal of Ethnic and Migration Studies*, 46(11), pp. 2258–2274. Available at: https://doi.org/10.1080/1369183X.2019.1596787.

Ceccorulli, M. (2019) 'Back to Schengen: The collective securitisation of the EU free-border area', *West European Politics*, 42(2), pp. 302–322. Available at: https://doi.org/10.1080/01402382.2018.1510196.

Cooper, A. (2015) 'Where are Europe's new borders? Ontology, methodology and framing', *Journal of Contemporary European Studies*, 23(4), pp. 447–458. Available at: https://doi.org/10.1080/14782804.2015.1101266.

Davis, D. and Gift, T. (2014) 'The positive effects of the Schengen agreement on European Trade', *The World Economy*, 37(11), pp. 1541–1557. Available at: https://doi.org/10.1111/twec.12158.

Deleixhe, M. and Duez, D. (2019) 'The new European border and coast guard agency: Pooling sovereignty or giving it up?', *Journal of European Integration*, 41(7), pp. 921–936. Available at: https://doi.org/10.1080/07036337.2019.1665659.

Eckhard, S. and Jankauskas, V. (2020) 'Explaining the political use of evaluation in international organizations', *Policy Sciences*, 53(4), pp. 667–695. Available at: https://doi.org/10.1007/s11077-020-09402-2.

Engelbert, J., Awad, I. and Van Sterkenburg, J. (2019) 'Everyday practices and the (un)making of "Fortress Europe": Introduction to the special issue', *European Journal of Cultural Studies*, 22(2), pp. 133–143. Available at: https://doi.org/10.1177/1367549418823055.

Fijnaut, C. (2015) 'The refugee crisis: The end of Schengen?', *European Journal of Crime, Criminal Law and Criminal Justice*, 23(4), pp. 313–332. Available at: https://doi.org/10.1163/15718174-23032076.

Fjørtoft, T.N. (2022) 'More power, more control: The legitimizing role of expertise in Frontex after the refugee crisis', *Regulation & Governance*, 16(2), pp. 557–571. Available at: https://doi.org/10.1111/rego.12373.

Franko, K. (2020) *The Crimmigrant Other: Migration and Penal Power*. Abingdon: Routledge.

Franko, K. and Gundhus, H.O.I. (2015) 'Policing humanitarian borderlands: Frontex, human rights and the precariousness of life', *British Journal of Criminology*, 55(1), pp. 1–18. Available at: https://doi.org/10.1093/bjc/azu086.

Frontex. (2012) *Common Integrated Risk Analysis Model: A Comprehensive Update*. Warsaw: Frontex.

Gülzau, F. (2021) 'A "new normal" for the Schengen area. When, where and why member states reintroduce temporary border controls?', *Journal of Borderlands Studies*. Epub ahead of print. Online on 17 November 2021. Available at: https://doi.org/10.1080/08865655.2021.1996260.

Gundhus, H.O.I. (2017) 'Discretion as an obstacle: Police culture, change, and governance in a Norwegian context', *Policing: A Journal of Policy and Practice*, 11(3), pp. 258–272. Available at: https://doi.org/10.1093/police/pax012.

Gundhus, H.O.I. (2018) 'Negotiating risks and threats: Securing the border through the lens of intelligence', in N. Fyfe, H.O.I. Gundhus, and K.V. Rønn (eds) *Moral Issues in Intelligence-led Policing*. London: Routledge.

Gundhus, H.O.I. (2020) 'Sorting out welfare: Crimmigration practices and abnormal justice in Norway', in M. Van der Woude and R. Koulish (eds) *Crimmigrant Nations: Resurgent Nationalism and the Closing of Borders*. New York: Fordham University Press, pp. 249–278.

Gundhus, H.O.I. (2021) 'Shaping migrants as threats: Multilayered discretion, criminalization, and risk assessment tools', *International Journal for Crime, Justice and Social Democracy*, 10(3), pp. 56–71. Available at: https://doi.org/10.5204/ijcjsd.2041.

Gundhus, H.O.I. and Franko, K. (2016) 'Global policing and mobility: Identity, territory, sovereignty', in B. Bradford et al. (eds) *The SAGE Handbook of Global Policing*. London: SAGE.

Gundhus, H.O.I. and Jansen, P.T. (2020) 'Pre-crime and policing of migrants: Anticipatory action meets management of concerns', *Theoretical Criminology*, 24(1), pp. 90–109. Available at: https://doi.org/10.1177/1362480619873347.

Hartwig, S. (2020) 'Frontex: From coordinating controls to combating crime', *Eucrim – The European Criminal Law Associations' Forum*, 4.

Hoerner, J.M. (2019) 'Adding fuel to the flames? Politicisation of EU Policy evaluation in national parliaments', *Politische Vierteljahresschrift*, 60(4), pp. 805–821. Available at: https://doi.org/10.1007/s11615-019-00213-6.

Horii, S. (2016) 'The effect of Frontex's risk analysis on the European border controls', *European Politics and Society*, 17(2), pp. 242–258. Available at: https://doi.org/10.1080/23745118.2016.1121002.

Høydal, Ø.S. (2021) 'Evaluation, framing and power', *Scandinavian Journal of Public Administration*, 25(3/4), pp. 137–153.

Huysmans, J. (2006) *The Politics of Insecurity: Fear, Migration and Asylum in the EU*. London: Routledge.

Kaasik, J. and Tong, S. (2019) 'The Schengen evaluation mechanism: Exploring the views of experts in the field of police cooperation', *European Law Enforcement Research Bulletin*, (18), pp. 1–18.

Karamanidou, L. and Kasparek, B. (2022) 'From exceptional threats to normalized risks: Border controls in the Schengen area and the governance of secondary movements of migration', *Journal of Borderlands Studies*, 37(3), 623–643. Available at: https://doi.org/10.1080/08865655.2020.1824680.

Lemke, T. (2002) 'Foucault, governmentality, and critique', *Rethinking Marxism*, 14(3), pp. 49–64. Available at: https://doi.org/10.1080/089356902101242288.

Mathiesen, T. (1997) *Schengen: Politisamarbeid, overvåking og rettssikkerhet i Europa*. Oslo: Spartacus forlag.

McMahon, S. and Sigona, N. (2018) 'Navigating the central Mediterranean in a time of "crisis": Disentangling migration governance and migrant journeys', *Sociology*, 52(3), pp. 497–514. Available at: https://doi.org/10.1177/0038038518762082.

Morris, M. and Clark, B. (2013) 'You want me to do what? Evaluators and the pressure to misrepresent findings', *American Journal of Evaluation*, 34(1), pp. 57–70. Available at: https://doi.org/10.1177/1098214012457237.

Neal, A.W. (2009) 'Securitization and risk at the EU border: The origins of FRONTEX', *JCMS: Journal of Common Market Studies*, 47(2), pp. 333–356. Available at: https://doi.org/10.1111/j.1468-5965.2009.00807.x.

Nordesjö, K. and Fred, M. (2021) 'Special issue introduction: The power of evaluation', *Scandinavian Journal of Public Administration*, 25(3/4), pp. 3–15.

Pallister-Wilkins, P. (2015) 'The humanitarian politics of European border policing: Frontex and border police in evros', *International Political Sociology*, 9(1), pp. 53–69. Available at: https://doi.org/10.1111/ips.12076.

Paul, R. (2017) 'Harmonisation by risk analysis? Frontex and the risk-based governance of European border control', *Journal of European Integration*, 39(6), pp. 689–706. Available at: https://doi.org/10.1080/07036337.2017.1320553.

Pinyol-Jiménez, G. (2012) 'The migration-security nexus in short: Instruments and actions in the European Union', *Amsterdam Law Forum*, 4(1).

Raimondo, E. (2018) 'The power and dysfunctions of evaluation systems in international organizations', *Evaluation*, 24(1), pp. 26–41. Available at: https://doi.org/10.1177/1356389017749068.

Rijpma, J. (2016) 'The proposal for a European Border and coast guard: Evolution or revolution in external border management?', in *Study for the LIBE Committee of the European Parliament*, PE 556.934. Brussels: Directorate General for Internal Policies.

Salomon, S. and Rijpma, J. (2021) 'A Europe without internal Frontiers: Challenging the reintroduction of border controls in the Schengen Area in the light of union citizenship', *German Law Journal*, pp. 1–29. Available at: https://doi.org/10.1017/glj.2021.60.

Somer, M.D. (2020) 'Schengen: Quo Vadis?', *European Journal of Migration and Law*, 22(2), pp. 178–197. Available at: https://doi.org/10.1163/15718166-12340073.

Steinhilper, E. and Gruijters, R.J. (2018) 'A contested crisis: Policy narratives and empirical evidence on border deaths in the Mediterranean', *Sociology*, 52(3), pp. 515–533. Available at: https://doi.org/10.1177/0038038518759248.

Stephenson, P.J., Schoenefeld, J.J. and Leeuw, F.L. (2019) 'The politicisation of evaluation: Constructing and contesting EU Policy performance', *Politische Vierteljahresschrift*, 60(4), pp. 663–679. Available at: https://doi.org/10.1007/s11615-019-00212-7.

Takle, M. (2012) 'The treaty of Lisbon and the European Border control regime', *Journal of Contemporary European Research*, 8(3), pp. 280–299.

Ulrich, S., Nøkleberg, M. and Gundhus, H.O.I. (2020) *Schengen Evaluation: An Educational Experience the Example of Norway*. Oslo: Politihøgskolen.

Van der Woude, M. (2020) 'A patchwork of intra-Schengen policing: Border games over national identity and national sovereignty', *Theoretical Criminology*, 24(1), pp. 110–131. Available at: https://doi.org/10.1177/1362480619871615.

Van der Woude, M. and Van Berlo, P. (2015) 'Crimmigration at the internal borders of Europe? Examining the Schengen governance package', *Utrecht Law Review*, 11(1), pp. 61–79. Available at: https://doi.org/10.18352/ulr.312.

Van der Woude, M. and Van der Leun, J. (2017) 'Crimmigration checks in the internal border areas of the EU: Finding the discretion that matters', *European Journal of Criminology*, 14(1), pp. 27–45. Available at: https://doi.org/10.1177/1477370816640139.

Votoupalová, M. (2020) 'Schengen cooperation: What scholars make of it', *Journal of Borderlands Studies*, 35(3), pp. 403–423. Available at: https://doi.org/10.1080/08865655.2018.1457974.

Wenger, E. (1998) *Communities of Practice: Learning, Meaning and Identity*. Cambridge: Cambridge University Press.

Wolff, S., Ripoll Servent, A. and Piquet, A. (2020) 'Framing immobility: Schengen governance in times of pandemics', *Journal of European Integration*, 42(8), pp. 1127–1144. Available at: https://doi.org/10.1080/07036337.2020.1853119.

Index

Note: Locators in **bold** indicate tables.

Kolibri 360 GmbH
Ferdinand-Jühlke-Straße 7
99095 Erfurt, Deutschland
produktsicherheit@kolibri360.de